The

DAN Guide

to

Dive Medical
Frequently Asked
Questions (FAQs)

By
Divers Alert Network

Cover Art and Illustrations by Rick Melvin

Design, Layout and Editing by Wesley Hyatt and Renée Duncan

DAN Reviewers:
  Frans Cronjé, M.D.
  Joel Dovenbarger, BSN
  Richard Moon, M.D.

ISBN :1-930536-18-6
Library of Congress Control Number: 2003109615

TABLE OF CONTENTS

To the Reader

Divers Alert Network (DAN), the world's leading organization for dive safety, receives more than 14,000 requests for medical and safety information each year through the DAN Dive Safety & Medical Information Line and via emails. In addition, DAN hosts between 5,000 and 6,000 medical webpage visits to the DAN website each month for medical information related to diving. These DAN benefits continue to grow as a vital part of the recreational scuba community.

Now, in order to better serve all recreational divers, DAN has put together the most commonly asked questions in one compact, portable source. Along with frequently requested articles from *Alert Diver*, this reference source offers more than 100 informative answers for divers, instructors and non-diving trained physicians to the top dive medical queries DAN receives.

This diverse resource is important to divers and diving, because the education process doesn't stop with a certification card: it is just the beginning. *The* DAN *Guide to Dive Medical Frequently Asked Questions* is a wonderful place to start for any diver. This book addresses the questions new divers often have about fitness and dive safety and gives experienced divers more detailed information about specific dive-related health and safety information.

For instructors, it is a quick reference for the many medical questions students have during their first open water class. In fact, instructors are encouraged to copy necessary pages to assist local physicians in evaluating divers, particularly physicians unfamiliar with dive medicine.

As always, the DAN Dive Safety & Medical Information Line is available to assist all callers with their questions, as are articles on the DAN website (visit www.DiversAlertNetwork.org) and emails. But when you're not near the computer and outside of normal business hours, we think you'll find this book very useful.

— *Joel Dovenbarger, BSN, Vice President, DAN Medical Services*

 *Vice President of DAN Medical Services Joel Dovenbarger has been with DAN since 1985. A medical professional for 27 years, Dovenbarger started work as a registered nurse in 1976 and began in hyperbaric and diving medicine at the F. G. Hall Lab at Duke University Medical Center in 1982.*

Section 1

General

Mask Squeeze

Not just a dilemma for new divers, DAN takes
an in-depth, in-your-face look at it

By Barbara Willingham, DAN Medic

Q: *I am a recently certified diver and have just completed my first offshore dive trip. I had what looked like a bright red patch of blood over the white of my eye when I looked in the rearview mirror on the way home. When I asked my instructor about it, he said it was probably due to mask squeeze. How does mask squeeze cause me to get a blood spot on my eye, and can this be a serious condition? What is the treatment for mask squeeze? Should I be concerned if this happens again?*

A: Each year DAN receives calls on both the Diving Emergency Hotline and the Dive Safety and Medical Information Line about mask squeeze. Most of these calls are from concerned divers who have unfortunately encountered one or more of the symptoms of mask squeeze. Although you may look like you've been badly injured, the condition is usually not serious. Here is some additional information about this diving dilemma.

What is mask squeeze?

Like the air spaces in your sinuses and ears, the air space in your face mask must also be equalized as you descend. Your internal body pressure and external water pressure need to stay in equilibrium. When you descend, remember to equalize, or add air to the air space in the mask, by exhaling through your nose. Failure to do so can create unequal pressure between the mask air space and the vascular pressure within the blood vessels of the face. This can result in various degrees of facial barotrauma, or injury to the soft tissues of your face contained within the mask.

If you've ever had a suction cup placed on your skin for even a short period of time, you may notice that after it is removed, the area can be red, slightly raised and may even have tiny red spots (petechia) if the suction, vacuum, is great enough. These are signs of barotrauma. Now imagine your face in a suction cup. The soft tissues beneath the mask and especially around the eye can be affected in the same manner, resulting in swelling (periorbital edema) and discoloration, such as redness or bruising (ecchymosis).

How can mask squeeze cause these symptoms?

"Remember Boyle's law,*" says Joel Dovenbarger, DAN Vice President, Medical Services. "We tend to think of Boyle's law in terms of a nice symmetrical container, contracting and expanding its volume as it goes up and down in the water. But what happens when that container is made up of your face mask and your face?

"As the air space volume of the face mask decreases, the mask is drawn closer to your face. Even when the mask is fully compressed the effects of Boyle's law continue unless the air space is equalized, just like a suction cup."

It is this kind of vacuum that is great enough to pull fluid to the surface of the skin. The delicate blood vessels near the eye may rupture and cause a bruised appearance. It can also create periorbital edema, or swelling around the eye. The result is blood pooling underneath the conjunctiva, the mucous membrane that covers the white part of the eye (sclera) and the inner surfaces of the eyelids. This blood (hematoma) is actually contained within the layers of the conjunctiva and will usually absorb after a period of time.

What treatment do I need?

Unless you are experiencing eye pain or visual problems, no treatment is required for facial barotrauma except time. Because it is a bruise, the effect of your mask squeeze will eventually be reabsorbed by your body.

Eye pain or visual disturbances such as blurred vision or loss of part of the visual field should be addressed by your physician or an eye specialist immediately. These symptoms would be extremely rare in mask squeeze, however. Opthalmologists may prescribe cortisone eye drops, and application of ice to the face may help ease swelling.

The signs and symptoms of mask squeeze can take up to two weeks or more to resolve. Unfortunately, it is one of those conditions where you will probably look worse than you'd like before it gets better. Not only will blood and edema need to be reabsorbed, but it tends to be gravity-dependent — which means it will spread downward on your face. Before you heal, you may look like a red-eyed black-and-blue marked creature in a B-grade horror flick or a boxer that took at least two too many punches.

---

* Boyle's Law states that at a constant temperature, the volume of a gas in inversely proportional to the pressure exerted on that gas. This means that when the pressure is doubled — as in descending in the water column — the volume is reduced to one half of its original amount.

Who gets mask squeeze?

Mostly new divers get squeezed — they tend to be overwhelmed by all the skills they need to remember, such as buoyancy control and equalizing their ears and sinuses, all while being mesmerized by the mysteries of the sea.

More experienced divers, however, are not immune to mask squeeze. They tend to have mask squeeze when they are concentrating on some new activity or focused in on a task which diverts their attention from clearing their mask. Changing to a new mask or to a low-volume mask may also lead to mask squeeze, because the diver may not be accustomed to when to add air. Also, divers who can clear their ears without using the Valsalva method (see page 77) tend to forget about their masks. Finally, poor-fitting masks or other issues such as facial hair may lead to problems with equalizing.

How do you prevent mask squeeze from happening again?

The solution to preventing mask squeeze is to remember to keep your nasal passageways open during descent. By exhaling through your nose and using a properly fitted mask, you will minimize the risk of facial barotrauma.

A face mask should fit comfortably against your face and you should be able to achieve an appropriate seal by gently placing the mask on your face and inhaling through your nose. The mask should seal to your face and not fall off even without the mask strap in place. It is not unusual for a small amount of leakage to occur while diving, especially if you have facial hair. Exhaling through your nose and tilting your face towards the surface while cracking the lower seal of the mask will generally remove any unwanted water from your mask.

— With reports from Dr. Richard Moon, Joel Dovenbarger, Kim Walker and Bruce Delphia

— From Alert Diver, July/August 1997

The Scuba Blues

DAN examines the possibilities behind flu-like symptoms following a dive

By Bruce Delphia, DAN Medical Information Specialist

Q: *I have been a certified diver since 1976. Over the past three years I have developed a condition related to diving: within two to four hours of my last dive on the first day of diving, I usually develop flu-like symptoms, including malaise, chills and fever. Although I don't experience other symptoms such as headache, trouble breathing or neurological symptoms, I do get a vague sense of irritation in my lungs and sometimes a dry cough. By the next day I am usually better. I have had a normal chest X-ray, EKG and blood chemistries, but no diagnosis has been made. Can you help?*

A: This malady has several possible explanations. Compressed gas breathing may result in pulmonary barotrauma; saltwater aspiration, directly or through a poorly functioning regulator, may also cause these symptoms. Mild decompression illness (DCI) can cause fatigue, but usually not chills and fever. This could be a condition that existed prior to the dive and coincidentally manifested itself afterwards (flu, perhaps).

It is possible that breathing air under pressure may spread microorganisms from the breathing apparatus into the lungs. This was described in "Proceedings of the Eighth Symposium on Underwater Physiology," A.J. Bachrach and M.M. Matzen, editors, Undersea Medical Society, Bethesda, 1984, pp. 113-180. This condition could possibly be prevented by routine regulator maintenance and cleaning.

DAN's records show similarities in calls concerning these otherwise unexplainable symptoms; and although this information is anecdotal, it deserves investigation. Unfortunately, most callers did not seek a medical evaluation while they were symptomatic, and reported symptoms after they had resolved. In each case the diver experienced flu-like symptoms within hours of the dive. This was always immediately after the first dive day or first dives in a series. Symptoms all resolved within 48 hours, many times within 24 hours.

The limited calls to DAN do not indicate that this is a widespread problem, but DAN needs more information on this malady and its relationship to diving. Post-dive symptoms must be carefully considered; continuing to dive with symptoms could cause additional problems.

DAN always recommends that you be examined by a physician or other healthcare professional. The possibility of decompression sickness must always be included in a differential diagnosis when a medical complaint is raised following a dive.

If you have experienced similar symptoms, please let us know. Include the following information: Age; previous / current health problems; whether you smoke; if so, how many packs daily, how many years have you smoked or, if you have quit, how long ago? current medications (prescribed / over-the-counter); diving location/environment (warm or cold, salt or fresh water; tropical, inland, U.S. or non-U.S. location), how long after the dive you began to feel ill; symptoms experienced; sequence of symptoms (i.e. headache first, then muscle aches, cough); how long symptoms lasted and what, if anything, you did to remedy the illness and the outcome. Did you fly prior to diving? If so, how many hours was the flight and how long after landing did you begin your dive? Please also advise us if these symptoms are present every time you dive, occurred once or sporadically. All replies are confidential.

— From Alert Diver, January/February 1997

Hand and Foot Edema After A Dive

By Joel Dovenbarger, Vice President, DAN Medical Services

Q: *After a recent dive, I noticed my right hand appeared swollen about an hour after my second dive. There was no pain or numbness, and I didn't notice any difference in strength. I've never injured this hand nor had this happen before diving. I've been diving about a year, and all my equipment is pretty new. I don't think this is decompression sickness (DCS), but why would my hand swell?*

A: Although it's not frequently reported, slight swelling in the hand or foot is not unusual — DAN periodically receives questions on this issue. Swelling, or edema, is not a typical symptom of DCS and would rarely occur alone. If it were related to DCS, it is more likely to occur with pain, numbness or change in skin sensation.

The most likely explanation for edema is a constrictive wet- or drysuit cuff. Prolonged or repeated exposure to a tight wetsuit cuff can produce swelling at the end of the extremity, which in this case is the hand. Even if you have worn the suit before, you may not have worn it long enough to get this effect.

Something as simple as a new wristwatch can add compression around that area. It's important that new suits fit correctly and not too tightly. It is equally important that you can still fit comfortably into your old wetsuit.

Cold water and wrist activity may add to a constrictive effect. If constriction is the cause, it should resolve shortly, with no other symptoms.

Other possible causes include:
• lymphatic decompression sickness (this usually affects the chest or abdomen rather than the extremities); and
• cold-induced angioedema (swelling that can occur in susceptible people, triggered by exposure to cold or water).

If the swelling occurs again, and does not appear to be due to a tight cuff or watch, you should seek evaluation by a physician while the swelling is present.

— *From Alert Diver, November/December 1996*

To Mix or Not to Mix

Is there a conflict with pseudoephedrine and enriched-air diving?

By Dr. E.D. Thalmann, DAN Assistant Medical Director

Note: *The decongestant pseudoephedrine is a commonly used drug by scuba divers, with mixed — though generally positive — reviews from sport divers, technical divers and diving professionals alike.*

DAN has received many inquiries for recreational divers who would like to know whether it is safe to take pseudoephedrine during enriched-air nitrox (EAN) diving. This inquiry is usually tied specifically to divers having read or heard the recommendation by diving organizations that pseudoephedrine be avoided with EAN.

The PADI "Enriched Air Diving Manual" says:

"Some drugs are CNS exciters believed to predispose you to CNS [central nervous system] toxicity. As reported at the October 1995 American Academy of Underwater Scientists (AAUS) workshop on enriched air, this includes the decongestant pseudoephedrine HCL (found in Sudafed™ and other decongestant products)."

Before answering the question of whether pseudoephedrine may predispose a diver to oxygen toxicity during enriched-air diving and whether it is safe for air diving, it is useful to look at the line of reasoning on which I based it.

The first question is: *How was it determined that there is an association between pseudoephedrine and CNS oxygen toxicity?* (For a discussion of CNS oxygen toxicity, see "If You Dive Nitrox, You Should Know About OXTOX," available on the DAN website medical articles section at www.DiversAlertNetwork.org/medical/articles/index.asp under the "Breathing Gases" category at the top). First, I needed to look at the American Association of Underwater Sciences (AAUS) workshop proceedings referenced in the statement by the certification organizations. So I went to work.

After a few phone calls and emails, I discovered that no proceedings for that workshop were ever published. The statement regarding pseudoephedrine was based on an article in a technical diving training association's journal. In this article, the author cites several incidents involving decongestants and diving listed below. After each incident from the journal I have put my own comments in italics.

1. A cave diver breathing a PO2 [oxygen partial pressure*] within limits (actual PO2 and depth not specified) died during a dive, the diver had a "high level" (*concentration not specified*) of pseudoephedrine in his blood. (*This incident could have been an overdose; taking more that the recommended dose of any drug is always dangerous. It could have also been an oxygen convulsion or any one of a number of other conditions unrelated to diving, but which causes sudden death. There is not enough information to decide.*)

2. A cave diver "bolted" from his dive buddies during an air dive and was later found dead. He had exhibited this behavior before. On both occasions he had taken pseudoephedrine before the dive.
(*This incident seems to have features of excitability, a known side effect of pseudoephedrine and a symptom of oxygen toxicity.*)

3. A diver accustomed to diving to 160 fsw went almost comatose during an dive (*breathing gas mixture not specified*). On that particular dive he had taken pseudoephedrine (*the article implied this was not usual*). (*This incident describes severe CNS depression, which is not a side effect of pseudoephedrine or oxygen toxicity.*)

4. A trimix diver (*breathing gas mixture and depth not specified*) felt he was "losing it" and aborted the dive. He had taken a pseudoephedrine before the dive (*the article implied this was not usual. This incident may be due to excitability, a known side effect of pseudoephedrine and a symptom of oxygen toxicity.*)

5. A diver experienced feelings of apprehension and was fighting to maintain consciousness after taking a 12-hour Sudafed capsule. A similar incident occurred on another dive after she took Benedryl (*an antihistamine*) for a jellyfish sting. (*The incidents described here are CNS depression, which is not a side effect of pseudoephedrine or oxygen toxicity. Benedryl, does cause drowsiness, so the diver's reaction to that drug is consistent with known antihistamine side effects. It is always recommended to avoid drugs that may cause drowsiness when diving.*)

6. On a Hydrolab dive in the '70s, one of Mount's dive partners was given Actifed (*pseudoephedrine plus an antihistamine*) for a cold. He went into a coma for two days before recovering. (*This incident is not likely due to oxygen toxicity or the pseudoephedrine in Actifed. However, the antihistamine can cause extreme drowsiness if taken in large doses. Another possibility is that the dive's somnolence was due to whatever was causing his "cold."*)

---

*The partial pressure of a gas is the measure of the number of molecules in a given volume. If a gas has only one component — 100 percent oxygen, for example — the partial pressure and the pressure are the same. With a gas mix, the partial pressure is the gas fraction times the total pressure. The physiological effects of a gas are due mainly to its partial pressure, no matter what the total pressure is. — E.D. Thalmann

7. On a shallow dive, a diver experienced symptoms of severe narcosis while using a breathing gas he considered unlikely to cause that severe a narcosis. He had taken pseudoephedrine prior to diving. (*This incident describes CNS depression, not a side effect of pseudoephedrine or oxygen toxicity.*)

8. A diver reported through a contact in Australia that Oceaneering International, a commercial diving company, banned pseudoephedrine more than 10 years ago because of "adverse effects." (*There is not enough information here to make any judgements about oxygen toxicity.*)

9. A contact in Australia reported incidents in recreational divers similar to those noted above to the author of the article in the technical diving journal. (*There is not enough information here to make any judgements about oxygen toxicity.*)

What can be made of these incidents? Starting with pharmacology, pseudoephedrine is a sympathomimetic (has effects similar to substances found in the sympathetic nervous system) whose major effect is to cause vasoconstriction in the lining of the nose and sinuses, thus reducing stuffiness and congestion. It is considered a mild central nervous stimulant, and its usual side effects are excitability, restlessness, dizziness, weakness and insomnia. Large doses (greater than those recommended) may induce several undesirable side effects including cardiovascular collapse and convulsions. Sounds like pretty ominous stuff could occur from simply taking a drug to relieve a stuffy nose, doesn't it? Well, first of all, drug manufacturers are required to report any and all side effects that may be associated with a drug, no matter how rare. Even aspirin in high doses can cause cardiovascular collapse and convulsions.

The reality is that adverse reactions to pseudoephedrine are rare in healthy people when it is used as directed. However, certain individuals may have an idiosyncratic reaction to the drug and experience undesirable reactions to a drug. For this reason, one should never use a drug for the first time just before diving and should make sure to use it long enough to determine that no hypersensitivity to the drug exists. What the author has presented in his article constitutes anecdotal evidence that pseudoephedrine may be associated with some undesirable side effects when taken before a dive. The issue, however, is this: Does this anecdotal evidence point to a predisposition to oxygen toxicity from taking pseudoephedrine?

While we have some evidence of an association between pseudoephedrine and these side effects, we really need to establish a cause-and-effect relationship. The following five criteria are used to make this connection:

1) statistical association;
2) strength of association;
3) timing of association;
4) consistency of response; and
5) biological plausibility.

"**Statistical association**" means that there is statistical evidence that symptoms that occur when pseudoephedrine is taken in association with certain types of dives are not a random occurrence. Mount did not provide enough information to establish a statistical association. "Strength of association" means that very frequently, when the drug is taken before a dive, some sort of untoward effect usually occurs during or after the dive: that is, the incidence of effects when pseudoephedrine is take in association with a dive is very high. Conversely, if no pseudoephedrine is taken, similar types of dives should almost never produce side effects. Since we don't know how many individuals take pseudoephedrine before diving with no effects, like those reported above, we can't measure the incidence.

"**Timing of association**" means that the reported side effects usually occur if the drug is taken before a dive, and not if it is taken afterward. Since only incidents in which the drug was taken before the dive were reported, we can't invoke this criteria.

"**Consistency of response**" means that the same effect is seen whenever the drug is taken, although the incidence may be rare. There does not seem to be any consistency in the symptoms reported above.

"**Biological plausibility**" means that there is some identified mechanism by which the drug could cause an undesirable side effect. In particular, we are interested in whether it may enhance susceptibility to oxygen toxicity. Here, we do have some evidence. In 1962, none other than DAN's Chief Executive Officer, Dr. Peter Bennett, while working as a research physiologist at the Royal Navy Physiological Laboratory in England, published a paper (Life Sciences; 12:721-727, 1962) testing the hypothesis that oxygen toxicity and nitrogen narcosis were caused by similar mechanisms. He found that in rats, sympathomimetics seemed to enhance oxygen toxicity. Pseudoephedrine was not tested specifically, but it is a sympathomimetic, so we might infer that it has a similar effect. In addition, our current understanding of the mechanisms which produce oxygen convulsions would predict that sympathomimetic drugs might enhance susceptibility to oxygen convulsions. It has been shown that drugs which inhibit sympathetic stimulation seem to reduce the likelihood of oxygen convulsions in animals. No human studies have ever been done. Thus, at least a theoretical reason exists why pseudoephedrine should be avoided while diving on high-PO2 dives.

What's the bottom line? In normal, healthy divers breathing air, occasional use of pseudoephedrine at the recommended dose is probably safe. This presumes that the drug has been taken during periods when no diving has occurred and that no undesirable reactions have occurred. However, one should avoid chronic (daily) use when diving, and it seems reasonable to avoid the drug entirely if diving while using oxygen-nitrogen mixes where the PO2 during a dive might exceed 1.4 ata, the current recommended "safe" open-circuit scuba limit.

Why the "long way around the barn" in reaching this conclusion? It is simply to present some tools and a logical process by which one can decide if anecdotal associations are due to an actual cause-and-effect relationship. Next time you hear that someone has suffered an undesirable effect from taking a drug or trying out some new dive gear, apply the five criteria given above to decide for yourself whether a cause-and-effect relationship exists.

— From Alert Diver, November/December 1999

A Tangled Question

Is there a connection between aluminum scuba tanks and Alzheimer's?

Q. **Dear DAN:**
Is there any information about aluminum tanks and their possible contribution to Alzheimer's disease?

A. **DAN Response**
A MEDLINE search going back to 1966 revealed some 67 papers addressing whether a link exists between ingested aluminum and Alzheimer's. This association was based on the fact that laboratory animals given large doses of aluminum salts develop neurofibrillary tangles in brain tissue similar to those seen in humans suffering from Alzheimer's.

However, there was no evidence that these aluminum-induced tangles were the same as those seen in humans or whether they were in fact the lesions that led to Alzheimer's. Studies looking at a relationship between Alzheimer's and aluminum levels in drinking water are not clear-cut: some show a weak association, others show none. In short, the evidence linking aluminum ingestion to Alzheimer's is very weak, and a cause-and-effect relationship has not been established.

DAN has not looked into this association, and no studies have ever been done to see if divers using aluminum tanks have a higher-than-normal incidence of Alzheimer's disease. Also, no evidence exists to show that inhalation of aluminum powder will significantly affect blood aluminum levels.

Whether there is significant corrosion in aluminum tanks, leading to the formation of aluminum salts, or whether these salts could then penetrate the filters in the first stage of scuba regulators and enter the lung is and enter the lung is a question for tank manufacturers.

— *Dr. Ed Thalmann, DAN Assistant Medical Director*

A. **Dive Industry Response**
As you know, cooks have been scraping the bottoms and sides of their aluminum cookware for nearly 100 years, with traces going into food. A study was funded several years ago at a medical school in the Midwest to address aluminum contamination and various diseases. The bottom line: the report stated that there was no connection.

Now to the contents of aluminum scuba and medical oxygen cylinders: as commonly happens, moisture entering a 3AL scuba cylinder allows corrosion and the formation of aluminum oxide or hydroxide, depending on whether the moisture is still present when you look inside. In bad cases, we have found more than five or six tablespoons of oxide moving around as powder in poorly maintained cylinders. At Professional Scuba Inspectors (PSI) Inc. we don't inspect regulator filters: our work is limited to cylinders and, to a much lesser extent, valves. We have no information as to whether trace amounts of corrosion product gets through to the diver's lungs.

In our visual cylinder inspector workshops, we do mention the importance of removing this material so that there is no opportunity for lung contamination. We have a material safety data sheet (MSDS*) for aluminum oxide that refers to it as "tumorigenic" (i.e., causing or producing tumors). We have not heard of any reports associating any disease with divers and aluminum cylinders.

Bill High, President, PSI, Inc.
Kenmore, Wash.

---

* An MSDS is a document that must be prepared by a manufacturer producing a chemical. All chemicals have such an information sheet with certain required information provided. There is even one for oxygen.

Tank Care Tips

Seawater combined with high pressure and temperature are a bad combination for the inside of scuba cylinders. If a cylinder is subject to this environment, severe corrosion that results in weakening of the cylinder walls can result in a relatively short period of time (a few months).

Beyond the physical damage, the air remaining in the cylinder can be affected as well, including depletion of oxygen and generation of carbon monoxide (CO). Although not nearly as pronounced a problem, the same conditions can also cause oxidation of aluminum cylinders. To avoid such problems, the following procedures are recommended.

• Avoid low air pressures when in the water. Any time the cylinder pressure is reduced to the ambient pressure, water can inadvertently enter. To be on the safe side, most instructors recommend exiting the water with 300-500 psi/21-35 bar of air remaining.

• When having your cylinder filled, make certain the technician blows any moisture from the fill connector before attaching it to your cylinder. This is a primary source for water entering cylinders.

• Steel cylinders should be stored with only enough excess interior pressure to keep out water and contaminant (20 to 50 psi/1.4 to 3.5 bar), and in an upright position if possible.
• Aluminum cylinders should be stored on their side (first choice) or upright (second choice) with low pressure (this is not as important as with steel cylinders).

• Only professionals in the dive industry following approved guidelines should repaint cylinders. Improper stripping and finishing can damage the cylinder. Experts at Catalina Cylinders warn against use of high temperature (above 265 degrees) for removing paint from aluminum cylinders, and recommend gel-type strippers as an alternative. High temperatures used in baked epoxy refinishing can weaken an aluminum cylinder, resulting in an explosion hazard. A cylinder should be hydrostatically tested following repainting to ensure its strength and integrity.

• Any time a problem is suspected (odors, sloshing, rattling, external damage such as gouges and dents, excessive heat, visible corrosion), have your cylinder inspected by a professional dive center.

• Although the industry guidelines call for an annual visual inspection, cylinders used in harsh environments (warm, humid climates with frequent fills) should be visually inspected every three to six months.

— *Bob Rossier, Alert Diver contributing author*

— *From Alert Diver, September/October 1999*

Post-Dive Symptoms

A DAN member asks: When something's 'not quite right,' when should you make the decision to be evaluated?

By Joel Dovenbarger, Vice President, DAN Medical Services

Q: *I am working in the Caribbean as a divemaster. It's not uncommon for my divers to come by the shop in the evening to talk and mention a symptom or say that something doesn't feel quite right.*

I am a DAN Oxygen Provider, and I've seen divers with the bends who have been treated locally. When I do the five-minute neurological exam I can tell if someone is bent. The people who come in to talk usually don't have symptoms like divers with the bends.

I don't want to tell these divers that it's probably nothing, but I also don't want to interrupt their vacation or have them see a local physician who is going to charge them. What's the best way to handle customer complaints about unusual symptoms?

A: You've just described the problem DAN has with getting injured divers to seek evaluation early and to call DAN for assistance. If you see a diver in obvious distress after diving (such as a convulsion), you can reasonably assume that this symptom may be related to their scuba diving.

Signs and symptoms of DCI are not always obvious, and they're often difficult for the diver to describe: the only indication you have may be a diver's complaint. The most common first symptom in DCI is pain in a joint, muscle or area of the body, such as forearm or the front of a thigh. And there is no single common definition for DCI pain — it's often difficult to describe, and frequently referred to as a "different type of pain" or something the diver has "never experienced before."

There are common factors that should make you suspect DCI in a diver. In the case of pain, it is most commonly, but not always, a constant pain with a gradual onset. In the majority of cases the pain does not come and go with movement and may be only minimally affected by using over-the-counter pain medication which divers often take for discomfort. The example of pain is a model for evaluating other symptoms, such as weakness, fatigue, dizziness or changes in skin sensation (numbness, coolness, stiffness), none of which will usually have any outward sign of injury.

Divers with discomfort may indeed be experiencing DCI, but that may not be the final diagnosis. Any sign or symptom is a call for action. If a symptom like pain or dizziness has already resolved, it still represents a reason for caution. Remember, a diver can only report a symptom they know they have: evaluation may still be necessary.

The best thing you can do for a customer or dive buddy with vague complaints is to listen. Don't try to diagnose DCI, hyperventilation, a strained muscle or the flu. Most importantly, don't dismiss or minimize diver's complaints — they wouldn't mention it if they weren't concerned. Get a clear idea about the nature of the symptom and suggest a call to DAN.

DAN's experience, knowledge and medical resources are as close as the telephone. After determining what has occurred and when, we can direct the caller to the next step. Many DAN calls turn out to be something other than DCI, but addressing concerns early can eliminate problems later.

Cost should not be a reason for not seeking an evaluation. That's why the majority of DAN members choose to purchase diver insurance: when you need the coverage, DAN is there for you.

— From Alert Diver, January/February 1998

Identifying the Problem

DAN offers assistance in helping the non-diving companion to determine when or if their partner needs to call DAN

By Joel Dovenbarger, Vice President, DAN Medical Services

Q: *As a diver's non-diving spouse, I read* Alert Diver *with great interest. However, I have yet to notice an article dedicated to the non-diving spouse in the event of an emergency. For example, if my husband goes diving while we're on vacation, and then we continue our travels (without diving buddies), how would I recognize symptoms of the bends? I do realize that divers typically deny initial symptoms, so what should I look for?*

A: This is a proactive question, and one that all non-diving spouses or companions should consider. Most of the answers you seek can be found in DAN's *Dive and Travel Medical Guide*. If the diving spouse is incapacitated with an injury, it is most likely you who will be calling DAN for advice and assistance.

There is no single set of signs that represent all decompression illness (DCI), but there are common symptoms that should make you (and your spouse or companion) suspicious when they occur after scuba diving.

Pain and Numbness

The two most common symptoms are pain and numbness. Pain is described in a variety of severities, from mild discomfort or a toothache-like sensation to a severe deep, boring pain anywhere in the body. It is commonly associated with the major joints of the body such as the shoulder, elbow, wrist, hip, knee and ankle. Pain can occur in any of these joints, but is also common in muscles and can appear at more than one site at the same time. DCS pain is almost always present at rest, and may or may not be made worse with movement.

Numbness, or paresthesia (prickling or tingling), is a catch-all phrase for a variety of altered or abnormal sensations usually confined to the skin. In most cases, it can be described as a loss of precise feeling. This may cause an inability to discriminate between a sharp or dull object when pressed against the skin. The altered sensory neuro pathway produces symptoms such as a tingling similar to that described when one's arm is "asleep," the funny bone has been struck or a constrictive band is placed around an extremity. Other associated complaints may be that a hand or foot feels swollen, heavy or cold.

Pain occurring in one or more locations may represent a diver's only complaint of DCI, but it is common for pain to occur with numbness and other symptoms. Numbness may also occur by itself but is seen more frequently with one or more other complaints.

Other Symptoms

According to DAN's *Report on Decompression Illness and Diving Fatalities* published each year, after numbness and pain, the other most common complaints associated with DCI are headache, dizziness, weakness, extreme fatigue and nausea. Any combination of these symptoms may represent DCI when they occur after a dive.

The injured diver may experience symptoms that appear mild but have serious implications. If you or your spouse ignore warning signals, more serious symptoms may develop.

Fatigue and/or itching are considered mild symptoms and may respond to treatment with oxygen first aid. Joint pain has sometimes been considered a mild symptom, but it does require recompression therapy.

A more ominous sign of DCS is muscular weakness and bladder abnormalities. If a diver complains of muscular weakness, has an abnormal gait, and/or difficulty with urination following a dive, then you must assume DCI until it can definitely be ruled out.

Denial

The most common symptom of decompression illness is denial. Part of this is because the symptoms of DCI often mimic those of other illnesses and diseases. For example, pain and numbness in specific locations are often the same or similar to symptoms produced from old injuries.

Divers often second-guess themselves as to whether current pain is different from the pain they occasionally have from an old injury. This confusion about symptoms may cause divers to delay calling DAN for help because they are reluctant to appear to be "complaining about nothing." There are even cases on record of divers who have denied symptoms as severe as muscular weakness and difficulty urinating.

Some divers simply refuse to admit that they have symptoms of decompression illness; they delay calling until they realize their symptoms won't go away. They may have been well within their computer or table guidelines, made the same dive many times before, or wonder why only they have symptoms out of 20 other divers who made dives using the same profiles. We hear these comments often on DAN's 24-Hour Diving Emergency Hotline. Remember, however, DCS can occur even when decompression procedures are followed meticulously.

Timing

Other clues on DCI are related to the time of symptom onset: half of all symptom onsets occur in the first 30 minutes after a dive. These figures are derived after excluding all cases of arterial gas embolism, and cases where altitude exposure occurred after diving. Ninety-five percent of all first symptoms will have occurred within the first 18-24 hours after diving.

When symptomatic divers call DAN's 24-Hour Diving Emergency Hotline or DAN's Medical Information Line with questions, we generally try to establish the relationship between symptom onset and the time of the dive. Further, we ask if the symptoms are new to the callers or if they have had similar symptoms in the past after diving or in relation to an injury or illness.

Most commonly, we try to find out if there is a history of old neck and back injuries from motor vehicle accidents or sports activities, or if an event recently occurred that may have contributed to the onset of symptoms, such as a recent fall or back strain from heavy lifting. Either way, a symptomatic diver must be referred for evaluation and proper diagnosis. Although we encourage divers to call when they have symptoms, we cannot diagnose someone's condition over the telephone. We can help identify common factors in a dive injury and make referrals to local health care.

Essential Information

Another important issue for the non-diving spouse is, simply, information. It is important for you to know what to do if there is any type of injury to your diving partner, and having that information close at hand is vital.

Keep all of your medical information and major insurance policy numbers with your DAN membership card. Before you go on a trip, take your DAN card out and review the appropriate numbers to call for information and assistance. On the back you will find numbers for:

• **Diving Emergencies** — the Hotline at +1-919-684-4326 (4DAN) or +1-919-684-8111; and +1-919-684-9111 for Latin America
• **Non-Diving Emergencies** — for DAN *TravelAssist* at 1-800-326-3822 (1-800-DAN-EVAC) or +1-919-684-3483;
• **Non-Emergency Diving Questions** — the Medical Information Line at +1-919-684-2948 or 1-800-446-2671 and press 2

DAN members also receive a Member Benefits Handbook that explains benefits and is useful for answering the most common member benefit and coverage questions. Remember to use the emergency lines only for emergencies, and call the Medical Information Line to request additional information.

Most important, be sure that you have current DAN membership coverage during your upcoming dive vacation. In an emergency situation, it is the non-diving spouse who may be making the decisions.

Physicians Reference

Here's a guide for physicians to use to help identify symptoms.

Post-Dive Symptoms of DCI:

Keep this in a safe place, with your DAN card and insurance information. You may want to provide this information to healthcare officials in the event of a diving emergency.

If, as a result of a dive, a diver has joint or muscle pain, skin rashes, hearing or vestibular problems, abnormalities of consciousness or higher mental function, personality changes, cerebellar abnormalities, disorders of sensation or muscle strength, or problems emptying the bladder:

Consider decompression illness in your differential diagnosis.

For assistance with diagnosis and/or arranging or conducting treatment, obtain information on reverse side and call DAN's 24-Hour Diving Emergency Hotline at +1-919-684-4326 or +1-919-684-8111.

For DAN membership or insurance information call 1-800-446-2671 and press 3.

If you suspect a diving accident and are unfamiliar with Dive Medicine, obtain the following information before calling DAN for assistance:

• For 48 hours preceding the injury, description of all dives: depths/times, ascent rates, intervals between dives, breathing gases, problems or symptoms.

• Relative to surfacing from last dive, symptom onset times and progression.

• Description of all first aid measures (including times and method of 100 percent oxygen delivery) and effect on symptoms since accident.

• A complete neurological exam including: higher mental function, cerebellar function (finger-nose, gait and tandem gait, or ability to walk barefoot heel-toe on a hard floor), strength of all major muscle groups, sensation (e.g., pin prick, light touch, and temperature), proprioception and coordination.

• Auditory and vestibular function including presence of hearing or balance deficits, tinnitus, nystagmus, and appearance of tympanic membranes.

• Description of all joint or other musculoskeletal pain including: location, intensity, changes with movement or weight bearing.

• Description and distribution of any rashes.

Divers Reference

Here's a quick guide non-diving spouses or companions can use to help identify symptoms.

Post-Dive Symptoms of DCI:

• joint or muscle pain

• skin rashes or mottling

• hearing problems, problems with balance or a sensation of the room spinning

• abnormalities of consciousness or higher mental function

• personality changes

• cerebellar abnormalities (balance and coordination)

• abnormal skin sensation (tingling, burning, or decreased feeling)

• decreased muscle strength

• problems emptying the bladder

If you have any suspicion that your spouse or companion may be experiencing signs and symptoms of DCS, call DAN's 24-Hour Diving Emergency Hotline at +1-919-684-4DAN (4326) collect from anywhere; or dial +1-919-684-8111.

— From Alert Diver, September/October 1998

Basic Instincts

DAN Explores A Hypothetical Underwater Emergency Using A Medical Perspective

By Joel Dovenbarger, Vice President, DAN Medical Services

Q: *Aboard the dive boat your dive buddy seemed relaxed and well prepared. Thirty minutes into the dive at about 50 feet / 15 meters, however, he panics and appears to be hysterical. He removes his mouthpiece.*

What emergency procedure should you perform?

1. Attempt to force the mouthpiece back into his mouth.
2. Cover his mouth and nose with your hand and take the panicked diver to the surface with you.
3. Release his weight belt, inflate his buoyancy compensation device and allow the diver to surface alone, in an uncontrolled ascent.

There could be many reasons for the diver's hysterical behavior. What is the best way to handle this situation?

A: Anytime a diver loses his regulator underwater he is at risk of drowning, loss of consciousness and, if he breath-holds on his way up, an arterial gas embolism. That's why we spend so much time in open-water training learning what it feels like to be underwater and working on equipment-related skills: it's to prevent the situation from occurring. Nonetheless, it does happen from time to time and for a variety of reasons.

Would You Know What to Do?

If you witness a diver panicking, try to determine what problem the diver is having. And remember, reminds Bill Clendenen, former Vice President, DAN Training, that every rescue attempt is unique, so be flexible and alert.

"Because each situation is different, one of the basic tenets of a rescue is 'Do What Works,'" notes Clendenen. As a rescuer, your first responsibility is to your own safety. The other basic rule is "Rescue Yourself First": attempting skills and techniques beyond your capability may make you a candidate for rescue.

Try to make contact with the diver. Do you know whether this diver has a history of anxiety-related issues when diving, or is he having a real problem with his regulator or air supply? For example, see if the tank is attached to the backpack. Is the regulator attached to the tank? Is the first stage leaking? Is the mouthpiece attached to the regulator? Does the regulator work? Is the regulator leaking? Does the octopus work? Can you see other equipment problems?

Consider Medical or Physical Problems

Has anything like this happened before? Does the diver have a significant medical history, such as high blood pressure or cardiovascular illness? Is there trauma — i.e., do you see any wounds?

A beginner is most likely to have problems using the regulator and other equipment when he is still new to diving; he has a lot of information to process the first few times he enters the water. During pool work or open-water training, the novelty of the experience can lead to high stress levels, anxiety and even panic. In some situations, instructors can offer the regulator to the student or new diver, perhaps even pushing the purge valve to show that air is coming out of the regulator. This action may offer some reassurance to an anxious diver, though a panicked diver may disregard it.

Many callers to the DAN Medical Information Line have said that just before they panicked, they had experienced the sensation of not getting enough air; others had noted that they felt like they were "breathing through a straw." It is difficult to communicate respiratory (breathing) distress underwater, and it very quickly turns to panic when the diver sees no real option except bolting to the surface for air.

Of the emergency procedure options listed above, trying to force the regulator into a panicky diver's mouth is not the answer. If he is unable to breathe at this point, he will continue to have difficulty breathing until the respiratory problem itself is resolved. Continuing to offer the regulator after the diver has refused it may waste precious time. Even your safe second regulator or other alternative air source is not going to work in this situation any more than the diver's own regulator would — the panicked diver will still most likely refuse the regulator.

Getting the Diver to the Surface

Time is a definite concern in a rescue like this. The panicked diver's tissues will consume oxygen, even while he is not breathing. This means that during the ascent, as oxygen concentrations in the lung decrease and gas expands, the diver is at risk of losing consciousness (called hypoxia of ascent, or "shallow-water blackout") and perhaps in danger of an arterial gas embolism from lung overexpansion.

On the other hand, if the diver is unconscious, he may relax the pharynx and allow passive exhalation. This will allow air to vent out of the lungs without over-pressurization and barotrauma.

The diver, whether conscious or not, may also experience laryngospasm, a reflex spasm that occurs when water enters the throat. Because the spasm may completely or partially close the airway, an ascending diver experiencing this reflex risks arterial gas embolism.

Dealing With Complications

The central task in the rescue of a panicked diver involves helping him make a normal ascent without inhaling water and holding his breath. Dropping the diver's weight belt, inflating his BCD and sending him rocketing to the surface would present the greatest risk for the unconscious diver. Assuming this is a standard no-decompression recreational dive, the best assistance is to hold onto the diver to help control the rate of ascent. A distressed diver in this situation will likely do everything in his power to hold his breath and not breathe in water voluntarily. Expanding lung volume usually forces some air to escape through the mouth and nose, but the risk of AGE still exists.

Drowning or near-drowning is also a possibility, but you shouldn't have to cover both the mouth and nose during the ascent. The diver may still have his mask. If he has panicked, however, both the regulator and mask may come off, making the situation grave indeed. We have a natural protective mechanism to continue to breathe after we lose consciousness. If that were to happen underwater, however, it could result in drowning or near-drowning.

The risk of injury and even death increases once a diver loses the regulator. In the best scenario, the diver takes it back immediately or the buddy will offer it to the diver and adjust the equipment, and the diver continues to breathe. If not, the buddy or dive guide will have to help the diver to the surface in a controlled emergency ascent, one would hope, without incident. If the diver can reach the surface safely, serious injury or death may be averted.

Other reasons besides equipment trouble or panic may cause the diver to spit out a mouthpiece. I have spoken to divers who experienced a medical problem, and they were on the verge of panic. Most said another diver assisted them to the surface.

Once you've reached the surface, establish positive buoyancy for both yourself and the panicked diver. If you haven't already removed the diver's weight belt, do it now. If you're diving in warm water without a wetsuit, you may have to inflate the diver's BCD to achieve positive buoyancy.

At this point, you should be able to get the diver back to the shore or the dive vessel.

A good diving buddy should be knowledgeable and skillful, should remain aware of the surroundings in the water, and should be aware of his partner's medical and diving history. That's what a buddy is for.

— From Alert Diver, November/December 2001

The Training Perspective

Dealing With the Injured or Panicked Diver at Depth

By Bill Clendenen, Vice President, DAN Training

Stay calm: Remember that major diving accidents — those which result in near-drowning, severe decompression illness or a fatality — are few. Yet the possibility exists.

Remain flexible. Every rescue attempt is unique, so do what works. And keep in mind that your first responsibility is for your own safety. Your actions underwater can make a significant difference in the outcome of the rescue.

Establish the diver's responsiveness. The first step in managing a panicked or struggling diver underwater is to evaluate his level of consciousness or awareness. Use the hand signal, *"Are you OK?"* If you don't get a reply, swim over and make physical contact with the diver. Gently shake the diver or squeeze an arm or hand. If he doesn't respond or appears dazed, bring the diver safely to the surface as soon as possible. Beware of startling a confused or panicked diver — he or she may suddenly strike out and place you in danger.

Assess the situation. Is the diver breathing? Watch for bubbles from the regulator. If the diver produces no exhaust bubbles within 10 seconds, he may not be breathing. If the diver is responsive and making efforts to breathe, check the air supply and / or offer your octopus if the situation dictates it.

Check the regulator. If the diver is unresponsive and the regulator is out of his / her mouth, don't waste time replacing it. Your main goal while the diver is in the water is to keep him from drowning, so make a controlled ascent as quickly and safely as possible.

Check the diver's airway. Is he breathing? Check for, and remove, any entanglements. Drop the injured diver's weights, but leave your own in place. Get a firm grip on the diver and make a controlled ascent to the surface. Remember, however, rescuer safety is your most important consideration. It is better to let the injured diver ascend to the surface alone than to risk injury to yourself, if the diver should begin to ascend uncontrollably. Different training organizations have different recommendations for the proper position for surfacing the unconscious injured diver. When bringing an injured diver to the surface, you should always follow your training.

Check weight and inflator. Locate and identify the diver's weight belt / weighting system and buoyancy control device (BCD) inflator / deflator mechanism. You need to establish positive buoyancy for both you and the diver. You have three options:

• use your own BCD to establish buoyancy;

• drop the injured diver's weight belt; or

• inflate the injured diver's BCD.

As a first preference, use your own BCD rather than the one belonging to the injured diver. Do this for two reasons: you're more familiar with your BCD, and there may be no air available to inflate the unconscious or panicked diver's device. However, if you're relying on your equipment to provide positive buoyancy, make sure you have a firm grasp on the diver you're rescuing: avoid losing contact on ascent if the panicked diver is negatively buoyant.

If you're having difficulty establishing positive buoyancy, remove the panicked diver's weight belt, and keep it clear of both of your bodies (sometimes, weight belts become entangled on gear or on an arm or leg). Otherwise, remove the weight belt on or near the surface. Be prepared, and avoid an uncontrolled ascent.

Keep a firm grip on the diver. Maintain a slow ascent rate. If your training dictates procedures involving head position during ascent, follow those and try to keep the diver's head in a neutral position or slightly extended back. This will reduce the risk of air being trapped in the airway and lungs. But don't lose precious time if you're having difficulties maintaining the correct head position — your biggest responsibility at this point is to get yourself safely to the surface while getting the diver to the surface as quickly and as safely as possible.

Your primary concerns are to do what works and to save yourself first. Beyond that, provide the best quality of assistance you can to the panicked diver. Taking a dive accident management class is one of the best ways you can improve your own diving skills.

Once trained, you'll need to practice your rescue skills regularly since they can diminish over time. When you know you can rescue another diver, your diving confidence and self-esteem improve. It's great for you and your buddy to know that you're prepared for diving's worst-case scenario.

Rescue and Dive Accident Management

Learning how to rescue divers in emergency situations is not difficult, but it does require training and frequent practice. This helps maintain proficiency with the skills you'll need and the array of situations you may encounter.

If you'd like to participate in training programs to develop and refine your diving accident management skills, contact your training association, or call DAN Training.

DAN Member Bill Clendenen is an avid diver, a PADI Course Director, and EMP Master Trainer. He has been teaching — and practicing — safe scuba diving for more than 17 years. A former emergency medical technician (EMT), Clendenen has served on many national and international first aid advisory committees.

— From Alert Diver, November/December 2001

Section 2

Cardiovascular

Cardiovascular Fitness & Diving

By James L. Caruso, M.D.

Before divers enter the water, they make decisions about how deep they will dive and how long they'll stay down. They check their own equipment and their buddy's, to ensure proper fit and assembly. Divers discuss what they wish to accomplish, evaluate the water and weather conditions and discuss emergency procedures prior to entry. This is the way well-prepared divers approach the risk of injury and reduce the probability of an unexpected incident during their dive.

Unfortunately, some diseases and illnesses that could threaten a diver's safety and health do not show themselves until the first symptom appears. Many people have hidden medical problems, such as those involving the cardiovascular system. The risk of cardiovascular disease increases as an individual ages, and some health problems, like valve disease, may not cause symptoms unless the individual exercises or becomes ill or stressed.

Individuals diving with some of the cardiac conditions listed in this article may be at an increased risk for injury. In fact, 20 to 30 percent of all diving deaths have a contributory cardiovascular condition.

There is a way to get a better handle on these medical risks, however. A regular medical evaluation with appropriate follow-up visits can help identify and control health problems associated with cardiovascular disease. To control risk factors for developing cardiovascular disease, it's important to: avoid smoking, eat a diet low in cholesterol and saturated fats, stay on a regular exercise program; and follow a doctor's advice.

This article by Dr. James Caruso answers the top 11 questions about cardiovascular conditions posed to DAN medics on DAN's Medical Information Line. Although you may not have experienced any of these conditions, the knowledge that they exist may benefit you in the future, or perhaps that knowledge may benefit a dive buddy right now. It is in every diver's best interest to manage personal health risks as well as assess conditions on dive day. An educated, well-informed diver who chooses to dive safely can minimize any health and safety risks associated with diving.

— Joel Dovenbarger, Vice President, DAN Medical Services

Hypertension

Description of Condition: Hypertension, or high blood pressure, is one of the most common medical conditions seen in the diving population — no surprise, really, since it is a common medical condition in the general population. Strict criteria for hypertension can vary depending on the reference cited, but normal blood pressure is generally accepted to be a systolic pressure below 140 and a diastolic pressure below 90 mm Hg, depending on age (cited as systolic first and diastolic second — e.g. "120 over 80," by your doctor). A thorough medical evaluation should be performed to find a treatable cause for hypertension; in most cases, however, none will be found.

Basically, two different sets of complications face a person with hypertension: short-term and long-term. Short-term complications are generally due to extremely high blood pressure; the most significant is the risk of a stroke due to rupture of blood vessels in the brain (called a cerebrovascular accident). Long-term detrimental effects are more common: they include coronary artery disease, kidney disease, congestive heart failure, eye problems and cerebrovascular disease.

Fitness and Diving Issue: As long as the individual's blood pressure is under control, the main concerns should be the side effects of medication(s) and evidence of end-organ damage. Divers who have demonstrated adequate control of blood pressure with no significant decrease in performance in the water due to the side effects of drugs, should be able to dive safely.

A recent report in a diving medical journal* citing several episodes of acute pulmonary edema (i.e., lungs congested with fluid) in individuals with uncontrolled hypertension while they were diving. Regular physical examinations and appropriate screening for the long-term consequences of hypertension such as coronary artery disease are necessary.

Medication Used in Treatment: Mild hypertension may be controlled with diet and exercise; however, medication is often necessary. Many classes of drugs are used to treat hypertension, with varying side effects. Some individuals must change medications after one drug appears to be or becomes ineffective. Others might require more than one drug taken at the same time to keep the blood pressure under control.

---

* Wilmshurst PT et al. Cold-induced pulmonary oedema in scuba divers and swimmers and subsequent development of hypertension. Lancet 1:62-5, 1989. See also: Hampson NB, Dunford RG. Pulmonary edema of scuba divers. Undersea Hyperb Med 24:29-33, 1997.

Classes of drugs known as beta-blockers often cause a decrease in maximum exercise tolerance and may also have some effect on the airways. This normally poses no problem for the average diver. ACE (angiotensin converting enzyme) inhibitors are the preferred class of drugs for treating hypertensive divers; a persistent cough is a possible side effect.

Calcium channel blockers are another choice, but light-headedness when going from a sitting or supine position to standing may be a significant side effect.

Diuretics are also frequently used to treat hypertension. This requires careful attention to hydration and electrolyte status. Most anti-hypertensive medications are compatible with diving as long as the side effects experienced by the diver are minimal and their performance in the water is not significantly compromised. Any diver with long-standing high blood pressure should be monitored for secondary effects on the heart and kidneys.

Coronary Artery Disease

Description of Condition: Coronary atherosclerosis is commonly described as "hardening of the arteries." It's the result of the deposition of cholesterol and other material along the walls of the arteries of the heart. The walls of the arteries, in response to the deposition of this material, also thicken. The end result is a progressively increasing blockage to blood flow through the vessel. Many factors contribute to the development of coronary atherosclerosis: a diet high in fat and cholesterol, smoking, hypertension, increasing age and family history. Women of reproductive age are generally at a lower risk due to the protective effects of estrogen. In the United States and other industrialized countries, coronary artery disease is the leading cause of death.

Fitness and Diving Issue: Symptomatic coronary artery disease is a contraindication to safe diving: don't dive with it. Coronary artery disease results in a decreased delivery of blood — and therefore, oxygen — to the muscular tissue of the heart. Exercise increases the heart's need for oxygen. Depriving myocardial tissue of oxygen can lead to abnormal heart rhythms and / or myocardial infarction, or heart attack.

The classic symptom of coronary artery disease is chest pain, especially when it follows exertion. Unfortunately, many people have no symptoms before they experience a heart attack. Cardiovascular disease is a significant cause of death among divers. Older divers and those with significant risk factors for coronary artery disease should have regular medical evaluations and appropriate studies (e.g., treadmill stress test).

Medication Used in Treatment: Medications typically used in the treatment of this disease include nitroglycerin, calcium channel blockers and beta-blockers. At some point, someone with coronary artery disease may need a revascularization procedure, or the re-establishment of blood supply, through bypass surgery or angioplasty. If the procedure is successful, the individual may be able to return to diving after a period of healing and a thorough cardiovascular evaluation (see "Coronary Artery Bypass Grafting" in this article).

Myocardial Infarction

Description of Condition: Myocardial infarction (MI), or heart attack, occurs when damage to the heart muscle cells results from interrupted blood flow to the tissue. Risk factors for heart attack are the same as those for coronary artery disease.

Most commonly, a myocardial infarction is the direct consequence of coronary atherosclerosis, or hardening of the arteries. The blocked arteries stop blood flow to the heart tissue and deprive the cells of necessary oxygen. Small areas of heart muscle may sustain damage, resulting in a scar; this may even occur without the individual experiencing significant symptoms. If larger areas of the heart are deprived of oxygen or if the cells that conduct the primary electrical impulses are within an area where blood flow is decreased, the heart may beat irregularly or even stop beating altogether. It is not unusual for sudden cardiac death to be the first symptom of coronary artery disease.

Fitness and Diving Issue: Cardiovascular events cause 20 to 30 percent of all deaths that occur while scuba diving. For many people, the real problem is that the first sign of coronary artery disease is a heart attack. The only realistic approach is to recommend appropriate measures to prevent the development of coronary atherosclerosis and to encourage regular medical evaluations for those individuals at risk.

Prudent diet and regular exercise should be habitual for divers. Older individuals and divers who have a family history of myocardial infarctions, especially at an early age, should receive appropriate evaluations to detect early signs of coronary artery disease.

Individuals who have experienced previous heart attacks are at risk for additional cardiac events in the future, and damaged heart tissue may have compromised cardiac function. The damaged left ventricle may not be able to pump blood as efficiently as it could prior to the MI.

Regardless of whether an individual has had a revascularization procedure (see "Coronary Artery Bypass Grafting"), strict criteria must be met prior to an individual's safe return to diving. After a period of healing —

six to 12 months is recommended — an individual should undergo a thorough cardiovascular evaluation, which includes an exercise stress test. The individual should perform at a level of 13 mets (stage 4 on Bruce protocol). This is a fairly brisk level of exercise, equating to progressively running faster until the patient reaches a pace that is slightly faster than running an eight-minute mile (for a very brief period of time). Performance at that level without symptoms or EKG changes indicates normal exercise tolerance.

Coronary Artery Bypass Graft

Description of Condition: Fortunately, for both patients and thoracic surgeons coronary artery disease affects the first part, or proximal end, of the artery much more frequently and severely than the downstream portion of the artery. This allows for a surgical procedure that uses a portion of a vein or another artery to direct blood around the blockage. Doctors perform this procedure hundreds of times daily around the country — more than 500,000 times annually. If the bypass is success-ful, the individual should become free of the symptoms of coronary artery disease, and the heart muscle should receive normal blood flow and oxygen.

A less invasive procedure, coronary angioplasty, consists of placing a catheter with a balloon on its tip into the area of the blockage and inflating the balloon to open the artery. This procedure does not require opening the chest and can be performed in an outpatient setting.

Fitness and Diving Issue: An individual who has undergone coronary artery bypass grafting or angioplasty may have suffered significant cardiac damage prior to having the surgery. The post-operative cardiac function of individuals dictates their fitness for diving.

Anyone who has had open-chest surgery needs appropriate medical evaluation prior to scuba diving. After a period of stabilization and healing (6-12 months is usually recommended), the individual should have a thorough cardiovascular evaluation prior to being cleared to dive. He or she should be free of chest pain and have normal exercise toler-ance, as evidenced by a normal stress EKG test (13 mets or stage 4 of the Bruce protocol — defined at the end of previous section on MI). If there is any doubt about the success of the procedure or how open the coro-nary arteries are, the individual should refrain from diving.

Mitral Valve Prolapse

Description of Condition: Mitral valve prolapse (MVP — called "click-murmur" syndrome, floppy-valve syndrome) is a common condition, especially in women. The problem arises from some excess tissue and loose connective tissue in the structure of the mitral valve in the heart: part of the valve protrudes down into the left ventricle during contraction of the heart.

An individual with MVP may have absolutely no symptoms, or the symptoms may vary from occasional palpitations, or unusual feeling in the chest arising from the heart beating, to atypical chest pain and a myocardial infarction. There is also a slightly increased risk of a small stroke or transient loss of consciousness.

Fitness and Diving Issue: Frequently mitral valve prolapse will not cause any symptoms or result in any changes in blood flow that would prevent an individual from diving safely. A diver with known mitral valve prolapse who has no symptoms and takes no medications for the problem should be able to safely participate in diving. The individual should require no medications and should be free from chest pain, any alteration in consciousness, palpitations and abnormal heartbeats. Individuals with abnormal cardiac rhythm, which can produce palpitations, should not dive unless these palpitations can be controlled with low doses of anti-arrhythmic medications.

Medication Used in Treatment: Beta-blockers are occasionally prescribed for mitral valve prolapse. These often cause a decrease in maximum exercise tolerance and may also have some effect on the airways. This normally poses no problem for the average diver, but it may be important in emergency situations.

Dysrhythmias

Description of Condition: The term "dysrhythmia" means abnormal heartbeat and is used to describe a wide range of conditions ranging from benign, non-pathologic conditions to severe, life-threatening rhythm disturbances. More familiar to many people is the term "arrhythmia," which literally means "no heartbeat."

The normal heart beats 60 to 100 times each minute. In well-trained athletes or even in select non-athletic individuals completely at rest, the heart may beat as slowly as 40 to 50 times each minute. Entirely healthy, normal individuals have occasional extra beats or minor changes in rhythm. These can be caused by drugs (caffeine), stress, or for no apparent reason. Dysrhythmias become serious only when they are prolonged or when they do not result in the desired mechanical contraction of the heart.

Physiologically significant extra heartbeats may originate in the upper chambers of the heart (supraventricular tachycardia or atrial dysrhythmia) or in the lower chambers of the heart (ventricular tachycardia). The cause may be due to a short-circuit or an extra conduction pathway for the impulse or secondary to some other cardiac pathology. People who have episodes or periods of rapid heartbeat are at risk for losing consciousness during these events. There are also conditions where the person has a fairly stable dysrhythmia (e.g., fixed atrial fibrillation), but they usually have additional cardiovascular and other health problems that coincide with their rhythm disturbance. A slow heart rate or heart block may cause symptoms, too.

Fitness and Diving Issue: The more serious dysrhythmias, like ventricular tachycardia and many types of atrial rhythm disturbances, are incompatible with diving. The risk for any person developing a dysrhythmia during a dive is, of course, losing consciousness while underwater. Supraventricular tachycardias are unpredictable in onset and are often triggered by immersing the face in cold water. Someone who has had more than one episode of this type of dysrhythmia should not dive.

An individual with any cardiac dysrhythmia needs a complete medical evaluation by a cardiologist prior to engaging in scuba diving. In some cases, thorough conduction (electrophysiologic) studies can identify an abnormal conduction pathway and the problem can be corrected. Recently, doctors and researchers have determined that people with some dysrhythmias (e.g., certain types of Wolff-Parkinson-White Syndrome) may safely participate in diving after a thorough evaluation by a cardiologist. Also, in select cases, some people with stable atrial dysrhythmias (e.g., uncomplicated atrial fibrillation) may dive safely if a cardiologist determines that there are no other significant health problems.

Medication Used in Treatment: Most dysrhythmias that require medication are medically disqualifying for safe diving. Exceptions may be made on a case-by-case basis in consultation with a cardiologist and diving medical officer.

Murmurs

Description of Condition: A heart murmur is an extra sound that can be heard during chest examination with a stethoscope. The opening and closing of the heart valves produce expected and predictable sounds in individuals with normal heartbeats. Murmurs represent extra sounds caused by turbulent or abnormal flow of blood past a heart valve, in the heart itself or in great vessels (i.e., aorta, pulmonary arteries).

Some murmurs occur strictly from increased flow. For example, pregnant women often have a functional murmur due to a greater blood volume and hyperdynamic metabolism; these are benign. Other murmurs are due to damaged heart valves and represent significant pathology. Damaged valves may either restrict blood flow (stenotic lesions) or allow blood to flow back into the chamber of the heart from which it had just exited (regurgitant lesions). Heart valves can be damaged due to infection, trauma, heart muscle damage (myocardial infarction), or an individual may be born with a structurally abnormal heart valve.

Fitness and Diving Issue: Stenotic lesions, such as aortic and mitral stenosis, restrict efficient blood flow and may have serious consequences during exercise. Significant aortic stenosis places an individual at risk for sudden cardiac death while exercising; it is a contraindication for diving. Mitral stenosis also limits the response to exercise and, over a period of time, can result in congestive heart failure.

Regurgitant lesions pose somewhat less of a risk during diving. Over a period of years, the heart will be taxed by the extra work necessary to pump blood, and heart failure may be the long-term result. Divers with these types of heart valve problems may safely participate in diving if they have no symptoms and have normal left ventricular structure and function, as evidenced by an echocardiogram.

Atrial And Ventricular Septal Defects

Description of Condition: An atrial septal defect (ASD) results from the incomplete closing of the wall that separates the right and left atria (the two upper chambers of the heart) during embryonic development. This is not an uncommon phenomenon in the general population, and, if the hole is small enough, the average person will experience minimal physiologic consequences. Women are affected more commonly than men.

Surgical correction of the defect may be undertaken, especially if the person is experiencing symptoms secondary to blood flowing from the normally higher pressure left atrium to the right atrium. Early in life, symptoms may be few, but over a period of years, complications, such as abnormal heart beats and shunting (bypassing) of blood from left to right may occur. On examination, the person with an ASD may have a significant murmur.

A ventricular septal defect (VSD) is a communication, or opening, between the right and left ventricles, the lower chambers of the heart. A fairly common developmental abnormality, VSD often merits surgical correction if the defect is large. Because of the large difference in pressures between the left and right ventricles, blood flow through the defect is nearly always from left to right. If this is the case, and the heart is otherwise performing normally, diving may be okay.

Fitness and Diving Issue: While the normal pressures in the chambers of the heart favor blood flowing from left to right through an ASD and VSD, periods in which this flow is reversed can occur, particularly for ASD. Although individual variations exist, Doppler studies have shown that most divers will have venous bubbles after a dive of significant depth and bottom time. These usually pose no significant threat, and the diver remains symptom-free.

Having a defect that allows bubbles to cross from the right side of the heart to the left is a whole different matter, however: once in the left side of the heart, bubbles may then be transported through the arteries to areas of the body where they can do some harm (e.g., to the brain, kidneys, and spinal cord). Several studies have demonstrated that a prevalence of ASD (and other defects in the wall separating the right and left sides of the heart) in divers treated for decompression illness was higher than expected, compared to the general population (see "Patent Foramen Ovale").

Someone with an ASD or VSD with a right-to-left shunt who wants to take up scuba diving should be discouraged from doing so. The diver with a known ASD or VSD should know of the potential increased risk of decompression illness and make an educated decision whether to continue diving. Individuals with a VSD, where the shunt is small and runs uniformly from left to right as determined by an echocardiogram, may be able to dive if it is determined to be safe by a physician knowledgeable in diving medicine. Surgical correction of ASD is now possible using an occluding device. This may be appropriate in some cases.

Raynaud's Syndrome / Phenomenon

Description of Condition: Raynaud's Syndrome is a condition where a person experiences episodes of decreased effective blood flow to the extremities, most significantly fingers and toes; this results in cold, pale fingers and toes, followed by pain and redness in these areas as blood flow returns. The underlying problem is constriction of the blood vessels in response to cold, stress or some other phenomenon supplying these areas. Symptoms are often mild. Raynaud's phenomenon may occur as an isolated problem, but it is more often associated with autoimmune and connective tissue disorders such as scleroderma, rheumatoid arthritis and lupus.

Fitness and Diving Issue: Raynaud's Syndrome poses a threat to a diver who is so severely affected that he or she may lose function or dexterity in the hands and fingers during the dive. If coldness is a trigger that causes symptoms in the individual, immersion in cold water will likely do the same. These individuals should avoid diving in water cold enough to elicit symptoms in an ungloved hand.

The pain may be significant enough that, for all practical purposes, the diver will not be able to use his or her hands. Less severely affected individuals may be able to function adequately in the water.

Medication Used in Treatment: Calcium channel blockers may be prescribed for individuals with severe symptoms; light-headedness when going from a sitting or supine position to standing may be a significant side effect.

Patent Foramen Ovale

Description of Condition: The foramen ovale is an opening that exists between the right and left atria, the two upper chambers of the heart. During the fetal period, this communication is necessary for blood to bypass the circulation of the lungs (since there is no air in the lungs at this time) and go directly to the rest of the body. Within the first few days of life, this opening seals over, ending the link between these heart chambers. In approximately 25-30 percent of individuals, this communication persists as a small opening, called a patent foramen ovale (PFO).

A PFO may be very small, physiologically insignificant, or it may be larger and occasionally a route for the bypass or shunting of blood. Usually, because the pressure in the left atrium exceeds that in the right atrium, no blood crosses the PFO (even though patent, or open, there is still a flap of tissue in the left atrium that overlies the opening of the PFO).

Fitness and Diving Issue: As in the case of atrial and ventricular septal defects, under certain circumstances, a PFO can result in shunting of blood from the right side of the heart to the left side. This is much more likely to occur in the atria than the ventricles because of the small pressure differences between the atria. Innocuous bubbles that may develop in the venous side of the circulation after a dive (see "Atrial and Ventricular Septal Defects") may be shunted to the left side of the heart and then distributed through the arteries. The result is that a paradoxical gas embolism or severe decompression sickness can result from a seemingly innocent dive profile.

Studies of divers with severe decompression sickness have shown a rate of patent foramen ovale higher than that observed in the general population. Special Doppler bubble contrast studies can identify a PFO. The diver with a known PFO should know the potential increased risk of decompression illness. A diver with a PFO who has suffered an embolism or serious decompression sickness after a low-risk dive profile should likely refrain from future diving.

At present, most diving physicians agree that the risk of a problem associated with a PFO is not significant enough to warrant widespread screening of all divers. An episode of severe decompression illness that is not explained by the dive profile should initiate an evaluation for the existence of a PFO. Surgical closure of a PFO with an occluding device is now possible for select cases.

Heart Valve Replacement

Description of Condition: Doctors in the United States perform more than 70,000 heart valve replacements each year. From birth, an individual may have an abnormal heart valve that requires replacement due to accelerated wear and tear (e.g., this happens with bicuspid aortic valves), or valve damage may occur following an infection or as an extension of damage to the adjacent heart muscle.

Most commonly, valve replacement develops from the consequences of bacterial throat infections, such as strep throat. In the body's attempt to fight off the bacterial infection, the heart valves, as innocent bystanders, sustain damage (called rheumatic heart disease). With the use of antibiotics, rheumatic heart disease occurs less commonly today, but individuals who had this problem during childhood may now, as adults, experience the consequences of the damage to the valves.

Fitness and Diving Issue: Anyone who has had heart surgery should be scrutinized a little more carefully regarding medical fitness to dive. With a properly functioning heart valve and no symptoms of cardiovascular disease, the real concern for a diver with an artificial heart valve is the anticoagulation (blood thinning) medication required to keep the valve functioning.

A mechanical valve (made of metal, polymer etc.) requires medication to keep blood clots from forming on the valve. This, of course, increases the risk of bleeding, and the diver needs to be aware of this risk, especially as it relates to trauma. Heart valves from pigs are also used to replace damaged native valves. These do not require anticoagulation medication, but they wear out sooner and require replacement earlier than mechanical valves.

Commander James Caruso (M.D.) is a Navy Flight Surgeon and Diving Medical Officer for the U.S. Navy at the Office of the Armed Forces Medical Examiner in Washington, D.C., and a consulting physician for DAN. These opinions are his own and do not reflect the official policy of the Department of the Navy, Department of Defense, or the U.S. government.

— From Alert Diver, July/August 1999

Pacemakers and Diving

DAN Offers Some Sage Advice on Mixing the Two

By Jim Caruso, M.D.

Q: *Is it safe to begin scuba diving — or to continue to dive — after having a cardiac pacemaker implanted?*

A: It was probably easier in the past to take an overly conservative approach to this question and provide an unqualified blanket statement like: "No one who has a cardiac pacemaker in place should ever scuba dive."

For military and commercial diving, a cardiac pacemaker is invariably considered a disqualification.

For sport divers, however, the limited medical literature available on the topic takes a more rational, but defensive approach. Each diver or dive student must be evaluated individually. The two most important factors to take into account are:

1. Why is the individual dependent on a pacemaker? and

2. Is the individual's pacemaker rated to perform at depths (i.e., pressures) compatible with recreational diving, including an added margin of safety?

As with any medication or medical device, the underlying medical problem determines one's fitness to participate in scuba diving after a cardiac pacemaker is implanted. Having a permanent pacemaker in place usually indicates a serious disturbance in the heart's own conduction system. If this is due to damage of the heart muscle itself, as is often the case when an individual suffers a large heart attack, the individual may lack the cardiovascular fitness to safely perform in the water.

Some individuals, however, depend on a pacemaker because of an identified rhythm disturbance or chronic abnormality in the conduction system. The area of the heart that generates the electrical impulse (resulting in the mechanical contraction that moves blood) may function inconsistently or inadequately.

Alternatively, the circuitry that conducts the electrical impulse to the rest of the heart may be faulty, resulting in improperly or irregularly conducted signals. Without the assistance of a pacemaker, the individual may suffer syncopal (fainting) episodes. Other individuals may have suffered a heart attack with minimal residual damage to the heart muscle, but the heart's conducting system remains unreliable.

If a diver's cardiologist determines that his/her level of cardiovascular fitness is sufficient for safe diving (i.e., exercising to a level of 13 mets or greater on a standard treadmill test) and the pacemaker is rated to function at 130 fsw equivalent pressures or greater, that individual may be considered fit for recreational diving. It is essential, however, that divers with cardiac issues check with their doctor before diving.

A cardiac pacemaker is implanted in the individual's subcutaneous tissue and will be exposed to the same ambient pressures as the diver. For diving, an adequate pacemaker must be rated to perform at least a maximum depth of 130 feet / 40 meters and must operate satisfactorily during conditions of relatively rapid pressure changes — e.g., ascent and descent.

All that being said, the most common reason people depend on pacemakers is underlying ischemic* heart disease. A significant number of recreational diving fatalities each year are attributable to coronary artery disease. Diving often takes place in remote locations far from facilities that provide emergency cardiac care.

While each individual's health status must be considered on a case-by-case basis, divers or dive students with significant cardiovascular disease and less-than-optimal exercise tolerance should be discouraged from participating in scuba diving. Remember, the individual must not only have adequate exercise tolerance for safe diving under routine conditions, but must also possess enough cardiovascular reserve to safely perform at the higher level needed in emergency situations.

Another device, the automatic implanted cardiac defibrillator, is not really a pacemaker, but it delivers a shock to the heart when a life-threatening rhythm disturbance occurs. Individuals with these devices are at a very high risk of sudden cardiac death and should be discouraged from participating in recreational diving.

* Having local decreased blood flow (therefore inadequate oxygen reaching the tissue) due to a mechanical obstruction, such as a narrowing of blood vessels.

Ref: Bove, AA. Bove and Davis' Diving Medicine. W.B. Saunders, 1997; and Divers Alert Network.

— From Alert Diver, August 2001

Vasovagal and Carotid Sinus Syncopes

DAN advises that you think twice before diving with either disorder

By James L. Caruso, M.D.

Q: *My 16-year-old daughter was diagnosed with "hairbrush syncope" by our family physician. Because she has episodes in which she faints or briefly loses consciousness, our doctor has told her that she cannot participate in scuba diving. Individuals with these conditions have a vasovagal response, he noted, and that is contraindicated for diving. Is this true, and will she be able to dive in the future?*

A: Syncope is the medical term for a fainting spell. The most common type of syncope is known as vasovagal syncope or a vasovagal response. These fainting episodes can be experienced by healthy individuals, tend to be recurrent, and often take place during periods of emotional stress.

Susceptible individuals may be especially prone to these fainting episodes if any of the following conditions are present: mild blood loss; anemia; fever; hypoglycemia; or injury. At times the person who experiences syncope has undergone prolonged bed rest. This is the mechanism that is at work when people faint at the sight of needles or blood. The person who experienced a fainting spell only when donating blood, however, is not likely to have a problem during a dive.

The decrease in cardiac output and blood pressure during a faint are responsible for the loss of consciousness, as the brain is the organ most sensitive to a decrease in oxygen, reacts to the situation with a fainting spell.

Carotid sinus syncope is a related phenomenon, which works through the glossopharyngeal and vagus nerves. Within the carotid arteries (large arteries in the neck) chemical and pressure receptors provide feedback on blood flow and blood pressure. When appropriate, the feedback results in a decrease in the heart rate and blood pressure. Some people have exquisitely sensitive carotid sinuses and may faint when pressure is applied directly to that area of the neck. Medical students are taught very early on not to check both carotid pulses at the same time, especially in the elderly, who may have atherosclerosis in these arteries.

For the rare person who faints with slight pressure to the carotid arteries, various terms are used to describe the phenomenon (e.g., hairbrush syncope, shaving syncope). These individuals may faint when simply turning their head to the side or wearing a tight collar. For those individuals who are more sensitive to pressure on the carotid, DAN advises caution before deciding whether to dive.

Any condition in which a person may suddenly and unpredictably lose consciousness should be considered disqualifying for safe diving. And for the rare individuals with such sensitive carotid bodies that they experience a syncopal episode with the slightest pressure to the carotid artery, they should be thoroughly evaluated by a physician and likely discouraged from diving.

Note: For more in-depth information on matters of the heart, see Dr. Caruso's article "Cardiovascular Fitness and Diving" starting on Page 36.

— From Alert Diver, July/August 1999

Section 3

Decompression Illness

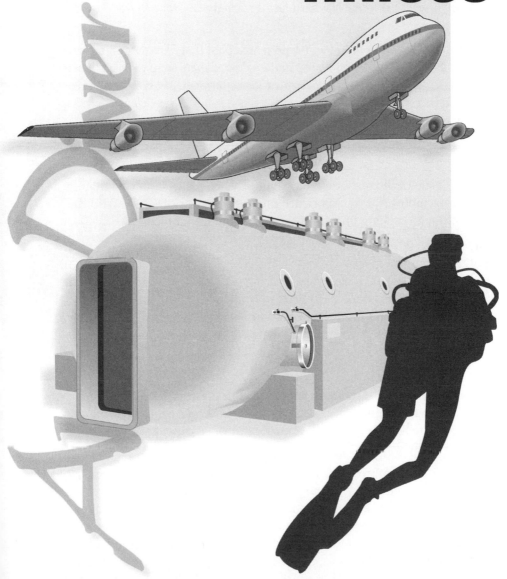

Return to Diving

DAN Takes A Look at Getting Back in the Water After Experiencing Decompression Illness

By Joel Dovenbarger, Vice President, DAN Medical Services

Q: *I was recently treated for decompression illness (DCI) after two days of diving. On my last diving day, two of my dives went to 40-50 feet / 12-15 meters for no longer than 35 minutes each. Minimum surface interval between dives was one and a half hours between the first two dives, and three hours before my final dive to 80 feet / 24 meters. During the ascent of my final dive, my weight belt came off, and I had a rapid ascent from 45 feet. I ended my dive at 8:45 p.m.*

At around 10 the next morning, I experienced pain that moved down my arm to my elbow, followed by numbness and tingling. I knew these were symptoms of DCI, and I was evaluated and treated that afternoon. My symptoms have completely resolved except for a soreness, like a bruise, in my elbow. I want to return to diving after I see my local physician.

What is the current recommendation for returning to diving after experiencing DCI?

A: One of the most difficult things divers face is admitting that symptoms they experience may be a result of DCI. You did the right thing in seeking immediate evaluation and treatment.

Divers often adopt a "wait and see" attitude before they accept the reality of DCI. In some cases, this delay in treatment can affect the outcome. In the [most recent] DAN *Report on Decompression Illness and Diving Fatalities: Year 2000 Edition*, only 50 percent of the injured divers analyzed received treatment within the first 20 hours they experienced symptoms. Several hundred DAN members are treated for DCI each year.

Regarding the return to diving after DCI, advice varies: it depends upon the specific symptoms a diver experiences, as well as their duration. Only 70 percent of injured divers experience an immediate and complete recovery; 30 percent will continue to experience either partial or temporary relief, from a few days to several weeks after treatment.

The response to treatment depends upon the severity of symptoms and the delay to recompression. The majority of mild residual symptoms, which are often due to inflammation, will resolve over a few days to a few weeks after an accident. Occasionally, persistent pain can be due to a bone infarct (i.e., a blood vessel that supplies a portion of the bone is occluded). If a portion of the joint is involved, then further diving is usually not recommended.

Although United States Navy "return to diving" policy was not written for recreational divers, it does give us the following guidelines to consider (specific Navy policy recommendations are in quotes):

1) "Divers with uncomplicated, pain-only DCI cases and whose symptoms resolve completely after 10 minutes breathing oxygen at 60 feet / 18 meters can return to diving after 48 hours of being symptom-free." This is probably a little too aggressive for recreational diving. Two to four symptom-free weeks is usually recommended for recreational divers.

2) "In uncomplicated pain-only DCI, divers who have had a completely normal neurological exam prior to recompression and whose symptoms took longer than 10 minutes to resolve, the Navy allows a two-week wait before a return to diving." This may be too soon for recreational divers, who may return to multiday repetitive diving. A minimum wait of four weeks is a more conservative option.

3) "If divers have had cardiorespiratory or neurological symptoms such as weakness or numbness, the Navy recommends a four-week waiting period." A six-week symptom-free minimum wait may be more appropriate for recreational divers.

4) "In more complicated DCI cases, in which symptoms seem to resist treatment or in which long treatment tables such as Table 4 or Table 7 are required, the Navy requires a minimum of a three-month layoff from diving. Diving may resume only after a thorough review by a Diving Medical Officer." This also applies to cases with multiple treatments. For recreational divers who experience DCI this severe, giving up diving altogether may be appropriate. At any rate, recreational divers should take a six-month hiatus from diving, followed by a thorough examination by a dive physician.

For recreational divers who want to dive after experiencing DCI, here is the best advice:

• Wait until you have been free of symptoms for four weeks; and

• Seek evaluation by a physician to determine whether there is some predisposition to decompression illness.

Remember, you're diving for fun and recreation — practice safe guidelines so you can enjoy it for many years to come.

— With reports by Dr. Ed Thalmann

— From Alert Diver, November/December 2000

Diving After Flying

By Joel Dovenbarger, Vice President, DAN Medical Services

Q: *It takes most tourists 24 hours to get to our resorts here in Thailand. I notice that many tourists begin diving immediately when they arrive and often start drinking quite a bit of alcohol. Aren't they at greater risk for decompression sickness after their long flight if they begin diving right after they arrive? Shouldn't they wait one day before they begin diving?*

A: Mild dehydration can occur on long flights, especially when travelers cross several time zones; alcohol consumption can also contribute to dehydration. Generally speaking, dehydration is thought to predispose a diver to decompression illness because the washout of inert gas (nitrogen, in diving) is less effective in a dehydrated individual.

If there were a relationship between diving after flying and DCI, we would expect to see a great deal of decompression illness on the very first day of diving — indeed, some data suggests that there are more accidents on the first day of a planned multiday dive trip. Of the 88 cases reviewed from the Caribbean for 1994, 33 — or 37.5 percent — occurred on the first day. The remainder occurred on days two through seven. Given that there are thousands of tourist divers who fly to Caribbean and Pacific dive sites, these numbers are far too small to establish a cause and effect.

Although no one can insist upon a 24-hour waiting period after flying, such a conservative approach to diving after flying is a reasonable idea - it gives divers an opportunity to rehydrate, adjust to a new climate and time zone, and rest up after a long flight.

— From Alert Diver, July/August 1996

The Industry Examines Flying After Diving

By DAN Medical & Research Staff

On May 2, 2002, DAN hosted a one-day workshop to review the state of the knowledge of flying after diving and to discuss the need for new flying after diving (FAD) guidelines for recreational diving.

The last FAD guidelines dated from an Undersea and Hyperbaric Medical Society (UHMS) meeting in 1991. Attended by 40 people representing the recreational diving industry, government agencies and Divers Alert Network, the May workshop was chaired by Dr. Paul Sheffield, organizer and leader of the 1991 UHMS meeting.

Discussions during the morning session reviewed the history of FAD, the development of FAD guidelines and the results of recent studies concerning the risk of decompression sickness in FAD. The afternoon session debated whether changes to the FAD guidelines were warranted by data presented in the morning and, if so, what should those changes be. The workshop concluded that changes were justified. The new guidelines are outlined below and will be formally published this spring in the workshop proceedings.

Provisional Flying After Diving Guidelines

The following recommendations, which apply to recreational divers, represent the consensus reached by attendees at the 2002 Flying After Diving Workshop. The recommendations are based on earlier published work and recent experimental trials as described in the Workshop Proceedings.

[The recommendations] apply to air dives followed by flights at cabin altitudes of 2,000 to 8,000 feet (610 to 2,438 meters) for divers who do not have symptoms of decompression sickness (DCS). The consensus recommendations should reduce DCS risk during flying after diving but do not guarantee avoidance of DCS. Preflight surface intervals longer than the recommendations will reduce DCS risk further.

Dives Within the No-Decompression Limits

• **A Single No-Decompression Dive:** A minimum preflight surface interval of 12 hours is suggested.

• **Multiple Dives per Day or Multiple Days of Diving:** A minimum preflight surface interval of 18 hours is suggested.

Dives Requiring Decompression Stops

• There is little experimental or published evidence on which to base a recommendation for decompression dives. A preflight surface interval substantially longer than 18 hours appears prudent.

— From Alert Diver, November/December 2002

Low Living, High Diving

DAN discusses living at a subsea level and diving above sea level

By Guy de Lisle Dear, M.B., FRCA, DAN Associate Medical Director

Q: *I am the medical officer for Peace Corps Jordan. While I am not a diver, many Peace Corps volunteers and staff dive in Aqaba, in the Red Sea, at the southernmost point of the country. Because of the difference in elevation between Aqaba and Amman, divers are advised to spend the night in Aqaba in order to avoid the bends.*

One of our volunteers is living in a village at the southernmost end of the Dead Sea, at approximately 365 meters / 1,197 feet below sea level. This young man is 29 years old, a diver, and in good health. My questions are:

1. What are the long-term side effects of living for a prolonged period of time (two years) at approximately 1,200 feet below sea level?

2. Would this person need to take any precautions before diving in the Red Sea in Aqaba?

3. If he would need to be transported via medevac for any reason from Jordan, would he not be able to fly within a specific time period?

A: 1. There is no evidence that living at depth, at least at such a small water-equivalent depth, has any deleterious effects. The barometric pressure at the surface of the Dead Sea is about 800mmHg (normal atmospheric pressure is 760mmHg). Prolonged subsea living, such as experienced by those divers exposed to saturation dives in underwater habitats (e.g., Tektite II at 50 feet / 15 meters, or 1,150mmHg), may have numerous side effects, ranging from decompression illness to dysbaric osteonecrosis (the death of portions of the long bones in the body in a proportion of those exposed to increased pressure). The dangers of Dead Sea living come more from exposure to the sun and the extreme salinity of the water.

2. The young man should consider himself to be diving at altitude in the Red Sea in Aqaba (when coming from his subsea home); this is a theoretical answer to the question as there is no data to support the following proposition. Standard tables were designed were designed for sea-level dives only.

The Theoretical Ocean Depth (TOD) concept was suggested by NOAA (National Oceanographic and Atmospheric Administration) to cope with diving at altitude. NOAA looked at the difference in barometric pressures at various altitudes and recalculated the dive tables based upon the new equivalent water depth, both for fresh water and sea water. This calculation converted for the Dead Sea would add about three feet (one meter) to any given dive. This in turn means he should count each dive as being one stop deeper. The U.S. Navy tables recommend, in fact, that no alteration be made for dives at altitudes lower than 2,300 feet / 701 meters.

A few dive computers use the Buhlmann correction for altitude, using the same principle as the TOD. Unfortunately, as they assume a sea-level starting point they would make an incorrect assumption for this diver.

3. DAN's research findings indicate that waiting to fly or go to elevation after diving requires at least a 12-hour wait after a single no-decompression dive and a 18-hour wait after multiple dives or multiple days of diving before flying. If the diver developed symptoms of decompression illness and required a medical evacuation, the aircraft cabin should be pressurized to a sea level equivalent.

In a dire situation in which the diver requires transportation over a mountain pass or other elevation to reach a medevac aircraft, then he should breathe 100 percent oxygen during the trip to prevent or lessen any effect that altitude may have on symptoms of decompression illness.

— From Alert Diver, March/April 1999

Section 4

Dbental

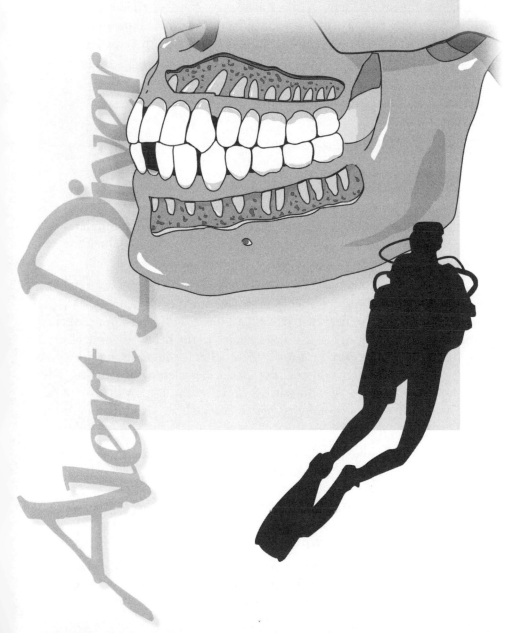

Dental Work & Diving

Putting the Bite on Jaw Fatigue, Tooth Squeeze and Dentures

By Karen Schwartz

When it comes to diving, the "Jaws" that we need be most concerned with are our own. Few of us put a trip to the dentist on the equipment checklist that might also include servicing our regulators, renewing our DAN membership or inspecting our tanks, but proper dental maintenance is an important part of responsible diving. Dental problems while diving can be irritating, painful and, in extremely rare instances, deadly.

There are three main dental conditions that can affect the diver:
• muscle and joint pain
• tooth squeeze
• the use of prosthetic appliances, such as dentures

Muscle & Joint Pain

Depending on whose estimates you believe, somewhere between 25 and 65 percent of divers suffer from problems with the temporomandibular joint (TMJ) — a small joint located just in front of the ears, to which the lower jaw is attached. No matter how you count it, that's a lot of unhappy divers.

Pain in this joint is a fairly common problem among the population as a whole. Some reports estimate that 10 million Americans suffer from TMJ dysfunction. Problems can result from accidents to the head, jaw or neck, or from diseases like arthritis, but it is believed that the most common cause is related to the teeth and bite. For instance, clenching or grinding the teeth can tire the muscles and cause them to spasm. But TMJ pain can also be caused by problems in the way teeth fit together — and it's here that divers are at risk.

The seemingly innocuous regulator and snorkel mouthpiece just wasn't designed ergonomically, and unfortunately, the design hasn't changed much over the past 50 years. Broken into its basic parts, most scuba mouthpieces have a labial flange that helps the lips seal against the water, and an interdental biting platform that is gripped between the teeth to keep the mouthpiece secure.

It serves its purpose, but very few people have an upper and lower jaw that line up exactly. That means that most divers must thrust their lower jaw, or mandible, forward in order to grasp the mouthpiece with the teeth — the incisors and the canines — at the front of the mouth. The awkward and unnatural position places an uneven load on the temporo-mandibular joint, increasing the stress and the risk of irritating the joint. Even if we don't have problems on land, holding a regulator mouthpiece for extended periods underwater is enough to help cause a TMJ problem or to aggravate an existing one.

"If you already have overloaded joints and muscles, one dive can do it," said Dr. Randall Moles, a Racine, Wis.-based dentist and author of the book *Ending Head and Neck Pain: The T.M.J. Connection*. "If you are someone who is coming in with a mild problem, it could take several dives before it acts up."

The signs of TMJ dysfunction include headaches and neck aches, pain in and around the ear, and tenderness of the jaw muscles. People with TMJ might also hear a clicking or popping noise when opening or closing their mouth, or have pain when yawning or chewing. They might have difficulty opening their mouth or find that their jaws get "locked" or "stuck" sometimes.

"The pain can vary from mild, being a little achy, all the way to a scream-ing headache," Moles said.

For those who continue diving with a TMJ problem, there are some real risks. The swelling and inflammation that occurs can result in the narrow-ing or blockage of the eustachian tubes and difficulty in clearing or equal-izing the ears. If severe enough, the inflammation can lead to vertigo and disorientation, obviously hazardous problems if they occur underwater.

The good news is that for most people, jaw fatigue and pain do not have to ruin a dive vacation. "Unless a patient has full-blown TMJ, where they're having facial pain, the vast majority can get relief" by using a better-designed mouthpiece, said Moles, who invented the SeaCURE mouthpiece.

In 1985, a British dentist, P.J. Mack, and his colleagues examined dental factors in mouthpiece design (*British Dental Journal*) and recommended that the mouthpiece have a bite platform of 4mm in thickness that can be gripped between the premolar and molar teeth. They also recom-mended palatal lugs on the biting platform to help keep the mouthpiece secure, but suggested ones that are small enough to not interfere with inserting and removing the mouthpiece.

In the last 15 years, a handful of mouthpieces, such as SeaCURE and Right Bite, have come on the market that incorporate some of these suggestions. Many divers swear by them, and they are inexpensive and available at most dive shops.

Still, even the most basic mouthpieces, those most often supplied with a regulator or snorkel, have some minor design differences, and divers might want to shop around for the best fit. Some dentists recommend trying a mouthpiece for at least 15 minutes to assess the comfort, then waiting an equal time before trying the next design.

For those with serious TMJ problems, a custom-made mouthpiece is the most likely solution. An article in the *European Journal of Prostethodontics and Restorative Dentistry* (September 1995) outlines a possible technique and construction suggestions.

Barodontalgia

All divers are familiar with the concept of barotrauma, or squeeze, that we most often feel in our ears and sinuses as a result of changes in pressure. But the compression and expansion of gas while diving can also cause pain in the mouth. Many times, that discomfort originates in the maxillary sinuses, which are close to the upper molars and bicuspids, and may apply pressure to the roots of the nearby teeth.

But in other instances, what we feel is tooth squeeze, or barodontalgia, that can occur when gas, soft tissue or blood becomes trapped in air spaces in the mouth. The pain may be felt on either descent or ascent, depending on the contributing factors.

Gas spaces in the mouth can be created by a number of conditions: cracked fillings; cavities; restorations that don't fit precisely, incomplete root canal treatments; or through a thin cementum — the hard tissue that forms the outer layer of the root of the tooth. Gas can also be forced into the tissue after oral surgery or dental extractions.

Tooth squeeze while diving or flying, like sinus squeeze, is the result of Boyle's law of physics: The higher the pressure, the smaller the volume — and vice versa. In many instances, the discomfort will disappear at normal pressure, but in some rare instances, the pressure difference that can develop while diving is sufficient to dislodge a filling or to crush or explode a tooth.

Just how often tooth squeeze occurs is unclear. Dr. Laurence A. Stein, a Miami-based dentist who wrote about a patient with a case of barodontalgia for *Alert Diver* (September/October 1993), said recently that in 25 years of practice, he has seen fewer than six cases. One patient developed barodontalgia in an old root canal, while another had a new silver filling that wasn't properly sealed. In every case, "It's something that was a pre-existing pathology," he said.

Still, the most common cause of what is perceived by the diver as being a toothache isn't a tooth problem at all.

"Almost any person who has ever come to my office having a toothache after a flight . . . it will almost always be a sinus problem rather than a dental problem," he said.

Not surprisingly, the extreme cases are the ones most often written about in medical books and journals. Dr. William E. Stein, a dentist in practice in Aitkin, Minn., wrote in *Northwest Dentistry* (November/December 1991) that he saw a case in which a diver had a full porcelain bonded molar crown shatter while ascending from a dive to 65 feet / 20 meters. Dr. John Parker wrote in *The Sports Diving Medical Guide* (1994) of an 18-year-old who had to abort a dive at a depth of 39 feet / 12 meters when a cavity imploded alongside a faulty filling.

It has been known since the 1940s that pressure changes may lead to barodontalgia. But few studies have been conducted since World War II.

R.S. Hobson of the Dundee Dental Hospital in Scotland sent question-naires to members of the British Sub Aqua Club and found that of the 74 respondents, two dozen reported tooth pain. Of those 24, 10 were suffering a cold or sinusitis, suggesting the maxillary sinus was a factor. Eight had a compromised tooth that required some sort of dental treatment ranging from a filling to an extraction, and six did not seek medical or dental treatment. Only one person reported a lost filling while diving. Hobson reported his findings in the *Journal of the South Pacific Underwater Medicine Society* (January-March 1987).

In Germany, researchers compared the dental records of 2,580 navy divers, frogmen and submariners to examine the effects of pressure on teeth. Normally, the navy divers are underwater for 200-300 hours annually, while the frogmen generally spend more time in shallower water. Submariners usually do service under normal pressure conditions.

After nine years, the navy divers and frogmen had more missing teeth and more teeth with crowns than did their submariner counterparts. W.H.G. Goethe and his colleagues wrote in the journal *Military Medicine* (October 1989) that the dental deterioration was probably due to the many years of barometric stress the divers experienced.

Another study exposed teeth to rapid decompression from a pressure of about 150 psi / 11 bar, which is about twice that acting on a scuba diver at a depth of 165 feet / 50 meters. I.M. Calder and J.D. Ramsey found that only carious teeth or those with deficient restorations failed under decompression (*Journal of Dentistry*, 1983).

The Bottom Line

So what does it all mean? It certainly doesn't suggest you need to give up diving if you don't have a perfect set of pearly whites. It just means that scuba divers should be conscientious about their oral health.

Neither Divers Alert Network, the American Dental Association nor the Undersea and Hyperbaric Medical Society has specific recommendations for divers as to their dental care. The ADA's international counterpart, the Federation Dentaire International, recommends annual checkups, with appropriate X-rays, by specially trained dentists. It also suggests waiting 24 hours before diving after a dental treatment under anesthetic, and waiting seven days after a surgical treatment.

The Search for a Diving Dentist

It may help to find a dentist in your area who is familiar with diving medicine. A good place to start is DAN's Dive Safety and Medical Information Line. Divers may also contact the UHMS (+1-301-942-2980, ext. 100) to see if any society members are in their area. And since not all dentists are necessarily on the lookout for diving-related dental concerns, it's good to let your dentist know that you scuba dive. Dentists who want more information on conditions that may affect divers may contact DAN's Information Line at +1-919-684-2948, 8:30 a.m. to 8 p.m. Eastern Time and the UHMS library at +1-301-942-2980, ext. 105. The ADA library also has articles on diving and dentistry.

Prosthetic Appliances

The problem with diving while wearing dentures is that the pressure a diver places on the front teeth while holding the regulator will pry the teeth loose in the back, causing slippage, irritation and pain. Even partial dentures can be troublesome. They can become dislodged easily, can be difficult to adjust and can be lost easily during an emergency resuscitation.

British pathologist Ian Calder tells of a 30-year-old who died in a swimming pool during a diving class when his false teeth became lodged at the back of his throat. Parker writes about a 34-year-old who jumped into the water and swallowed his partial denture when it dislodged. It came out the other end two days later.

Some medical experts, including Drs. Peter Bennett and David Elliott, authors of *The Physiology and Medicine of Diving*, advise that full dentures must be removed while diving, while partial dentures can be worn if secured by clasps or other attachments to the adjoining teeth.

Diving without dentures can be difficult. Holding a regulator in the mouth will likely cause soreness along the ridge, TMJ pain, and muscle fatigue and pain. One option is a custom mouthpiece, in which an impression of the patient's arch is connected directly to a mouthpiece.

A variation on that theme is the special diver's denture, developed by Dr. Thomas Hurst, a former Navy dentist, for a diver who had his upper molars and lower front teeth. The device is an acrylic insert that fits against the molars and the front of the upper jaw. A small, narrow ridge in the front holds the mouthpiece against the lower teeth when the mouth is closed. The ridge is narrow enough to allow air to pass along either side. Hurst, a professor at the University of Texas Health Science Center-Houston, shares his technique in the May 1986 *Journal of Prosthetic Dentistry*. Hurst also recommends that the diver's dentures be made of amber-colored acrylic resin so that they can be more easily seen if they become dislodged at depth.

Another option is the full face mask, which covers the face from forehead to chin. It has a built-in second-stage that eliminates the need for the diver to hold anything in his or her mouth.

Divers with braces or other types of fixed orthodontic appliances may also have trouble with commercial mouthpieces. A 15-year-old had to abort his dive when he lost some of the bonded brackets in his mouth while diving. Colwyn Jones and colleagues at the Dental School in Glasgow, Scotland, recommend customizing a mouthpiece, and give their technique in the *British Journal of Orthodontics* (1990).

Appraising the Risks

The frequency of serious dental problems while diving is relatively small. Divers Alert Network gets perhaps a half-dozen calls a year from divers suffering from TMJ problems, according to Joel Dovenbarger, Vice President, DAN Medical Services. It's likely, however, that most divers don't call DAN for dental matters.

So remember to brush between meals, floss regularly and keep smiling — secure in the knowledge that proper dental care and a good dentist will help you ensure safe, comfortable dives.

Karen Schwartz is a Portland, Oregon-based writer. She has been a certified diver since 1980 and a DAN member.

— *From Alert Diver, July/August 1996*

Realignment

DAN talks with divers about diving with dental braces

By Joel Dovenbarger, Vice President, DAN Medical Services

Q: My 14-year-old son will be making his scuba certification dives to 45 feet / 13.7 meters. He is in good health, athletic and has worn braces on his teeth for about nine months. Can scuba diving or the depth of his dives create any safety problems?

A: Scuba diving with dental braces in a young adolescent should pose no problem. Neither teeth nor braces are compressible, so the depth of a dive, or the pressure that is exerted on a body air space, like a sinus, should not present a problem.*

That is not to say that a new diver with braces won't have some soreness or aches after scuba diving. Braces gradually realign the position of an individual's teeth over the course of many months. At any given time, most of the teeth are still mobile.

The act of biting down on the bite block of a scuba regulator mouthpiece for a prolonged period of time may produce a little extra stress or tension on a young diver's teeth that are still being realigned. This may produce a little soreness or tenderness after a couple of dives and perhaps a little jaw fatigue in a new diver. Any diver should be able to properly grasp a regulator mouthpiece for the duration of a dive or series of dives without difficulty in order to dive safely.

*Note: there have been reported incidents of tooth squeeze in divers when an air pocket has developed in a loose filling or through tooth decay; the air expands upon ascent and can cause pain and even break through a filling. For more information on this, see page 62.

— From Alert Diver, January/February 1999

Root Canal

Can this procedure affect diving?

By Joel Dovenbarger, Vice President, DAN Medical Services

Q: *I recently returned from a dive vacation where I enjoyed a fair amount of diving. I experienced trouble with a tooth about a week after my return, and three days later required a root canal. My dentist said he knew another diver who had required root canal work; my wife has a friend whose husband, also a diver, required a root canal. Is this a coincidence or is it a problem related to diving? Will it affect my diving in any way?*

A: There has been no established cause-and-effect relationship between root canals and scuba diving. It is possible that the repetitive action of clenching a scuba regulator with your teeth may have exacerbated an underlying problem. Root canal therapy is generally necessary after a tooth nerve has been damaged from a direct blow to the dental area or the result of decay, abscess, or infection.

Most root canals are done in patients who are over 50 years of age and who have had one of these events occur after a lifetime of using their teeth. In the thousands of certified divers over age 50, who have made millions of dives, root canals are rarely reported. In all likelihood, the problem was just coincidental and would most likely have occurred even if you had not participated in scuba diving.

There is a small risk of infection immediately after a root canal, but once you are released by your dentist, you should have no problem when diving.

— *From Alert Diver, May/June 1994*

Toothy Wisdom

DAN Sinks Its Teeth Into Dental Issues and Diving

By Joel Dovenbarger, Vice President, DAN Medical Services

Q: *My wife had oral surgery about six weeks ago for the removal of a wisdom tooth. The dentist said that there is no infection, and the wound is healing nicely. But it was deeply rooted, and the nerve was traumatized. She's still taking painkillers. The problem is that we are going on a trip to Hawaii next week, where we planned to make a few — i.e., two to four — dives. Her oral surgeon, who's not a diver, said that it's probably not a very good idea for her to dive. What's your read?*

A: First, let's state what might be obvious. If your wife's surgery had been routine, with normal healing, uncomplicated by infection or pain and she could hold a regulator without discomfort, then it would be hard to advise her to wait any longer than she has already waited — i.e., six weeks. Normally, four to six weeks is sufficient time to allow for the risk of infection, provided there has been good healing and gum tissue has begun to fill in the empty socket. However, the nerve trauma may indicate that her case may be different. I had to consult with two of DAN's referral oral surgeons with experience in dive medicine for assistance on this issue.

Occasionally, proper healing is delayed, often in smokers or older people. In such cases, air can be forced into the subcutaneous tissues by the increased pressures in the mouth during a dive. This condition could further delay the healing process and can be uncomfortable.

Pain can impede the ability to hold the mouthpiece in place; a loosely held regulator during submersion can present a possible drowning hazard. One consultant also cautioned on returning too early to diving based on the softness of the lower jawbone (mandible) after a wisdom tooth extraction. The end of the mandible remains fragile until it's fully healed. Additionally, it is subject to fracturing when pressure is placed on the bone, such as when gripping a regulator in place.

Theoretically, if there is still some localized swelling (edema), offgassing of nitrogen from the area during decompression could be impaired. Although decompression illness in a small area of the jaw seems unlikely, we have insufficient data to be sure.

Finally, some types of pain medicine (those containing codeine, oxycodone or other narcotics) could promote nitrogen narcosis and impair performance and judgment underwater. Both consultants agreed that if a diver still has symptoms, diving is not a good idea.

Guidelines for diving after most dental surgery include waiting for:

1) A minimum of four to six weeks or until the tooth socket or oral tissue has sufficiently healed to minimize the risk of infection or further trauma;

2) Medication to control pain resulting from the surgery has been discontinued and there is no risk of drug interaction with nitrogen; and

3) The diver can hold the regulator mouthpiece without pain or discomfort for a period of time sufficient to perform a planned scuba dive.

— From Alert Diver, January 2002

Section 5

Ear, Nose & Throat

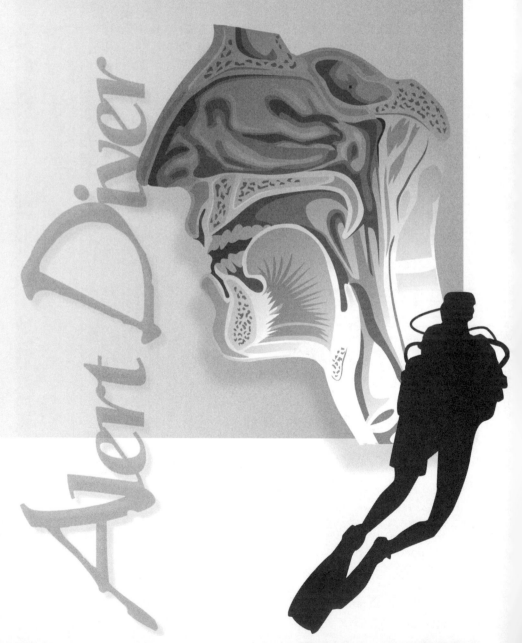

Guide to Dive Medical FAQs ✴DAN

Before the Pressure Gets Too Great, Equalize

A DAN doctor discusses how to equalize and answers queries of the ear, nose and throat

By Allen Dekelboum, M.D.

Although not the most serious of diving problems, those related to ear, nose and throat conditions are the most common. They probably account for more time away from diving and for the majority of calls to the DAN Diving Emergency Hotline than any other area.

In our basic scuba courses, we were subjected — both physically and via our dive texts — to diving physics and particularly the gas laws. We learned from Boyle's Law, for example, that an inverse relationship exists between pressure and the volume of gas in the gas-filled spaces: increasing pressure on descent reduces the gas volume and decreasing pressure on ascent increases the gas volume proportionately. Because of this pressure differential, we learn to equalize pressure on descent to allow the air-filled spaces to equalize. If we don't, we are subject to barotrauma or pressure damage. And until damaged areas heal, divers must stay out of the water — a fact that's true for the ear and the sinuses as well as other gas-filled spaces.

'Sinus'

Q: *Doc, I got 'sinus.' Can I dive?*

A: "Sinus": This is a term used by many individuals to categorize a wide spectrum of conditions, the chief characteristics of which are nasal congestion and nasal discharge, either from the front of the nose or the back. Actual sinus disease is uncommon, but the nasal congestion of allergic and non-allergic rhinitis (inflammation of the nose's mucous membrane) is widespread. Certainly, if congestion is significant and affects the sinus openings and the Eustachian tubes, then sinus and / or ear squeezes can be a consequence if you're scuba diving.

The sinus ostea (openings) are usually clear and are blocked only by severe congestion, by mucus or polyps. The Eustachian tube is usually closed, and requires some effort to open. To prevent congestion, treat your allergies. Follow your physician's advice, try antihistamines, decongestants, nasal sprays, and / or allergy desensitization.

Many of the newer antihistamines do not produce drowsiness, but they are available only by prescription. Decongestants may have side effects that can speed up the heart rate, keep you awake and sometimes produce a rebound effect, causing greater congestion. Decongestants might also affect you if you have high blood pressure or heart disease — they are cardiovascular stimulants and may speed up the heart and increase blood pressure. Over-the-counter nasal sprays can produce this rebound congestion, too. The newer steroid nasal sprays do not cause this side effect and are quite useful, though available only by prescription. (See #7 in "Instructions for Equalizing Ears and Sinuses," Page 77.)

Combinations of antihistamines and decongestants are useful in both allergic and non-allergic rhinitis. After discussion with your physician, these medications can be very useful in controlling the "sinus" problem.

Tympanic Membrane Rupture

Q: *Is it safe to dive with a perforated eardrum?*

A: A perforated tympanic membrane (eardrum or TM) can occur from diving as well as from non-diving causes. Most traumatic perforations heal spontaneously and, following an appropriate time after they have healed — usually about two months — you can return to diving if your physician feels the healing is solid and there is no evidence of problems with your Eustachian tubes.

If the perforation does not heal, an ear surgeon can repair it. After healing, the same rules cited in the paragraph above apply about when you may return to diving. If you have a belated healing process, it's important to check for chronic nose and sinus problems.

Chronic perforations that do not heal, however, are a contraindication to diving. Some have advocated the use of earplugs for these individuals, but if there is any water leakage, a severe infection could occur. (See "Unplugged," Page 80.)

ENT Surgery

Q: *Is it safe to dive after ear or sinus surgery?*

A: This is a broad question. The final decision on returning to diving depends on the nature of the problem and how well it heals. However, in general, individuals who have had external canal surgery can return to diving as soon as the canal skin has completely healed.

Middle ear surgery is more complicated. Problems with the middle ear are frequently caused by Eustachian tube dysfunction, and this must be cleared up before the diver can go under pressure. If the individual has received prostheses (artificial ear bones), there is controversy between otologists (specialists dealing with the ear and its diseases) about returning to diving. In cases like this, divers should consult with their surgeon for an individual assessment.

After inner ear surgery involving removal of the stapes bone or the placement of a stapes prosthesis (as in otosclerosis), scuba diving is generally discouraged. Also, if you have had surgery for inner ear barotrauma, many diving physicians advise against any further diving. Another group of diving physicians would allow the return to diving if there is no significant residual hearing loss, no balance problems and the middle ear can be easily equalized.

After sinus surgery, the surgical site should be completely healed, and there should be clearing of the sinus problem. Any residual sinus disease might lead to a worsening of the original problem or significant complications.

Ultimately, you should follow the advice of your surgeon.

Tinnitus (Ringing)

Q: *Will tinnitus prevent me from diving?*

A: Tinnitus, or ringing in the ears, has many causes. The underlying cause should be investigated if the problem is acute as well as chronic. Gradual progressive tinnitus can be due to noise exposure as well as advancing age, and it is usually associated with a hearing loss. If the underlying reason for tinnitus is not serious, there is no reason to curtail diving.

Menière's Disease

Q: *Can I dive with Menière's disease?*

A: Menière's disease is a recurring group of symptoms, characterized by episodes of fullness in the ear, tinnitus (ringing) and vertigo, sometimes with nausea and vomiting and fluctuating hearing loss. The episodes of vertigo can occur without warning, and if they occur underwater, could lead to panic. This could lead to a possible uncontrolled ascent or even drowning. Recurring episodes of vertigo from any cause should be a contraindication to diving.

Deviated Septum

Q: *Is a deviated nasal septum a reason not to dive?*

A: If there is no difficulty with the sinuses or ears with diving, then a deviated nasal septum (sometimes due to a broken nose in the individual's past) is of no consequence. But straightening of the septum can often relieve chronic ear and sinus problems if they exist, and might also eliminate difficulty with ear and sinus equalization, preventing squeezes.

Temporomandibular Joint (TMJ) Syndrome

Q: *What is TMJ? Can it occur in divers?*

A: TMJ, or temporomandibular joint syndrome, is an inflammation of the jaw joint just in front of the ear. It is usually caused by abnormalities of occlusion (the way your teeth come together) or by jaw tension and teeth grinding. The chief symptom of TMJ is pain in the ear with a normal ear examination. Tinnitus and vertigo can also occur.

TMJ can occur in novice divers who clench their teeth, occasionally biting through the mouthpiece. It frequently goes away with diving experience and reduction in tension.

Treatment includes bite adjustment, management of dental problems and the use of orthodontic mouthpieces. Heat and anti-inflammatory drugs are helpful. Custom mouthpieces on scuba regulators can help with jaw fatigue, but TMJ often requires medical / dental intervention

Hearing Loss / Deafness

Q: *I have a hearing loss in one ear. Is it safe for me to dive?*

A: Although it's not common, it is possible for a diver to suffer a significant hearing loss in an ear from a diving accident. Generally speaking, if your original hearing loss is severe and loss of hearing in your remaining ear would cause you to become deaf, then my advice would be not to dive. This is an individual decision for each diver to make, however, assisted by counsel from your physician.

This advice is particularly true if you regularly have difficulty equalizing. Most physicians are very conservative, even diving doctors. Severe hearing loss in both ears is a great handicap and should be avoided, if at all possible.

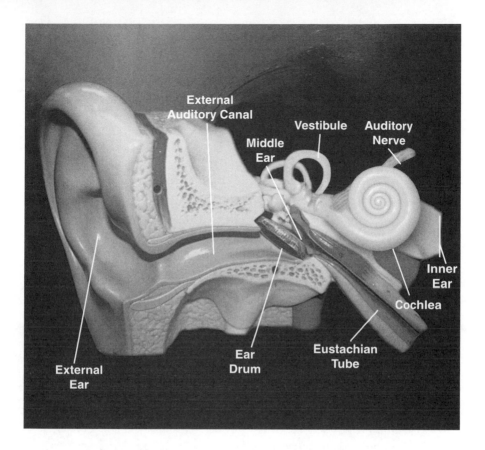

External Auditory Canal

Vestibule

Auditory Nerve

Middle Ear

Inner Ear

Cochlea

Ear Drum

Eustachian Tube

External Ear

Difficulty Equalizing

Q: *It takes me a long time to equalize my ears when descending in the water. How can I avoid this so that my diving buddies will not have to wait for me?*

A: As we mentioned in the introduction, Boyle's Law dictates that on descent, the air in the middle ears is reduced in volume by the increasing surrounding (ambient) pressure. Some divers are able to equalize their middle ears easily, but on occasion every diver has had some trouble. Others always have difficulty.

The culprit is the inability of the Eustachian tubes to open. The tube extends from the middle ear to the back of the throat, above the palate (see diagram, above). It has the same kind of mucous lining as the nose and sinuses and is subject to any inflammation that can occur in those areas. If there is enough swelling or mechanical obstruction, then all attempts at equalizing can be difficult, if not impossible.

In order to avoid difficulty, control all acute nasal and sinus problems. If you're cleared by your physician, the use of decongestant medications may be helpful. Equalize early and often. Use proper techniques (see following). Don't let your buddies rush you. If you do, you may incur permanent damage.

INSTRUCTIONS FOR EQUALIZING EARS AND SINUSES

Middle ear and sinus barotrauma are the most common injuries associated with exposure to increasing and decreasing pressure. Descent in the water adds approximately one-half pound per square inch of pressure for each foot of descent and diminishes a similar amount on ascent.

According to Boyle's Law, as the pressure increases on descent, the volume of a gas in an enclosed space decreases proportionately. As the pressure decreases on ascent, the volume of the gas increases proportionately: on descent, it is imperative that all enclosed air-filled spaces be equalized actively or passively. On ascent, the increasing volume usually vents itself naturally.

In order for equalization to be effective, the diver should be free of nasal or sinus infections or allergic reactions. The lining of the nose, throat and Eustachian tubes should be as normal as possible. If this is true, then the following techniques are effective in reducing middle ear and sinus squeeze:

1. Prior to descent, gently inflate your ears with one of the techniques listed on page 77. This gives you a little extra air in the middle ear and sinuses as you descend.

2. Descend feet first, if possible. This allows air to travel upward into the Eustachian tube and middle ear, a more natural direction. Use a descent line or the anchor line.

3. Inflate gently every 2 feet / 60 centimeters for the first 10-15 feet / 3-4.5 meters, then every 4 feet / 120 centimeters or so, as required.

4. Pain is not normal! If there is pain, you have descended without having equalized adequately.

5. If you do not feel your ears opening, stop, then try again. Ascend a few feet to diminish the pressure around you and try again. Do not bounce up and down. Try to tilt the difficult ear upward.

6. If you are unable to equalize, abort the dive. The consequences of descending without equalizing could ruin an entire dive trip or produce permanent damage and hearing loss.

7. If your doctor agrees, decongestants and nasal sprays may be used prior to diving to reduce swelling in the nasal and ear passages. Decongestants should be taken one to two hours before descent and last from eight to 12 hours, so that a second dose need not be taken prior to a repetitive dive during that time. Nasal sprays should be taken 30 minutes before descent and usually last 12 hours. Use caution when using over-the-counter nasal sprays, since repeated dosages over several days can cause a rebound reaction, with worsening of congestion and possible reverse block on ascent.

8. If at any time during the dive you feel pain, have vertigo or note sudden hearing loss, abort the dive. If these symptoms persist, do not dive again and consult your physician.

EQUALIZING TECHNIQUES

a. Passive — Requires no effort

b. Valsalva — Increase nasopharynx pressure by holding nose and breathing against a closed glottis (throat)

c. Toynbee — Swallowing with mouth and nose closed (good for ascent)

d. Frenzel — Valsalva while contracting throat muscles with a closed glottis

e. Lowry *(Valsalva plus Toynbee)* — holding nose, gently trying to blow air out of nose while swallowing (easiest and best method)

f. Edmonds — Jutting jaw forward plus Valsalva and/or Frenzel (good method)

g. Miscellaneous — Swallowing, wiggling jaws (good for ascent)

Dr. Dekelboum is a retired ear, nose and throat physician and surgeon who was board certified in Otolaryngology and Head and Neck Surgery 1965. He is a Clinical Professor at the University of California and trained in diving medicine (NOAA/UHMS 1983). He is a NAUI Instructor Trainer (1982), a DAN Instructor Trainer in all programs and is certified in SCC rebreather, extended-range nitrox and deco and a full cave diver. He has extensive lecture experience on all aspects of diving and technical diving medicine

— From Alert Diver, January 2001

The Trauma of Barotrauma

DAN discusses the consequences of additional damage to existing ear injuries

By Joel Dovenbarger, Vice President, DAN Medical Services

Q: *I am in good health and have had occasional problems clearing my ears because I had a broken nose with a deviated septum. I was diving recently and had a little trouble clearing my ears during my dives. I also had sinus congestion from a recent cold.*

After surfacing from my final dive, my ears felt blocked (like they had cotton in them), and voices seemed muffled. I began taking decongestants. They helped, but as the blocked / pressure sensation got better I noticed a ringing in both of my ears. I saw an ear, nose and throat physician who put me on prescription medication, including steroids and a strong decongestant. I have had excellent hearing in the past, but a recent test showed that I had severe to moderate hearing loss in both ears.

The doctors told me that the ringing may be permanent and that I should not continue scuba diving, but he is not a diver. Can I continue to dive with ringing in my ears?

A: Your doctor is probably correct — you should consider discontinuing diving. Sinus- and middle ear barotrauma are the most common dive-related injuries. Injury to the soft tissue lining of these air spaces in the body is an inherent problem in scuba diving because of the changing volumes of gas while descending and ascending.

Improper clearing (equalizing technique) can lead to these types of injuries and is the most common contributing factor among new divers. Other contributing factors may be a history of sinusitis, allergies and childhood ear infections. Any chronic irritations or infections may damage the soft tissue lining (mucous membrane) of the sinuses and especially the Eustachian tube, connecting the middle ear with the pharynx. A deviated septum can also cause difficulty in clearing.

Divers who continue to descend when they cannot equalize pressure risk several consequences: pain, fluid accumulation and bleeding into the cavity, whether it is the ears or the sinuses. Infection of the fluid can ensue; and persistence of fluid in the middle ear is one possible reason for impaired hearing. Rupture of the eardrum can also occur, and more serious is damage to the small membranes in the inner ear: the round or oval windows. Although spontaneous healing of these structures can occur, and surgical repair may be possible, permanent loss of hearing can result.

Over-the-counter medication used for the symptoms of congestion can be very effective for some divers and can help with pressure equalization. However, the mucous membrane may not fully recover from a viral infection or head cold for several weeks after initial symptoms begin — this is why DAN advises divers not to dive with any symptoms of a cold.

When barotrauma has occurred in the middle ear, it is not unusual for the diver to have a sensation of pressure or fullness and decreased hearing. Ringing (tinnitus) represents the stimulation of the nerve fibers responsible for interpreting sound.

In your case, a similar episode of barotrauma could lead to further damage and additional impairment. Your physician may probably feel that this risk is not worth taking, and you will have to consider whether some degree of permanent hearing loss is an acceptable risk for you.

DAN recommends that divers wait until symptoms of viral illnesses and head colds have completely resolved before planning a dive. Although decongestant medications may be helpful in salvaging a diving vacation if symptoms are mild, they do not necessarily prevent serious sinus or ear barotrauma. If you cannot equalize pressure in the middle ear cavities or sinuses, you should not dive or continue a descent.

— From Alert Diver, May/June 1999

Unplugged

DAN Examines the Use of Earplugs In Scuba Divers, Noting the Pros and the Cons

By Wesley Hyatt, DAN Communications and
Joel Dovenbarger, Vice President, DAN Medical Services

Q: *I have had trouble clearing my ears, and recently had an eardrum (tympanic membrane) rupture. My ENT (ear, nose and throat) doctor found no problems that would lead to clearing trouble. I never had a broken nose, nor suffer from allergies or ear infections. Even though my eardrum has healed completely, he has advised caution in returning to diving.*

Is this something that I should consider using an earplug for in the future? If I have another ruptured eardrum, can I dive if I use an earplug? I have heard a lot of pros and cons. What's the main issue with earplug use?

A: Once a ruptured tympanic membrane (TM) has healed, a diver usually can return to diving. Divers with this injury should exercise caution, however, because a small scar is left in the layer of tissue that makes up the TM. Forceful clearing could cause repeated problems with the membrane.

Although your doctor found no ENT problems, it is possible for you to irritate the Eustachian tube (which connects the middle ear with the back of the throat and regulates air pressure on both sides of an eardrum) when you're trying to clear your ears and sinuses. You may even have small Eustachian tubes, sensitive to rapid pressure changes. Descend slowly, clearing often, and you may avoid future injury.

As for the use of earplugs, opinions differ on their use in scuba diving. In general, they are not recommended. However, some divers use earplugs in special situations. Divers should also know special considerations before trying them. We asked several referral doctors for DAN to address this issue; we also discussed it with a doctor who created vented earplugs that some divers endorse.

Dr. Allen Dekelboum, an ENT and DAN consulting physician in California, reiterated the common view that earplugs create an air pocket in the ear canal, preventing equalization and resulting in differences in the pressure between the water and a diver's ear canal. This situation could lead to serious injury, he said.

"With an intact tympanic membrane, the increasing water pressure against the earplug and the decreasing volume of air between the plug and the tympanic membrane would have a tendency to drive the plug against the TM," Dekelboum said. "The increasing water pressure also could wedge the plug in the ear canal. If this occurs, there is risk of external ear barotrauma."

To address these concerns, some manufacturers promote the vented earplug, which has a small hole for venting between the water and the ear canal. The holes typically have a valve for pressurization without letting water enter the ear canal.

Dr. Robert Scott, creator of Doc's Proplugs, said his vented earplugs are safe for divers to use. It has one chief advantage, he said: "They make pressurization easier."

Most manufacturers of vented plugs emphasize the ease at which their products equalize. Doc's Proplugs website (www.proplugs.com) recommends that divers, to maintain proper pressurization, clear their ears frequently while wearing the earplugs. According to the website, those having trouble clearing with the plugs should check if earwax is pushing against the plug vent or blocking the canal. The website also says that if the vent is fouled by debris while a diver ascends, it is best to remove the Proplug, and if it is fouled during ascent, there is no problem: the air and water under pressure can escape around the Proplug.

However, Scott acknowledged that these assertions have not been proved scientifically, that no outside medical authority has endorsed the product or tested it under laboratory conditions to prove the veracity of its alleged capabilities. Scott said the claims are backed up through the use of plugs with hundreds of divers. "I guess you'd call it anecdotal, divers saying they've been good," he said, adding that some 10,000-20,000 divers have bought his earplugs. "That would be a conservative guess," he said.

Said Dekelboum: "I know Dr. Robert Scott, who invented Doc's Proplugs, feels that his vented plugs will keep water out of the ear. I believe he feels that the surface tension of the water against the vent prevents water from getting in. He also believes that the plugs make it easier to equalize the ears. The ProEar 2000 (a dive mask designed to keep the ears dry) people also believe this as well. I was unable to demonstrate that characteristic since I do not have difficulty equalizing. There is much anecdotal claim for both, but I have not seen any data for either."

Longtime DAN consulting physician Dr. Cameron Gillespie said divers could wear vented earplugs, yet he has significant reservations. "I believe earplugs can be used in diving, if vented, but I see little value in using them," he said. "Perhaps earplugs could arguably keep warmer water in the ear canal for comfort and, by reducing thermal conductivity, reduce chill to the canal walls, drum and semicircular canals." Dr. Scott echoed this belief.

However, Gillespie noted, "A wetsuit hood vented over the ear canals would accomplish the same things, and more (such as a significant conservation of the core body temperature), while not reducing surface hearing more than about 5 decibels (dBs) by eliminating the gain normally provided by the external ear."

Gillespie added that "earplugs make surface communication more difficult, because the small vents tend to retain water in the canals, causing up to a 35-dB conductive hearing loss. This could adversely affect safety."

Dr. Ernest Campbell, webmaster of Diving Medicine Online, said he had had several divers write to him, saying the Proplug allows them to dive comfortably after years of difficulty with equalizing and many episodes of middle ear barotrauma.

"I have no personal experience, and the only reason that I can see that they would be beneficial is that they might slow the rate of pressure change on the external surface of the eardrum," Campbell said. "It certainly has no ability to alter the pressure inside the middle ear or the Eustachian apparatus."

Campbell said that one diver claimed that he was even able to dive with a perforated eardrum, an activity that is not recommended, since the possibility of middle ear infection is great. "The usual vertigo from water in the middle ear is not as severe — apparently due to the warming effect of the external ear canal on water between the plug and the eardrum," he said.

Dr. Shannon Hunter, an ENT physician at Duke University Medical Center, N.C., also expressed reservations. "I have reviewed the limited information on the vented plugs, and it appears that there is too much of a chance for failure — "Too many 'ifs'," Hunter said. "If the plug vent is occluded by wax or debris, it should be removed — at depth? In cold water, where the temperature in the ear canal is warmed by the presence of a plug?

"An influx of cold water to the vestibular system is a setup for vertigo, nausea and even vomiting — this is duplicated every day in vestibular testing procedures used to test patients for balance disturbances. Cold water stimulation of the inner ear (cold calorics) through the ear canal is also reproducible in normal, healthy people and often renders them unable to stand or balance for a period of minutes.

Nausea and vomiting are also common side effects of this testing. A similar situation at depth is possible if a fouled earplug were removed and allowed for an abrupt influx of cold water into a warm ear canal. The resultant effects of nausea, vomiting and vertigo could be deadly.

"I concur with Dr. Dekelboum in that there is just not enough data or evidence to recommend the use of plugs for divers. The risks of complications underwater from malfunction or removal of an earplug are real and can potentially place the diver at increased risk for injury."

— From Alert Diver, January 2001

Section 6

Fitness To Dive

Exercise Training and Scuba Diving

By Joel Dovenbarger, Vice President, DAN Medical Services

Q: *My wife and I are going on a dive vacation. We will probably make 10 dives. My wife is also in training for a 25K event and is following a training schedule. She is extremely fit, has been a runner for a number of years, and she does regular strength training.*

Our concern is information we had read in dive magazines relating to the onset of decompression sickness (DCS) when divers take part in physically challenging activities (such as beach volleyball). While she's on vacation, my wife does not want to give up running completely. She realizes that she would log fewer miles on her dive trip, compared to what she would do if we were not diving. To keep her conditioning up, she would like to be able to do a few shorter runs, and I would like to join her for them.

We are advanced divers who do not push decompression limits. Do you feel some running during vacation would be relatively safe and, if so, what time of day would be best? To enjoy the morning, we often get up at 6 a.m. while we are on vacation. Would this be a better time to run prior to diving?

A: This is a question that comes up more frequently because many DAN members are also active in other sporting and exercise activities. The short answer is this: there is no real data on heavy exertion, such as a prolonged (or short) run, when you are also scuba diving.

We can, however, note several relevant studies. In 1949, the Navy found that two hours of post-dive exercise increased DCS incidence significantly for dives more stressful than we would normally perform today. In the '70s and '80s, during diving research at the Center for Hyperbaric Medicine and Environmental Physiology (F.G. Hall Lab) at Duke, several divers developed severe DCS during dives shortly after heavy weight lifting.

NEDU Data

Dr. Edward D. Thalmann, a retired Navy Diving Medical Officer and now DAN Assistant Medical Director, relates how he handled a similar situation while serving at the Navy Experimental Diving Unit (NEDU). He was conducting decompression table trials involving Navy Seals and Army Special Forces divers. These divers, very conscious of maintaining themselves in peak physical condition at all times, had a vigorous daily physical training regimen. They were told that while participating in the decompression trials they should exercise only to maintain conditioning.

They were also advised to exercise at the levels that they had been doing for the two weeks before the trial. They were instructed that, during the trial, they should not increase their levels of exercise or seek to increase their levels of conditioning (i.e. increase the amount they could bench press, shave another few seconds of time off their two-mile run, etc.). In addition, any exercise should not result in any prolonged (>30 minutes) soreness. Exercise should be either completed two hours before diving or started two hours after completing their dives.

In one NEDU decompression study, divers actually exercised by running three miles during repetitive-dive surface intervals. This simulated actual missions in which combat swimmers would have to perform exercise between repetitive dives. While no increase in decompression sickness was seen, these divers did experience normal aches, pains and skin sensations. Changes associated with running were not easily distinguished from symptoms of DCS. Thus, while exercising soon after a dive may not cause DCS, it may produce symptoms leading to unnecessary treatments.

Physiological Considerations

Nitrogen absorption and elimination is largely a matter of temperature and circulation. Gas exchange works very well at a constant temperature. After diving, when body tissues have taken up nitrogen, activities such as running, weight lifting or a heavy work load can "shake up the soda," so to speak. If you're planning to exercise after a diving day, it's advisable to rest after your dive(s). Rest allows tissue nitrogen levels to drop and reduces the likelihood that bubbles will be generated in the tissues.

You should always start off a dive well rested, with muscles that are cooled down and not calling for more oxygen and increased blood flow.

Exercise before diving may be your best bet. We all enter the water warm and take on nitrogen at a similar rate. Once in the water, we begin to cool, blood vessels constrict, and although we take on less nitrogen, we tend to retain excess nitrogen more easily. This means that after the dive, we are still cool and not offgassing as a mathematical model may predict. This would appear to favor a diving-after-exercise procedure. (For additional information, see "Thermal Facts: Dr. Bennett explores the relationships between cold, exercise and DCS risks" in the January/ February 2000 issue of *Alert Diver.*)

In the 1990s, an altitude study by Mike Powell, Ph.D., showed that if you waited two hours to go to altitude after doing a series of deep knee bends, the number of Doppler bubbles produced at altitude decreased to a baseline level after a two-hour wait.

There is, in the final analysis, no definitive answer about diving after exercise. One might consider at least a two-hour wait as a guide for diving after exercise. A more conservative suggestion would be four hours to allow your body to gradually warm up and rest after a nitrogen exposure.

We have documented cases of decompression illness in divers who exercise, work out or perform a strenuous task too soon after diving. Remember also to rehydrate after exercise. Although dehydration doesn't cause decompression illness, increased fluid losses may contribute if a problem occurs, so be sure to get plenty of water on dive and exercise days.

— *From Alert Diver, May/June 2000*

Fitness Issues for Divers With Musculoskeletal Problems

By James Chimiak, M.D.

Can abnormalities in your musculoskeletal system prevent you from scuba diving? Can fractures, osteoarthritis, rheumatoid arthritis, tendonitis, sprains, dislocations, bursitis, scoliosis, carpal tunnel syndrome, muscular dystrophy, joint replacement, disc surgery or amputation halt your watery pursuits?

The answers are yes, no and maybe; it comes down to specifics such as the type of injury or other abnormality you may have experienced as well as the degree of healing that may have already taken place.

Here's a look at musculoskeletal issues. Remember to call DAN if you believe you're injured as a result of a scuba diving injury; and keep in close contact with your physician on medical matters that can affect your diving.

Condition: Osteoarthritis

Description: Osteoarthritis (OA), is a disease of the bone and cartilage. Specifically, it affects the hyaline cartilage, the most common type of joint cartilage, and sub-chondral bone, located beneath cartilage.

Osteoarthritis is linked to aging; it most often shows up as joint pain and can result in a significant decrease in the range of motion. By age 40, almost everyone has some evidence of OA; by age 60-70, most individuals have symptoms. Scientists have even seen OA in whales and dolphins, our mammalian kin.

Fitness and Diving: Keep alert to your body. An individual's progressive loss of function due to arthritis requires ongoing evaluation: simply turning a valve can become impossible for those with severe OA. The restricted range of motion in joints can make certain maneuvers difficult or impossible. This requires adequate pre-dive training and suitable gear modifications such as bigger knobs, tabs and zippers. It may also necessitate a change in the position of equipment to allow easier access.

Altered tissue blood flow may alter normal inert gas exchange in two ways: inflammation increases blood flow, while degenerative changes and scarring can result in little or no blood flow. Either of these changes affect the way nitrogen is taken up and released.

Many individuals find a reduction in pain when exercising through the distraction of the activity — i.e., keeping the mind busy with another activity rather than concentrating on pain. Exercise also strengthens muscles and supporting structures for a given joint or for the spine and thereby reduces pain, and it releases endogenous pain killers, or endorphins, which provide pain relief. The pain can return, however, or even increase afterward

Painful joints can pose a diagnostic dilemma: it may be difficult to discern the difference between the joint pain of arthritis and the joint pain of decompression sickness after a dive.

Immobilization worsens OA, while a well-planned exercise program is essential to preserving joint function. Diving and other water activities are particularly beneficial for persons with OA: the buoyancy of a body in water reduces the weight-bearing capacity of the affected joints.

Medication Used: Aspirin and non-steroid medications, though helpful in reducing pain, impair platelet function. Properly functioning platelets are essential for adequate hemostasis, or clotting. The most obvious sign is bruising, but a theoretical risk includes increased bleeding at injury sites that include those affected by barotrauma as well as neural tissue.

Condition: Rheumatoid Arthritis

Description: Rheumatoid arthritis (RA) is a progressive disease, OA, but with more vascular effects. It causes symmetrical joint inflammation (involving both the left and right sides of joints) that can lead to their eventual destruction.

Rheumatoid arthritis can become systemic — that is, it can involve far more than bones and joints. A vasculitis, or blood vessel inflammation, may result in fever, skin breakdown, ulceration and infection. The mechanism of vasculitis is not completely understood, but in some conditions there is actual attack by the body's immune system on its vascular components

Other ailments that can come with RA include:
• mononeuritis multiplex — the inflammation of separate nerves in unrelated parts of the body;
• pleural and cardiac effusions — the escape of blood or lymphatics into tissues or a cavity of the body;
• lymphadenopathy, or diseases of the lymph nodes;
• Sjogren's syndrome — immunological disorder of tear and salivary glands, usually occurring in post-menopausal women, and presenting with dry mouth and dry eyes;
• episcleritis — inflammation of the eye; specifically, in the subconjunctival layers of the sclera.

RA can also cause spinal cord compression — due to destabilization of the vertebral joints — and carpal tunnel syndrome, described later in this article. Inflammation of a blood vessel (vasculitis), in combination with vasoconstriction, a narrowing of the blood vessels, can literally starve a limb of oxygen.

Fitness and Diving: As with osteoarthritis, an individual's progressive loss of function due to RA requires ongoing evaluation, and the restricted range of motion in joints can make certain maneuvers difficult or impossible. This requires adequate pre-dive training and suitable modifications, as described in the section on osteoarthritis.

Generally, it's advisable to minimize active exercise during periods of inflammation: altered blood flow can affect normal inert gas exchange. Joint pain that increases during a dive trip, for example, due to lifting and carrying of dive equipment, can be difficult to differentiate from DCI.

Medication Used: Aspirin and non-steroid medications, helpful in reducing pain, can impair platelet function and hence blood-clotting ability. Steroid medications affect electrolyte balance and cause edema (accumulation of excess watery fluid in cells, tissues or cavities). Gold preparations, used for treatment of RA, can cause lung irritation.

Cytotoxic drugs (cancer-fighting agents) such as methotrexate and azathioprine are used in severe cases because they help combat ongoing cartilage destruction. However, they, too, can cause a pneumonitis as well as affect the bone marrow or liver due to their toxic effects.

Condition: Tendonitis

Description: This acutely painful inflammation of the tendon may result from overuse or trauma. Often, however, there is no specific cause or event that can be linked to tendonitis. Usually, with a period of rest and anti-inflammatory medication, tendonitis will run its course. It also helps to evaluate possible positions or repetitive motions that may be causing or aggravating the condition.

Fitness and Diving: Because tendonitis is an injury or inflammation of the connective tissue between a muscle and another part of the body — and tendons transmit the force of movement — pain can significantly decrease the function of joints and muscles.

Remember to give it a rest: continued use of the inflamed tendon can perpetuate or even worsen the condition. There is even the danger of rupture, or a tear in the connective tissue, with subsequent loss of function. And as with arthritis, tendonitis can be difficult to distinguish between the pain of decompression sickness after a dive.

Medication Used: Non-steroid medications, though helpful in reducing pain, alter platelet function hence blood-clotting ability. Steroid medication, often injected, is effective in reducing inflammation.

Condition: Sprains

Description: This traumatic injury to a joint damages the surrounding soft tissues and ligaments. The degree of disruption of the joint and supporting elements determines the severity of the injury.

Fitness and Diving: A sprain can cause a measurable decrease in function, which is secondary to the injury. It also causes mechanical impairment of the joint, which is secondary to ligament tear, connective tissue disruption and swelling.

After a sprain, soft tissue swelling may be severe, resulting in a diver's inability to comfortably fit into dive equipment. It can also result in a decrease in blood flow perfusion and alter the inert gas exchange.

Any change in the pain presents a diagnostic dilemma after a dive: is it the pain of a sprain or DCS? After a sprain, diving should be avoided until the injury has healed and the prospective diver can effectively perform all expected diving and swimming maneuvers without pain. A good test is to try maneuvers in a pool, swimming with fins.

Medication Used: Non-steroidal anti-inflammatory drugs (NSAIDs) affect platelet function. Rest, elevation of the injured limb and icing are the initial treatments, which are incompatible with diving.

Condition: Dislocations

Description: Joint dislocations are temporary or persistent displacements of articulating joint surfaces. Usually the dislocated joint is very painful and can cause swelling and loss of function. Once swelling is reduced or the joint is placed back in its anatomic location, the individual with a dislocation should take a prescribed a period of rest and rehabilitation before resuming normal activity. Due to structural abnormalities and stretching of the ligaments, some individuals may be subject to recurrent dislocations: under conditions of minimal stress from routine physical activity, the joint may be prone to dislocation. Some cases may require surgical repair.

Fitness and Diving: Diving may need to be avoided if a diver is subject to recurrent joint dislocation, especially if this may result in sudden incapacitation while under water. An orthopedic surgeon may allow a return to diving after a period of rest and rehabilitation and if the diver can engage in strenuous exercise.

As with sprains, soft tissue swelling can hamper the normal exchange of inert gas and result in DCS. The resulting chronic joint pain can be confused with decompression sickness post-dive. In addition, scars from corrective surgery pose a remote theoretical risk of impaired inert gas exchange.

Medication Used: NSAIDs, often helpful in pain reduction, result in decreased platelet function and hamper blood clotting ability.

Condition: Bursitis

Description: A bursa is a collection of tissue and fluid that decreases the friction between opposing bony surfaces of the body. Bursitis is the inflammation of this structure due to overuse or trauma. As with tendonitis, there is often no identifying cause. The pain and swelling can be severe; an individual can experience a considerable loss in a joint's range of motion. Often, with rest and anti-inflammatory medication, the condition is self-limiting — i.e., like tendonitis, it will run its course.

Fitness and Diving: Increased tissue swelling secondary to the inflammation carries the theoretical risk of hampered inert gas exchange and, subsequently, the development of DCS. Extreme pain can cause a loss of function. If the pain or loss of function worsens, the individual with bursitis should postpone diving and other strenuous athletic activity until the condition resolves and the joint is pain-free during activity.

Medication Used: Anti-inflammatory drugs are helpful in pain reduction, but NSAIDs affect platelet function and hamper blood clotting ability. Corticosteroids may be injected into the bursa but can cause systemic glucocorticoid effects — i.e., fluid or electrolyte abnormalities, associated with osteoporosis — with repeated use.

Condition: Scoliosis

Description: This condition is an abnormal curvature of the spine due to asymmetric growth. Depending of the extent of the deformity, scoliosis may result in a variety of symptoms including pain, neurological problems and difficulty in breathing.

Fitness and Diving: Severe scoliosis can result in pulmonary compromise, making even moderate exercise impossible. The abnormal posture seen in individuals with scoliosis may require equipment modification to allow donning and optimal balancing, with special weight-bearing considerations or restrictions.

With scoliosis, the individual may experience neurological abnormalities continuously or intermittently. Muscles near the spine can develop asymmetrically with scoliosis: overuse leading to muscle strain can result in significant back pain and spasm. The spasm can cause a pinching in the nerves coming out of the vertebral column, resulting in a new neurological deficit.

Correction of severe scoliosis can employ the placement of steel rods to support vertebral column when it is straightened to improve function and symptoms. Once healed, an individual may resume diving, but with sensible restrictions including considerations of bumpy boat rides and weight bearing of equipment. Mild cases of scoliosis are found sometimes during routine exams and have little or no impact on the person. Before making plans to dive, individuals with severe scoliosis should be evaluated by a physician knowledgeable in dive medicine.

Medication Used: NSAIDs affect platelet function. Muscle relaxants are incompatible with diving because of their sedating effects.

Condition: Carpal Tunnel Syndrome

Description: This mechanical entrapment of the median nerve — as it travels through a tunnel bordered by bones and ligaments at the wrist — results in paresthesias (altered sense of touch or numbness) of the thumb, index and middle finger. Severe, long-standing cases result in the wasting of muscles at the thumb. For these individuals, surgery is the treatment of choice.

Carpal tunnel syndrome results from overuse of the hands and wrists, abnormal positioning of the hands for extended periods, and soft tissue swelling; in some cases, however, there is no identifiable cause. Tingling of the hands can occur with hyperventilation and also during recompression therapy. These conditions should be distinguished from carpal tunnel syndrome.

Fitness and Diving: Severe cases can cause a weakness in grip. The numbness common to most cases is difficult to evaluate after a dive, particularly if new or worsening symptoms are discovered post-dive.

Medication Used: If conservative rest and redesign of the working environment are ineffective, surgery is the treatment of choice. Edema associated with CTS can cause sensory changes, as the fluid may actually compress an area where the nerve passes. Renowned dive physician Dr. Carl Edmonds has reported the gradual onset of the condition when a diver stopped taking her diuretic (medication to relieve edema) during a week of diving.

Condition: Muscular Dystrophy

Description: This condition is characterized by generalized weakness of skeletal musculature associated with various muscle diseases: Landouzy-Dejerine, Leyden-Mobius, Duchenne and Becker are the most common. The condition can affect the ability to swallow, stand erect, maintain balance, walk, swim, or even hold a regulator in the mouth.

Many individuals with MD require a wheelchair by their late teens. These individuals can also have cardiac dysrhythmias, or irregular heartbeats. An active exercise program can benefit them, aiding in maintaining function.

Fitness and Diving: The most critical considerations are whether or not a diver can enter and exit the water safely and function effectively under water. Weakness not only impairs the diver's ability to react to emergency situations, but it also demands significant gear and routine modification during diving. The disease, often progressive and ongoing, requires careful expert evaluation, but diving may prove impractical.

Unfortunately, diving may frequently prove to be impractical, although it may be therapeutic if it can be integrated as part of an exercise program rather than only a recreational activity. Just as trained personnel assist the therapy of the individual on land, the underwater environment requires no less attention to detail. Careful planning should include modifying both gear and operating procedures. Guidelines are available for diving with disabilities, and these should be observed in the interest of the diver's safety (visit the website www.hsascuba.com).

Medication Used: Corticosteroids have been used in aiding joint movement, but they also cause fluid or electrolyte abnormalities.

Condition: Joint Replacement Surgery

Description: Destruction of a joint for whatever reason may require its replacement by an artificial joint. After surgery, aquatic activities are excellent sources of exercise, because they decrease weight-bearing stress.

Fitness and Diving: Theoretical concerns exist as to altered blood flow to the joint, resulting in impaired inert gas exchange. After a period of rehabilitation and subsequent authorization by an orthopedic surgeon for return to strenuous activity, individuals can dive, but they must document episodes of post-op neurological deficits. If severe pain or neurological symptoms persist, the individual should stop diving. Physicians should assess individually the loss of function or range of motion, noting appropriate changes to enhance underwater safety.

Medication Used: None required.

Condition: Disc Surgery

Description: The disc is a shock-absorbing structure that lies between two successive vertebrae. When injured, it can be a source of severe pain and neurological abnormalities. A herniation of the disc may result in the expulsion of disc material into the spinal canal, often causing excruciating pain and neurologic deficits.

The condition may require surgery for the removal of part of the vertebrae and the injured disc. The surgery, which can result in remarkable relief of the symptoms, can allow return to full activity after a period of rest and rehabilitation. To prevent re-injury, individual should use a regular program of back exercise. A small percentage of such persons may experience no symptom relief or even worsening of the pain or neurological deficit even after surgery.

Fitness and Diving: Once a person has fully recovered and is symptom-free, a surgeon might authorize a return to strenuous exercise. Those individuals whose symptoms remain should be cautious. An increased risk for DCS theoretically exists if persistent inflammation causes impaired inert gas exchange. Also, persistent neurological abnormalities pose a diagnostic dilemma, especially if they worsen or a new deficit shows itself after a dive.

The diver must be careful not to re-injure his back while balancing himself or lifting his equipment on a shifting boat: this advice is easier said than done. Expert evaluation and detailed neurological examination is recommended for anyone wishing to return to diving after back surgery.

Medication Used: NSAIDs help relieve pain but impair platelet function. The need for narcotic medications may indicate a degree of pain that precludes diving. Narcotics, anticonvulsants, membrane stabilizers, muscle relaxants and tricyclic antidepressants (all commonly prescribed for significant back pain) may have an adverse effect on the central nervous system and even work synergistically with the effects of nitrogen to further impair performance and judgment while diving.

Condition: Amputation

Description: Loss of limb due to trauma or surgical removal, as well as the congenital (existing since birth) absence of a limb, pose obvious challenges to a person's overall function. Adaptation by the diver, however, can greatly decrease that impact. Both task modification and prosthetics have enhanced the lives of amputees.

The effects of amputation vary: some amputees are able to regain near complete return to full function, whereas others may be completely incapacitated. Traumatic amputations usually occur in previously healthy, young individuals. Unless the trauma has also caused other injuries that may affect diving safety – such as head injuries or lung damage – diving may be permitted if the diver can effectively function underwater. Guidelines are available for diving with disabilities (www.hsascuba.com). However if the amputation due to a medical condition, such as peripheral vascular disease, specialists should evaluate the diver's cardiovascular status, general health and use of medication. Chronic phantom sensations and phantom pain can adversely affect quality of life, whereas delayed wound healing precludes exposure to water and robust activity.

Fitness and Diving: Diving safety requires an ability to function effectively in preparation to, during, and after diving. Guidelines are available for diving with disabilities and these should be considered, not only for the benefit of the disable diver, but for their buddy or buddies as well. Even the most motivated diver with an amputation will have difficulty with some aspect of the dive, but it is usually possible to manage such difficulties with gear modifications and individualized diving procedures. Many professional divers with amputations have made adaptations in order to continue diving. After amputation, divers should define their limitations and risks – both for themselves and their buddies.

Medication Used: Many medications used to treat pain may cause sedation and are not recommended for diving. Any medications used for associated conditions must also be examined before diving under their influence.

Medications Used in the Treatment of Musculoskeletal Disorders

Diving while using medication is generally discouraged due to the potential for side effects. Certain medications may be relatively safe but the reasons for taking them may not be: The use of aspirin for a headache may be relatively benign, but its use to avoid a second stroke or heart attack presents a completely different set of risks. Medication should never be taken for the first time prior to diving. Unpredictable effects or allergic reactions may prove life-threatening under water. Even so-called "safe" medication should be taken well before an active dive. The following drugs are commonly used for musculoskeletal disorders.

• **NSAIDs / Aspirin:** The use of anti-inflammatory medications for musculoskeletal problems is common. Allergic reactions to aspirin and non-steriodal anti-inflammatory drugs (NSAIDs) have been reported. Aspirin and NSAIDs (such as Motrin®, Naprosyn®, etc.) can impair platelet clotting capability that can last up to one week. Theoretically, impaired platelet function may cause in increased bleeding in the event of barotrauma or neurological DCS. This has occurred in hemorrhagic lesions identified during the microscopic examination of spinal cords of animals experiencing DCS.

Some divers purposefully take aspirin to decrease the ability of platelets to clot around bubbles in the case of DCS. This has been prompted by the former use of aspirin in the treatment of acute DCS. Today, neither aspirin nor NSAIDs are recommended by most dive physicians in treatment of DCI.

• **Corticosteroids:** The use of these drugs may result in electrolyte and fluid imbalance, mood changes and muscle weakness.

• **Narcotics, muscle relaxants and benzodiazapines:** These are potent medications used to relieve moderate to severe pain and muscle spasm. Conditions requiring this level of pain relief generally precludes diving. The effects of these medications on the user's mental status restrict their use. Their interaction with nitrogen narcosis can result in significant mental impairment, which can lead to loss of consciousness, even in those with well-controlled pain.

DAN referral physician James Chimiak, M.D., is Chief of Anesthesiology at the Naval Hospital in Camp Lejeune, N.C., a Navy Diving Medical Officer and a Hyperbaric Medicine Adviser.

— *From Alert Diver, March 2002*

Healthy, But Overweight

DAN Discusses the Issue of Fitness and Diving

By Joel Dovenbarger, Vice President, DAN Medical Services

Q: *I have a friend who wants to learn to scuba dive. Although he does not have any major illnesses, he is overweight — he is 5 feet 6 inches / 168 centimeters tall and weighs about 250 pounds / 112.5 kilograms. He is on a diet recommended by his doctor, does not take any medication and he walks a mile or more every evening. Before I encourage him to dive, what are the chances he can be approved for diving?*

A: Fitness for scuba diving is a complex issue. Certainly, excessive weight can be a reason to restrict diving. We have discussed the issue in past *Alert Divers**.

Consider two questions:

(1) Will an overweight individual suffer any ill health effects by diving? and

(2) Will this individual be able to perform all of the necessary skills to dive successfully?

There is no strong body of evidence to suggest that overweight individuals have a greater risk of DCI or that they suffer more dive-related injuries that divers who are within 10 percent of their ideal body weight. Obesity by itself does not restrict diving.

The best indicator of diving fitness is the individual's general health and level of physical fitness. Keep in mind that divers who are overweight can have a greater risk for cardiac incidents. Consider the exercise regimen — or lack of it — in an overweight individual. Diving requires a diver to lift and carry scuba equipment, swim both underwater and on the surface.

When evaluating a candidate for scuba, a dive physician will consider these factors as well as the "reserve" factor: the increased cardiovascular and respiratory response required when a sudden need arises. In an emergency situation, unfit divers may end up in a near-drowning or fatal dive incident.

* Past issues of Alert Diver contain other articles: "Obesity and Diving Fitness," by Hillary Viders, September/October 1998; "Are You Ready to Dive? Diving Fitness Involves More Than Just Getting Into Good Physical Condition," by Glen H. Egstrom, Ph.D., May/June 1995; "Fitness and Diving: Buddied up, they make a safer, more enjoyable pastime — and contribute to the overall quality of your life," by G. Yancey Mebane, M.D., DAN Associate Medical Director, September/October 1994.

The second question considers an individual's ability to perform self-rescue in the open water and assist a buddy. Both skills are vital to the scuba buddy system. Will your partner's physical conditioning and stamina allow him or her to provide assistance to you at the surface?

These are good questions to ask any dive buddy. Remember, it is difficult to get a heavy person out of the water and onto the back of a boat for cardiopulmonary resuscitation (CPR): you can lose vital minutes. While very obese individuals with limited exercise tolerance may be able to dive in a tranquil sea, when things go wrong or when circumstances change, they may not have sufficient reserves.

Fitness for diving depends on more than just one criterion like weight. Physical fitness and ability are major factors to consider. Other experiences in life don't always prepare a new diver for the potential physical exertion he or she can encounter underwater. For some, lacking physical fitness and endurance and being overweight may be a barrier to dive training. Also, divers who have gained weight over the years might now be considered unfit. These divers do have the advantage of experience, however. Perhaps this can help them avoid situations that can stymie new divers.

Each individual is different, and that's the way diving fitness decisions should be made. Individuals who want to learn to dive should join introductory scuba programs through local dive stores: they could see how they handle themselves with equipment in the water. Equally important, they can get the opinion of a professional instructor who can speak realistically about the physical abilities needed for diving.

For more information on fitness and diving, visit www.DiversAlertNetwork.org/medical for information on: asthma and scuba diving; bone considerations in young divers; cytotoxic drugs, cancer effects; hepatitis; medication while scuba diving; and demographics and illness prevalence in recreational scuba divers.

— *From Alert Diver, July 2001*

Section 7

Gastrointestinal

Gastrointestinal Issues
Consider Them Before Returning to Diving

By David Vote, M.D.

Introduction

Specific medical problems with the gastrointestinal tract (GI system) do not generate many calls on the DAN Medical Information Line. But each year, however, callers ask DAN about fitness-to-dive questions involving the GI system.

Since the GI system contains air spaces, we should view them in relation to scuba diving, along with diseases of the esophagus, stomach, small and large intestines. Like diseases of other body systems, GI problems can weaken individuals and restrict them from certain types of physical activity.

In this series of frequently asked questions, physicians have determined which disease conditions might not be compatible with the physiology of scuba diving. Many individuals with chronic, long-term disease stop diving altogether, while others experiencing more acute disease may only have to wait out their current illness to resume diving. Physicians use their experience and theory to make the most prudent decision when or if one should return to diving. That is what DAN tries to provide with this article and others like it.

More and more individuals with special health concerns are considering scuba for their recreational activity; others may wish to remain in scuba after they develop a medical condition. These articles help address this need for new divers and aid the instructors and stores that are responsible for providing training. Although study data linking medical illnesses to diving is limited, we will continue to do our best to find answers for some of these difficult questions.

— Joel Dovenbarger, R.N., Vice President, DAN Medical Services

Don't Overlook It

Fitness to dive with gastrointestinal conditions doesn't have as high a profile as other conditions, but divers should not be complacent about obtaining such a medical evaluation. Several GI conditions can significantly affect dive safety.

The No-Nos

Two classes of conditions can contain absolute contraindications:

1) those that can cause gastric and intestinal gas-trapping at depth; this can lead to subsequent expansion — and possible rupture — on ascent; and

2) conditions that increase the risk of vomiting underwater, which can lead to panic, rapid ascent, aspiration or drowning.

Relative contraindications involve conditions that can be surgically repaired or have a pattern of acute episodes followed by long symptom-free periods. Many factors prevent patients with such gastrointestinal conditions from diving:

1) Scuba diving in remote locations or from a boat with minimal or no definitive medical care for emergencies;

2) Fluid and electrolyte losses that can occur with acute conditions and rendering the individual more susceptible to DCI and heat stroke;

3) Head-down positions, common in diving, which increase tendency to regurgitate; and

4) Chronic bowel inflammation, which can cause poor nutrition and hence a general lack of cardiovascular fitness, as well as requiring medication incompatible with diving.

Those with either condition should recover general strength and fitness and then resume diving.

COMMON ACUTE CONDITIONS

Gastroenteritis — with Vomiting / Diarrhea

Condition: This irritation of the large and small bowel can lead to diarrhea, vomiting, fever, abdominal pain and cramping, loss of appetite and general weakness. Caused by various bacteria or viruses, it may also indicate other gastrointestinal disease. Often mild and lasting only a day or two, it can be severe and cause life-threatening dehydration.

Fitness and Diving: Malaise and dehydration can both adversely affect divers; one should postpone diving until symptoms have subsided and hydration is normal. To maintain or regain hydration, take extra fluid as tolerated. Divers should remember that medications used to control nausea, vomiting and diarrhea may have some adverse side effects, such as sedation.

Small Bowel Obstruction

Condition: Obstruction of the small bowel refers to the intestinal blockage due to adhesions (external bands), scarring, external compression, twisting or entrapment of the bowel within a hernia (see Hernias). Vomiting and abdominal pain are symptoms.

Fitness and Diving: Almost all individuals with bowel obstruction will be hospitalized. Because of possible over-distension and rupture, those with such an obstruction should avoid diving until the underlying problem has been corrected.

CHRONIC CONDITIONS

These conditions are lifelong or of long duration.

Gastroesophageal Reflux ("Heartburn" or "Waterbrash")

Condition: "Reflux" is a backward flow of acid or food from the stomach into the esophagus. Symptoms include burning upper abdominal or chest pain, sour taste or food regurgitation, which can happen when divers are in the head-down position. Symptoms can be exacerbated by:
• drinking alcohol;
• smoking;
• an ulcer or hiatal hernia;
• certain medications such as aspirin or non-steroidal anti-inflammatory drugs (NSAIDs); or
• a tight-fitting belt or wetsuit.
Physicians treat reflux with medications or through surgery.

Fitness and Diving: While most people may experience occasional mild heartburn, if reflux of gastric contents occurs while one is diving, a diver could be at significant risk. Aspirating food or acid into the lungs or into the regulator could be fatal. Individuals with significant reflux should not dive.

Achalasia

Condition: A disorder of the esophageal smooth muscle, achalasia has two components: the lower esophageal sphincter that does not relax with swallowing and abnormal contractions that replace the normal movement of the esophagus.

Fitness and Diving: Food and secretions can collect in a pool in the lower esophagus and cause regurgitation when the diver is in the head-down position. As with reflux, diving is not recommended.

Inflammatory Bowel Disease

Condition: Inflammatory bowel disease (IBD) can result from ulcerative colitis or Crohn's disease. The major symptoms are diarrhea, which can be bloody; abdominal pain; nausea; and vomiting, often with fever and weight loss.

Commonly, IBD usually occurs to divers aged 20 to 40 years and who experience the following:

1) Intermittent disease with long periods of normal bowel functioning; and

2) Complications including anemia, electrolyte disturbances, dehydration, poor absorption of fluids, liver disease and generalized fatigue.

Drug treatment often involves corticosteroids, which can impair one's ability to fight infections.

Fitness and Diving: Someone with symptomatic IBD should not dive until treatment has caused remission and they do not need medication. A person experiencing no significant complication of IBD or its treatment and has adequate cardiovascular fitness could consider diving.

Abdominal Surgery

Condition: This is a surgical procedure in which a portion of the intra-abdominal contents or the abdominal wall has been removed, manipulated or repaired.

Fitness and Diving: Diving in the ocean exposes the skin to innumerable microorganisms. To minimize infection, divers should allow surgical wounds to heal fully before diving. A small proportion of abdominal wounds may develop into incisional hernias, leading to bowel entrapment. One should avoid swimming or lifting heavy objects such as scuba tanks until the abdominal muscles have fully recovered from surgery (4-6 weeks). As for when to resume swimming and diving, a surgeon can best assess the wound's status.

And, the fatigue and lack of general fitness present after any surgery can limit a diver. Gradual exercise under the direction of a doctor may help the diver regain cardiovascular performance and general fitness.

Hernias

Condition: A hernia is the protrusion of a loop or portion of an organ or tissue through an abnormal opening, usually in the abdominal wall (in the groin, or inguinal region, alongside the artery supplying the thigh, through an unhealed, surgical incision) or in the diaphragm. Hernias can also occur internally, when the bowel protrudes through a narrow opening or pocket in the peritoneum, the abdomen's internal lining.

Bowel protruding into a hernia can become entrapped, causing an obstruction or damage to the bowel. Surgical repair is usually recommended for hernias.

Fitness and Diving: During an ascent, a trapped segment of bowel containing gas will expand; it could rupture and compromise its blood supply. For this reason, individuals should not dive with an unrepaired hernia.

Hiatal Hernia

Condition: In a hiatal hernia, part of the stomach protrudes into the chest cavity through the diaphragm's esophageal opening. Two main types of hernia are distinguishable, since they have different implications for fitness to dive.

In a sliding hiatal hernia, the upper portion of the stomach slides upward in the space occupied by the esophagus. This hernia, found in a large percentage of North American adults, can cause gastroesophageal reflux, but it often has no symptoms. A paraesophageal hernia is a protrusion of the stomach through a separate opening of the diaphragm.

Fitness and Diving: Significant gastroesophageal reflux should be treated before diving, but a sliding hiatal hernia does not by itself contraindicate diving. Part of the stomach can become trapped within a paraesophageal hiatal hernia, and could rupture during ascent. Thus, paraesophageal hiatal hernia is considered a contraindication to diving.

A few who have had surgical repair of their hiatal hernia (e.g., fundoplication) can suffer from gas-bloat syndrome, which is associated with gaseous distension of the stomach. This is believed to occur due to one's inability to expel swallowed air by belching. During an ascent, this distension can also lead to gastric rupture. The symptom usually resolves within a few weeks. If the distension persists, however, diving is not advised.

Peptic Ulceration

Condition: A peptic ulcer is a breakdown of the inner lining of the stomach or duodenum, the first part of the small intestine. Acid and pepsin, the chief active ingredient in gastric juice with acid, play major roles in creating and developing this ulcer. Peptic ulcer includes duodenal ulcer (DU) and gastric ulcer (GU); both are chronic diseases, often caused by a bacterium *Helicobacter pylori*. They may be caused by stress or by ingesting drugs, most commonly, aspirin and non-steroidal anti-inflammatory drugs such as ibuprofen and naproxen. Peptic ulcer is caused when defenses provided by the mucous membrane fail to protect the lining of the stomach from the corrosive effects of acid and pepsin.

Fitness and Diving: Symptoms can be sudden, severe and disabling. Usually consisting of pain in the upper central abdomen, it is often described as a sharp, burning or gnawing pain. Complications include bleeding, which can cause anemia, general fatigue and a reduced tolerance for exercise. Other complications include perforation, which requires immediate surgery, and obstruction of the duodenum.

Diving is not recommended for individuals with symptoms of peptic ulcer disease. However, one who is symptom-free for more than a month may consider diving.

Some medications used to control stomach acids may cause side effects. Check with your physician. Peptic ulcer may also be corrected by surgery. After abdominal surgery and all activities have returned to normal, one may consider scuba diving (see "Dumping Syndrome").

Dumping Syndrome

Condition: Following peptic ulcer surgery, some patients experience wide-ranging symptoms called dumping syndrome. Symptoms often occur in the early post-surgery period. Experienced within 30 minutes after eating, these symptoms include palpitations, light-headedness, sweating and a drop in blood pressure upon standing. Late dumping syndrome, which occurs 30 minutes to three hours after eating, can involve any of these symptoms or additional confusion and even loss of consciousness.

Fitness and Diving: For obvious reasons, diving is not recommended with these symptoms.

Ileostomy and Colostomy

Condition: An "ostomy" is an opening created surgically to allow the bowel to empty through the abdominal wall. Connection of the end of the small bowel and the large bowel in this manner are known, respectively, as ileostomy and colostomy.

The continent, or moderate, ileostomy is a loop of small bowel fashioned under the skin with a nipple valve to prevent spillage. Ileal effluent collects in this reservoir, which must be emptied with a soft rubber catheter. The second type opens directly onto the abdomen, requiring an external ileostomy or colostomy appliance.

Fitness and Diving: The direct type of ileostomy and colostomy poses no danger to the diver. Ensuring a secure fit of the external bag can prevent spillage of fecal material. A continent ileostomy poses theoretical risk if gas swallowed during the dive cannot escape through the ileostomy site.

For one with continent ostomy, an gastroenterologist or surgeon should make an individual assessment.

Esophageal Diverticulae

Condition: Diverticula, protrusions of the esophagus wall, can occur at various sites, causing a number of symptoms, ranging from halitosis, or offensive breath, to regurgitation of saliva and food particles and difficulty in swallowing.

Fitness and Diving: Because of the risk of aspirating pooled secretions and food debris when one dives in the head-down position, esophageal diverticula may disqualify one for diving.

Diverticular Disease of the Colon

Condition: Diverticulae consist of herniations, or saclike protrusions of the inner lining through the outer muscular wall. Most common in the large bowel, these diverticulae become more common with advancing age. The incidence ranges between 20 and 50 percent in Western populations over 50. The most frequent complication, diverticulitis, is inflammation in or around the diverticular sac. Such inflammation may vary from small, localized abscesses to generalized peritonitis or inflammation of the stomach lining.

Fitness and Diving: Uncomplicated small or large bowel diverticula should pose no problem to diving. Anyone with symptoms indicating a complication should have prior medical evaluation before clearance to dive.

Liver Cirrhosis

Condition: Liver cirrhosis, a destructive process resulting from fibrosis of liver tissue, is most commonly due to toxic substances (alcohol) or viral infections (hepatitis). Complications include bleeding from the esophagus or stomach, impaired blood coagulation, accumulation of fluid in the abdomen and impaired ability to detoxify medications.

Fitness and Diving: If otherwise fit, divers who, have a normal response to exercise, can dive if they have mild cirrhosis, with no symptoms or secondary complications. Before diving, they should be evaluated by their physicians. In cases where cirrhosis is more severe, the rigors of scuba and the effects of the disease could impair a diver's ability. In such cases, scuba is not recommended.

Chronic Pancreatitis

Condition: Chronic pancreatitis is a progressive and destructive process resulting in fibrosis and calcification of pancreatic tissue. Loss of pancreatic function can reduce or eliminate the production of insulin. Chronic pancreatitis (70-80 percent) has many causes, including chronic alcohol use and gallstones. Endemic in tropical parts of the world, it can be hereditary as one ages, and it can be caused by other illness and disease.

It may present as indigestion, nausea or stomach pain; it can be triggered by eating or drinking alcohol. While this disease can cause chronic malabsorption of nutrients leading to severe weight loss, it can also lead to diabetes.

Fitness and Diving: Scuba diving depends on the level of fitness and health of the individual. If a diver's condition has not progressed to the point of needing medication control for chronic pain, if the diver can eat without the gastrointestinal side effects of pancreatitis, including diabetes, and if the diver can perform exercise without unusual fatigue, then scuba may be permitted. However, the manifestation of continuous and chronic symptoms of pancreatitis would make diving with symptoms unwise.

Dr. David A. Vote, MB, BS, FANZCA, DipDHM, is an anesthesiologist working at St. Vincent's Hospital in Melbourne, Australia. During his two years at Duke University Medical Center and DAN (1998-2000), he completed two fellowships in Diving and Hyperbaric Medicine and Pediatric Anesthesiology. Currently, he assists DAN South East Asia-Pacific, based in Australia, with ongoing diving medicine research.

— From Alert Diver, April 2001

Section 8

Hematology (Blood)

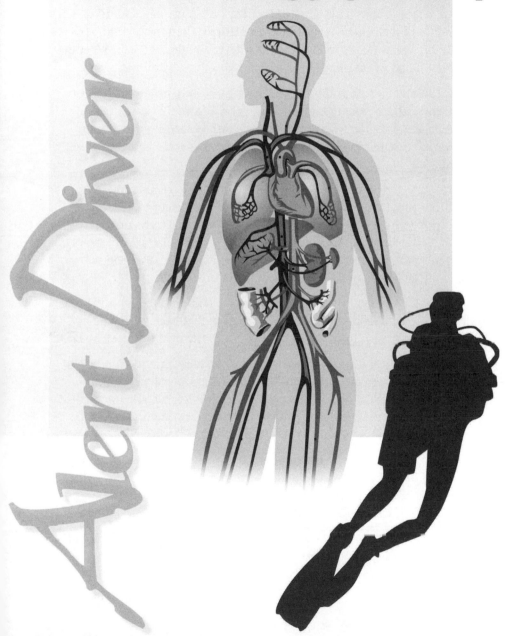

Risks of Diving with Hemophilia

By Joel Dovenbarger, Vice President, DAN Medical Services

Q: *I recently worked with an adult tourist who wanted to do a "Discover Diving" course while he was vacationing on the island. He listed hemophilia on his diving medical check-out form. Isn't scuba diving contraindicated for people with hemophilia?*

A: Hemophilia is an inherited disorder of blood coagulation, which can range from a very severe problem to a relatively mild, controllable bleeding disorder. Persons with the highest risk for bleeding would not be good candidates for scuba diving for several reasons.

The most likely risk areas for a scuba student with hemophilia are sinus, middle ear and pulmonary barotrauma. While a sinus or ear squeeze may result in a small amount of inconsequential bleeding in a person with normal coagulation, such bleeding could be severe in a person with hemophilia.

Certain types of decompression illness (DCI) can also cause bleeding. DCI of the spinal cord can cause bleeding within the cord itself, and inner ear decompression sickness can cause bleeding in the organs responsible for hearing (cochlea) and balance (vestibular apparatus, or semicircular canals). As yet, the response to therapy in a person with a blood clotting disorder after such bleeding is unknown.

Finally, many individuals with hemophilia have had repeated bleeding into joints, causing pain and joint damage. In such individuals it may be difficult to distinguish pain due to bleeding from the pain triggered by DCI.

Individuals who are well-informed about their disorder and who have undergone proper treatment to minimize bleeding problems can probably dive. Still, they should use conservative profiles, be able to equalize middle ear and sinus pressures, and be instructed on the possible risks of bleeding into these areas.

One final concern is that many popular dive sites are remote locations where the appropriate level of medical care may not be available. Individuals with any chronic disease requiring specific medication cannot always rely on local medical facilities.

If you have a chronic ailment, have a contingency plan before diving at a remote site. A prospective diver with hemophilia should be evaluated by a physician with these specific issues in mind.

— *From Alert Diver, November/December 1997*

Section 9

Marine Life

I've Been Stung: What Should I Do?

By Paul S. Auerbach, M.D., M.S.

Editor's Note: We asked DAN consulting physician Dr. Paul Auerbach to compile a "short list" of DAN's most frequently asked questions in the treatment of marine animal injuries. The result is this informative article.

Coral Scrapes

Q: *I was snorkeling in Bonaire over a patch of elkhorn coral and dove down to get a closer look at a sea fan. A dive boat zoomed by and I got shoved by the swell. My knee scraped against a horn of coral. I was surprised that it stung. Rubbing it didn't help. When I got back to the hotel, one of the cooks told me to rub it with meat tenderizer, but we didn't have any. Now it's been two weeks and the skin on my knee doesn't seem to be healing. What should I do?*

A: Coral scrapes are the most common injuries from marine life incurred by divers and snorkelers. The surface of coral is covered by soft living material, which is easily torn from the rigid (abrasive) structure underneath, and thus deposited into the scrape or cut. This greatly prolongs the wound-healing process by causing inflammation and, occasionally, initiating an infection. Cuts and scrapes from sharp-edged coral and barnacles tend to fester and take weeks or even months to heal.

The Treatment

1. Scrub the cut vigorously with soap and water, and then flush the wound with large amounts of water.
2. Flush the wound with a half-strength solution of hydrogen peroxide in water. Rinse again with water.
3. Apply a thin layer of neomycin (neosporin), and cover the wound with a dry, sterile, and non-adherent dressing. If no ointment or dressing is available, the wound can be left open. Thereafter, it should be cleaned and re-dressed twice a day.
4. If the wound shows any sign of infection (extreme redness, pus, swollen lymph glands), the injured person (particularly one with impairment of his or her immune system) should be started by a qualified health professional on an antibiotic, taking into consideration the possibility of a *Vibrio* infection. *Vibrio* bacteria are found more often in the marine environment than on land, and can rapidly cause an over-

whelming illness and even death in a human with an impaired immune system (e.g., someone with AIDS, diabetes or chronic liver disease).

Coral poisoning occurs if coral abrasions or cuts are extensive or are from a particularly toxic species. Symptoms include a wound that heals poorly or continues to drain pus or cloudy fluid, swelling around the cut, swollen lymph glands, fever, chills and fatigue. If these symptoms are present, the injured person should see a physician, who may elect to treat the person with an antibiotic or corticosteroid medication.

Sea Urchin Spine Punctures

Q: *I was chasing a big marble ray underwater near Cocos Island — I wanted to photograph it — and wasn't paying attention to my buoyancy. I brushed by a rock wall and suddenly felt severe burning in my arm and elbow. There were 15 black sea urchin spines sticking out of my forearm. The spines had gone right through my diveskin. I remembered hearing that it helps to urinate on a sea urchin sting, so I tried it, but it didn't help. Most of the black spots on my arm have disappeared, but I still can see two, and my wrist is starting to swell. What should I do?*

A: Some sea urchins are covered with sharp venom-filled spines that can easily penetrate and break off into the skin. Others (found in the South Pacific) may have small pincerlike appendages that grasp their victims and inoculate them with venom from a sac within each pincer. Sea urchin punctures or stings are painful wounds, most often of the hands or feet. If a person receives many wounds simultaneously, the reaction may be so severe as to cause extreme muscle spasm, difficulty in breathing, weakness and collapse.

The Treatment

1. Immerse the wound in non-scalding hot water to tolerance (110 to 113° F / 43.3 to 45° C). This frequently provides pain relief. Other field remedies, such as application of vinegar or urine, are less likely to diminish the pain. If necessary, administer pain medication appropriate to control the pain.

2. Carefully remove any readily visible spines. Do not dig around in the skin to try to fish them out — this risks crushing the spines and making them more difficult to remove. Do not intentionally crush the spines. Purple or black markings in the skin immediately after a sea urchin encounter do not necessarily indicate the presence of a retained spine fragment. The discoloration more likely is dye leached from the surface of a spine, commonly from a black urchin (*Diadema* species). The dye will be absorbed over 24 to 48 hours, and the discoloration will disappear. If there are still black markings after 48 to 72 hours, then a spine fragment is likely present.

3. If the sting is caused by a species with pincer organs (see "A" in this section), use hot water immersion (#1 in this section), then apply shaving cream or a soap paste and shave the area.

4. Seek the care of a physician if spines are retained in the hand or foot, or near a joint. They may need to be removed surgically, to minimize infection, inflammation and damage to nerves or important blood vessels.

5. If the wound shows any sign of infection (extreme redness, pus, swollen regional lymph glands) or if a spine has penetrated deeply into a joint, the injured person (particularly one with impairment of his or her immune system) should be started on an antibiotic by a qualified health professional, taking into consideration the possibility of a *Vibrio* infection (see #4 under "Coral Scrapes").

6. If a spine puncture in the palm of the hand results in a persistent swollen finger(s) without any sign of infection (fever, redness, swollen lymph glands in the elbow or armpit), then it may become necessary to treat the injured person with a seven- to 14-day course of a non-steroidal anti-inflammatory drug (e.g., ibuprofen) or, in a more severe case, oral prednisone, a corticosteroid medication.

Lionfish, Scorpionfish & Stonefish Envenomations

Q: *Last week I got a saltwater aquarium with an anemone and a small lionfish. I saw the lionfish swimming through the anemone and thought it was going to hurt the anemone, so I reached in the tank and pushed the lionfish away. It nailed me on the fingers, and now they're all swollen and blistered. Is there anything I can do?*

A: Lionfish (as well as scorpionfish and stonefish) possess dorsal, anal and pelvic spines that transport venom from venom glands into puncture wounds. Common reactions include redness or blanching, swelling and blistering (lionfish). The injuries can be extraordinarily painful and occasionally life-threatening (in the case of a stonefish).

The Treatment

Soaking the wound in non-scalding hot water to tolerance (110 to 113° F / 43.3 to 45° C)
• may provide dramatic relief of pain from a lionfish sting,
• is less likely to be effective for a scorpionfish sting, and
• may have little or no effect on the pain from a stonefish sting, *but it should be done* nonetheless, because the heat may inactivate some of the harmful components of the venom.

If the injured person appears intoxicated or is weak, vomiting, short of breath or unconscious, seek immediate advanced medical care.

Wound care is standard, so, for the blistering wound noted previously, appropriate therapy would be a topical antiseptic (such as silver sulfadiazene [Silvadene] cream or neomycin ointment) and daily dressing changes. A scorpionfish sting frequently requires weeks to months to heal, and therefore requires the attention of a physician. There is an antivenin available to physicians to help manage the sting of the dreaded stonefish.

Stingray Envenomation

Q: *My daughter was walking in the surf near Panama City, Fla., when she got stung. She was barefooted and said something wrapped up around her foot right before she felt the pain. One of the lifeguards pulled out a small spine, and then she saw a doctor. He put her on an antibiotic, but the cut on her foot doesn't seem to be healing. What should she do?*

A: A stingray does its damage by lashing upward in defense with a muscular tail-like appendage, which carries up to four sharp, swordlike stingers. The stingers are supplied with venom, so that the injury created is both a deep puncture or laceration and an envenomation.

The pain from a stingray wound can be excruciating and accompanied by bleeding, weakness, vomiting, headache, fainting, shortness of breath, paralysis, collapse and occasionally, death. Most wounds involve the feet and legs, as unwary waders and swimmers tread upon the creatures hidden in the sand.

The Treatment

1. Rinse the wound with whatever clean water is available. Immediately immerse the wound in non-scalding hot water to tolerance (110 to 113° F / 43.3 to 45° C). This may provide some pain relief. Generally, it is necessary to soak the wound for 30 to 90 minutes. Gently extract any obvious piece of stinger.
2. Scrub the wound with soap and water. Do not try to sew or tape it closed — doing so could promote a serious infection by "sealing in" harmful bacteria.
3. Apply a dressing and seek medical help. If more than 12 hours will pass before a doctor can be reached, start the injured person on an antibiotic (ciprofloxacin, trimethoprim-sulfamethoxazole or doxycycline) to oppose *Vibrio* bacteria.
4. Administer pain medication sufficient to control the pain.
5. Some wounds remain chronic, eventually requiring excision of the wound.

Prevention of Stingray Injuries

1. Always shuffle your feet when wading in stingray waters.
2. Always inspect the bottom before resting a limb in the sand.
3. Never handle a stingray unless you know what you are doing or unless the stingrays are definitely familiar with divers and swimmers (e.g., the rays in "Stingray City" off Grand Cayman Island in the British West Indies). Even then, respect them for the wild creatures they are — the less you handle them the better for them and for you, too.

Sea Bather's Eruption, Seaweed Dermatitis & Swimmer's Itch

Q: *I was swimming for exercise out in front of my hotel in Cozumel when my entire body started to tingle. I didn't see anything in the water, so I kept swimming. A few minutes later, I swam into a swarm of tiny pulsating brown blobs. They didn't have any tentacles that I could see. The stinging got pretty bad, especially underneath my bathing suit. I hosed off on the beach and jumped in the shower, and that seemed to help. Now I have an ugly red rash under my neck and where my bathing suit goes. I'm having trouble sleeping, and it seems like I'm tired all the time. What should I do?*

A: Sea Bather's Eruption

Often misnamed "sea lice" (which are true crustacean parasites of fish, and which inflict miniscule bites), sea bather's eruption occurs in sea water and involves predominately bathing suit-covered areas of the skin, rather than exposed areas. The skin rash distribution is very similar to that from seaweed dermatitis (read below), but no seaweed is found on the skin.

The cause is stings from the nematocysts (stinging cells) of the larval forms of certain anemones and thimble jellyfishes. The injured person may notice a tingling sensation under the bathing suit (breasts, groin, cuffs of wetsuits) while still in the water, which is made much worse if he/she takes a freshwater rinse (shower) while still wearing the suit. The rash usually consists of red bumps, which may become dense and confluent (i.e., run together in a mass). Itching is severe and may become painful.

The Treatment

Treatment consists of immediate application of vinegar, rubbing alcohol, or papain solution (for decontamination), although these may not be very effective. Some persons note topical papain (e.g., meat tenderizer) solution to be the most effective. This is followed by hydrocortisone lotion 1 percent twice a day, noting that a physician would likely prescribe a more potent topical steroid. Topical calamine lotion with 1 percent menthol may be soothing.

If the reaction is severe, the injured person may suffer from headache, fever, chills, weakness, vomiting, itchy eyes and burning on urination, and should be treated with oral prednisone.

The stinging cells may remain in the bathing suit even after it dries, so once a person has sustained sea bather's eruption, the clothing should undergo machine washing through a hot cycle or be thoroughly rinsed in alcohol or vinegar, then be washed by hand with soap and water.

A: Seaweed Dermatitis

Sea bather's eruption is easy to confuse with "seaweed dermatitis." There are more than 3,000 species of algae, which range in size from 1 micron to 100 meters in length. The blue-green algae, *Microcoleus lyngbyaceus*, is a fine, hairlike plant that gets inside the bathing suit of the unwary aquanaut in Hawaii and Florida waters, particularly during the summer months. Usually, skin under the suit remains in moist contact with the algae (the other skin dries or is rinsed off), and becomes red and itchy, with occasional blistering and / or weeping. The reaction may start a few minutes to a few hours after the victim leaves the water.

The Treatment

Treatment consists of a vigorous soap-and-water scrub, followed by a rinse with isopropyl (rubbing) alcohol. Apply 1 percent hydrocortisone lotion twice a day. If the reaction is severe, oral prednisone may be administered.

A: Swimmer's Itch

Also called "clamdigger's itch," swimmer's itch is caused by skin contact with *cercariae*, which are the immature larval forms of parasitic schistosomes (flatworms) found throughout the world in both fresh and salt waters. Snails and birds are the intermediate hosts for the flatworms. They release hundreds of fork-tailed microscopic *cercariae* into the water.

The affliction is contracted when a film of *cercariae*-infested water dries on exposed (uncovered by clothing) skin. The *cercariae* penetrate the outer layer of the skin, where itching is noted within minutes. Shortly afterwards, the skin becomes reddened and swollen, with an intense rash and, occasionally, hives. Blisters may develop over the next 24 to 48 hours.

Untreated, the affliction is limited to 1 to 2 weeks. Persons who have suffered swimmer's itch previously may be more severely affected on repeated exposures, which suggests that an allergic response may be a factor.

The Treatment

Swimmer's itch can be prevented by briskly rubbing the skin with a towel immediately after leaving the water, to prevent the *cercariae* from having time to penetrate the skin. Once the reaction has occurred, the skin should be lightly rinsed with isopropyl (rubbing) alcohol and then coated with calamine lotion. If the reaction is severe, the injured person may be treated with oral prednisone.

Because the *cercariae* are present in greatest concentration in shallow, warmer water (where the snails are), swimmers should try to avoid these areas.

Jellyfish Stings

"Jellyfish" is the term commonly used to describe an enormous number of marine animals that are capable of inflicting a painful, and occasionally life-threatening, sting. These include fire coral, hydroids, jellyfishes (including "sea wasps") and anemones. The stings occur when the victim comes into contact with the creature's tentacles or other appendages, which may carry millions of small stinging cells, each equipped with venom and a microscopic stinger.

Depending on the species, size, geographic location, time of year and other natural factors, stings can range in severity from mild burning and skin redness to excruciating pain and severe blistering with generalized illness (nausea, vomiting, shortness of breath, muscle spasm and low blood pressure). Broken-off tentacles that are fragmented in the surf or washed up on the beach can retain their toxicity for months and should not be handled, even if they appear to be dried out and withered.

The dreaded box jellyfish (*Chironex fleckeri*) of northern Australia contains one of the most potent animal venoms known to man. A sting from one of these creatures can induce death in minutes from cessation of breathing, abnormal heart rhythms and profound low blood pressure (shock).

The Treatment

BE PREPARED TO TREAT AN ALLERGIC REACTION FOLLOWING A JELLYFISH STING. If possible, carry an allergy kit, including injectable epinephrine (adrenaline) and an oral antihistamine.

The following therapy is recommended for all unidentified jellyfish and other creatures with stinging cells:

1. If the sting is believed to be from the box jellyfish (*Chironex fleckeri*), immediately flood the wound with vinegar (5 percent acetic acid). Keep the injured person as still as possible. Continuously apply the vinegar until the individual can be brought to medical attention, unless you are able to apply the pressure-immobilization technique. If you are out at sea or on an isolated beach, allow the vinegar to soak the tentacles or stung skin for 10 minutes before attempting to remove adherent tentacles or to further treat the wound. In Australia, surf lifesavers (lifeguards) may carry antivenin, which is given as an intra-muscular injection a first aid measure.

2. For all other stings, if a topical decontaminant (e.g., vinegar, isopropyl [rubbing] alcohol, one-quarter-strength household ammonia or baking soda) is available, apply it liberally onto the skin.

If it is a liquid, continuously soak a compress. (Be advised that some authorities advise against the use of alcohol because of scientific evaluations that have revealed that some nematocysts discharge because of this chemical's application.) Since not all jellyfish are identical, it is extremely helpful to know ahead of time what works for the stingers in your specific geographic location.

Apply the decontaminant for 30 minutes or until pain is relieved. A paste made from unseasoned meat tenderizer (do not exceed 15 minutes' application time, particularly upon the sensitive skin of small children) or papaya fruit may be helpful. Do not apply any organic solvent, such as kerosene, turpentine or gasoline.

Until the decontaminant is available, you may rinse the skin with sea water. Do *not* rinse the skin with fresh water or apply ice directly to the skin. Although a brisk freshwater stream (forceful shower) may have sufficient force to physically remove the microscopic stinging cells, fresh water is likely to cause the cells to fire, increasing the envenomation. A non-moist ice or cold pack may be useful to diminish pain, but take care to wipe away any surface moisture (condensation) prior to the application.

3. After decontamination, apply a lather of shaving cream or soap and shave the affected area with a razor. In a pinch, you can use a paste of sand or mud in sea water and a clam shell.

4. Reapply the primary decontaminant for 15 minutes.

5. Apply a thin coating of hydrocortisone lotion (0.5 to 1 percent) twice a day. Anesthetic ointment (such as lidocaine hydrochloride 2.5 percent or a benzocaine-containing spray) may provide short-term pain relief.

6. If the victim has a large area involved (entire arm or leg, face, or genitals), is very young or very old, or shows signs of generalized illness (nausea, vomiting, weakness, shortness of breath or chest pain), seek help from a doctor. If a person has placed tentacle fragments in his mouth, have him swish and spit whatever potable liquid is available. If there is already swelling in the mouth (muffled voice, difficulty swallow-ing, enlarged tongue and lips), do not give anything by mouth, protect the airway and rapidly transport the victim to a hospital.

Ciguatera Poisoning

Q: *We were on a liveaboard in Fiji, and the cook served us a meal of jack from a real monster someone hauled up during our crossing. In retrospect, I probably shouldn't have eaten it, because when I asked him whether it was safe, he said: "Sure, because when the flies are attracted to the fish, it's OK." About an hour after we ate, most of us got sick, throwing up and having diarrhea. I felt like I was floating and my lips started burning. Now I feel dizzy and generally miserable. What happened?*

A: Ciguatera fish poisoning involves a large number of tropical and semitropical bottom-feeding fish that dine on plants or smaller fish, which have accumulated toxins from microscopic dinoflagellates, such as *Gambierdiscus toxicus*. Therefore, the larger the fish, the greater the toxicity. The ciguatoxin-carrying fish most commonly ingested include the jack, barracuda, grouper and snapper.

Symptoms, which usually begin 15 to 30 minutes after eating the contaminated fish, include abdominal pain, nausea, vomiting, diarrhea, tongue and throat numbness, tooth pain, difficulty in walking, blurred vision, skin rash, itching, tearing of the eyes, weakness, twitching muscles, incoordination, difficulty sleeping and occasional difficulty in breathing. A classic sign of ciguatera intoxication is the reversal of hot and cold sensation (hot liquids seem cold, and vice versa), which may reflect general hypersensitivity to temperature.

Persons can become severely ill shortly after they are poisoned, with heart problems, low blood pressure, deficiencies of the central and peripheral nervous systems, and generalized collapse. Unfortunately, many of the debilitating, but not life-threatening, symptoms may persist in varying severity for weeks to months.

The Treatment

Treatment is for the most part based upon symptoms without any specific antidote, although certain drugs are beginning to prove useful for aspects of the syndrome, such as intravenous mannitol for abnormal nervous system behavior and abnormal heart rhythms. A physician must undertake these therapies.

Prochlorperazine may be useful for vomiting; hydroxyzine or cool showers may be useful for itching. There are chemical tests to determine the presence of ciguatoxins in fish and in the bloodstream of humans, but not yet a specific antidote. If a person displays symptoms of ciguatera fish poisoning, he/she should be see a physician promptly.

During recovery from ciguatera poisoning, the injured person should exclude the following from the diet: fish, fish sauces, shellfish, shellfish sauces, alcoholic beverages, nuts and nut oils.

Diving While on Medications for Stings

In general, it is safe to dive while taking an antibiotic or corticosteroid medication. If a wound infection is more than minor or is expanding, however, diving should be curtailed until it becomes minor, is no longer progressing and can be easily covered with a dressing.

Most injuries from animals result from chance encounters. Be an alert diver, and respect their personal space. If you're injured, follow the advice you find here, and call DAN.

Be aware that there is a new combination sunscreen-jellyfish sting inhibitor product, Safe Sea, on the market, which appears to be quite effective in preventing or diminishing the intensity of stings from certain jellyfishes, including those that cause seabather's eruption.

Paul Auerbach, M.D., M.S., is a consultant on hazardous marine life to DAN, medical editor for Dive Training magazine, advisor to numerous medical, recreational and scientific organizations and recognized internationally as a leading expert on the clinical management of hazardous marine encounters.

— *From Alert Diver, January/February 1998*

Taking the Sting Out Of Jellyfish Envenomations

Knowing First Aid Basics is a Necessity for Divers

By Joseph W. Burnett, M.D.

A close encounter with a jellyfish, often sudden and painful, can occur before a diver realizes it. To successfully treat a severe jellyfish stings — jellyfish envenomation — you should first know how to recognize the animal.

The diver, swimmer or snorkeler who cannot identify the offending stinger should draw the creature, then document the location, time and water conditions in which the sting occurred. These particulars help pinpoint certain species, aiding subsequent treatment.

First Aid Basics

Regardless of the species of the stinger you encounter, some basic first-aid guidelines will aid in treating jellyfish stings:

• To stabilize the injured person's vital signs is top priority. First check the ABCs — Airway, Breathing and Circulation. If necessary, proceed with CPR or artificial resuscitation.

• Keep the injured diver/swimmer/snorkeler quiet and comfortable. Stings from some jellyfish can be very painful, and, if left unchecked, the pain and excitement will stimulate muscular activity, circulating the venom — in larger doses — through the body. Depending on the injured person's condition, you might need to administer analgesic drugs.

• Treat the affected areas. The jellyfish releases a stingingapparatus contained within nematocysts or cnidocytes which can result in a painful injury. Many stingers can remain on the person's skin and, unless removed or neutralized, they will continue to sting, especially when they're rubbed.

• Apply vinegar or use a 50-50 mixture of water and baking soda on the affected area. In the waters of the Gulf and Atlantic coast below the Chesapeake Bay, a good rule of thumb for neutralizing jellyfish nemato-cysts is to apply vinegar in liberal amounts. For stings along the Atlantic Coast north of the Chesapeake Bay and in the central and northern Pacific regions, applying a thin mixture — 50 percent water and 50 percent baking soda — is the recommended application.

What's Next?

These measures, though essential, don't always stop the pain or swelling. The venom-coated nematocyst thread has already penetrated the outer layer of skin, where topical agents exert their action. Topicals are ineffective in pain relief. Ointments generally do not work.

A physician should treat signs of post-envenomation. The doctor may order blood serum studies to check for antibodies produced after the sting or take skin scrapings for microscopic examination to pinpoint the nematocysts characteristic of individual species.

The doctor may counteract hyperpigmentation (skin discoloration) with topical hydroquinone bleaches, may relieve persistent nodular lesions by injectable corticosteroid or may address urticaria, or allergic swelling, by using antihistamines, with subsequent itching controlled by topical antipruritic (anti-itch) lotions containing menthol.

Stinging creatures seem to like some beaches more than others, especially the Australian coastline, where barrier nets have been set up to discourage their visits. While partially successful against adult jellyfish, such nets permit the younger, smaller larval and medusa forms of these and other stinging animals to pass through. Even at a beach with a jellyfish net, you should remain alert for the creatures.

Every day, somewhere in the world, divers, swimmers, snorkelers and others enjoying water sports report incidents with stinging animals, making the study of marine envenomations both an active and continually changing field. Doctors believe that in the future they will use species-specific measures in both the first aid and the treatment of these injuries.

Dr. Joseph W. Burnett is professor and acting chairman of the Department of Dermatology, University of Maryland. A leading authority on jellyfish stings, Burnett is also editor of "The Jellyfish Newsletter."

— From Alert Diver, March/April 2000

No Fish Tale

If You Eat Fish, It's Good to Know About Ciguatera — Before You Get Sick

By Joel Dovenbarger, Vice President, DAN Medical Services

Q: *My dive buddy had quite a scare last year when we went diving in the Caribbean. After four days of diving, she developed numbness in her hands and her face. We thought she had decompression illness, but we had stayed well within our dive computer limits and completed safety stops on all our dives. She then experienced nausea, vomiting and diarrhea. The bottom line: she was treated for ciguatera fish poisoning. Is this a common problem in the Caribbean?*

A: Each year DAN handles from 6-12 calls about ciguatera. Generally found between 35 degrees north latitude and 35 degrees south latitude around the globe, ciguatera is not a major complaint by divers, but it can be a very serious illness when someone eats sufficient amounts of toxin-laden fish. The toxin attacks the neurological, gastrointestinal and cardiovascular systems, and it causes a variety of generalized symptoms. When physicians diagnose decompression illness, ciguatera is one of the illnesses that must be ruled out. Many ciguatera symptoms are similar to decompression illness and can make diagnosis difficult.

Divers should remember some general information about ciguatera poisoning. First, how do you contract ciguatera?

Ciguatera is reportedly more common in reef fish and larger, older fish that are higher up on the fish food chain. The most notable culprits are red snappers, amberjacks, groupers, surgeonfish and barracudas. Cooking does not affect the toxin, which is undetectable by odor, color or taste. Although the toxin is not commonly found in the United States, it's advisable to avoid eating the organ meats of any fish, as these concentrate the toxin.

One can experience symptoms shortly after ingesting the fish, or they can begin in the hours following. Rarely do they occur after 24 hours. The most common gastrointestinal symptoms are abdominal cramps, nausea, vomiting and diarrhea, symptoms not generally associated with DCI.

Numbness in the face, hands and feet are common neurological signs, but they are not limited to these areas. When facial numbness occurs, we at DAN always ask if the diver has numbness around the mouth (perioral) or in the tongue. This particular sign occurs in ciguatera poisoning, but it is not usually reported in DCI. Another common sign of ciguatera poisoning is temperature reversal in the hands and mouth, where cold feels hot to touch and hot feels cool — also not a sign reported with DCI. Additionally, once ingested, ciguatoxin is reported to makes foods have a metallic taste. Other generalized symptoms are muscle and joint pain, weakness, fatigue, rash and, less commonly, chills, itching, headache and dizziness.

If enough ciguatoxin is ingested, severe cardiovascular symptoms may occur. The toxin can produce both hypertension and hypotension, with a very slow heart rate. And although it's rare, ciguatera poisoning can be fatal.

For a full recovery, one must get immediate treatment. When used early, Mannitol, an intravenous solution, has been effective in preventing some of the neurological symptoms. Other medications are used largely to decrease the severity of symptoms such as the pain, itch, burning sensation and rash that can accompany ciguatera poisoning.

The duration of symptoms can vary, although the most severe signs and symptoms usually occur between six and eight days. No specific treatment exists for continuing and intermittent symptoms. Little information exists about the duration of such symptoms, but they can last for extended periods. With some people, the symptoms can recur whenever they eat fish or fish products.

As with DCI, it is best to call DAN if you have questions, and report symptoms as early as possible. Restaurants in the Caribbean carefully screen fish that can have the ciguatera toxin. Still, exercise caution in what you eat and take notice of any unusual symptoms after eating fish.

Ciguatera: Self-Limiting or Chronic?

By Cassandra Misunas

Note: Author and DAN Member Cassandra Misunas contracted ciguatera poisoning in October 1996. In February 1999, she created a website for people with the same malady. Ciguatera Support* offers a listening ear and a group "cyber-setting" for people who wish to connect with others who have experienced the disease. The following is anecdotal information gleaned from her web-based discussion groups.

* www.ciguaterasupport.org — Although this URL is no longer active, Ms. Misunas plans to reinstate Ciguatera Support. When this happens, we'll announce it in Alert Diver. — Ed.

If you're a fisherman or a diver, chances are you've heard about ciguatera poisoning. And chances are, you believe it is a particularly nasty case of food poisoning that you don't want to get; not necessarily a life-changing illness but definitely undesirable. Chances are, you could be wrong.

Of the fishermen and divers I have spoken to in Florida, not one of them truly knew the full effects of ciguatera. They knew you could get it from fish, but they had no idea of its impact. In addition, of the many doctor's offices I polled in my area, not one of them had a full understanding of what ciguatoxin can do to the human body, and none of them realized how enduring the condition can be.

Statistically, only a tiny percentage of people who get ciguatera poisoning suffer from long-term effects, but for some, ciguatera poisoning has been life-changing. Some people have reported symptoms for one, two, three and even more years. Some have reported milder symptoms for much longer.

Sadly, physicians who don't understand how long the effects of ciguatera poisoning can last brush some sufferers aside. This lack of understanding may come from the diversity of answers from researchers who are working specifically with molecular studies or from researchers who don't have any real access to adequate follow-up data. Estimates from the CDC and other sources suggest that only 2-10 percent of United States ciguatera cases are reported.

Every researcher I have spoken to, from Florida to Hawaii to Australia, had a different answer to the longevity question: one year; two years; six months. This can send confusing signals to doctors, who then diagnose their patients with conversion reaction or depression. Such a diagnosis may devastate the patient who, in fact, may still feel the effects of a powerful neurotoxin.

Follow-up is critical in helping researchers and doctors understand the broader scope of ciguatera poisoning. But with so many cases of ciguatera poisoning going undiagnosed and with a lack of understanding in the medical community, follow-up is difficult. Ciguatera Support seeks to maintain a connection for follow-up and to provide an outlet for people who have had, or still feel the effects of, ciguatera poisoning.

So, how long can ciguatera last? "Two years to infinity," said one researcher. "We just don't know enough about it to say for certain." Most people, however, experience symptoms from six to eight days, as noted in the accompanying article.

To understand ciguatera, education is key.

References
• http://www.cigua.com
• "Fruits of the Sea," Louise Sweeney, July/August 1996 *Alert Diver*
• DAN's Dive and Travel Medical Guide, 1999 edition
• Dr. Paul Auerbach's "A Medical Guide to Hazardous Marine Life," third edition, 1997
• Undersea and Hyperbaric Medicine, Fall 1999, Vol 26, No. 3.
• DAN Pocket Guide to First Aid for Hazardous Marine Life Injuries, by Dan Orr and Bill Clendenen, 1999.

— From Alert Diver, January/February 2000

Section 10

Musculoskeletal

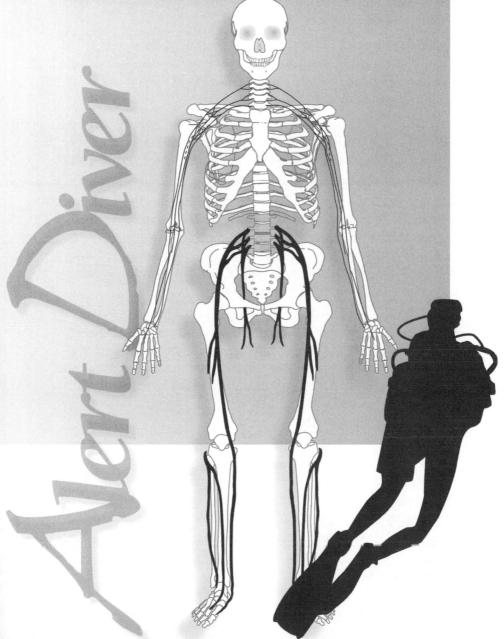

Fitness & Diving with Chronic and Long-Term Illnesses

As scuba diving's appeal broadens to all ages, more individuals with some type of health concern are asking about fitness requirements for scuba diving. Many years ago, when physicians trained in diving medicine began discussing recreational scuba fitness requirements, a "model diver" was created.

This model diver was the accumulation of medical expertise, diving physiology and known disease processes. Restrictions to scuba diving included medical conditions and illnesses that might impair or limit a diver's ability to perform underwater.

Unfortunately, very little research data existed to support many of these theoretical restrictions to scuba diving. Now, as it was then, it would be unethical to place individuals at risk of injury just to prove actual risk is less than what we might expect.

Some restrictions have changed over the years, however. For example, 10 years ago the fear of hypoglycemia kept any person taking medication for diabetes out of scuba diving. Today, individuals who control their diabetes with oral medication may dive; and perhaps, once DAN's research on diving with diabetes is completed, the scuba training agencies may accept a select group of insulin-requiring persons with diabetes.

There are still prospective students who are going to be turned away because of a medical condition, not just because they have a medical problem but because of the severity of their symptoms. In general, any condition that may impair mental or physical performance, induce pain or loss of consciousness, or cause nausea or vomiting must be evaluated before diving. Additionally, there are some medical conditions that may be affected by diving physiology.

This article presents some very difficult frequently-asked questions that concern chronic and long term illness. Dr. Guy Dear, one of DAN's Associate Medical Directors, has put together some very detailed answers to help explain these medical concerns to divers and their physicians so that, together, they can make an informed decision about scuba diving.

This is one way we at DAN strive to increase general medical knowledge in the scuba diving community and prevent injuries and deaths related to these medical conditions.

— *Joel Dovenbarger, Vice President, DAN Medical Services*

Diving & The Body Systems

Diving with conditions of the endocrine, pulmonary and cardiac systems

By Dr. Guy de Lisle Dear, M.B., FRCA, DAN Associate Medical Director, With Additional Reports From Joel Dovenbarger

Continuing the series of DAN's most frequently asked questions, DAN's Associate Medical Director Dr. Guy Dear explores the topic of scuba diving and various conditions of the endocrine, pulmonary and cardiac systems.

Body System: Endocrine

DIABETES

Condition: Diabetes mellitus (DM) is a disorder of the endocrine system, manifested by one of two things: an insufficient production of insulin or the resistance of the body's cells to the actions of insulin despite normal or high levels. People with DM often have excessively high blood glucose (BG), called hyperglycemia, or an excessively low BG, better known as hypoglycemia.

Diabetes mellitus itself has two major forms: Insulin-requiring diabetes (IDDM, Type 1),* for which insulin must be given by injection to control blood sugar levels; and non-insulin-dependent diabetes (NIDDM, Type 2), which may be controlled by diet or by oral medications (oral hypoglycemic medications).

The main risk to the diver is the occurrence of hypoglycemia, that can manifest itself as confusion, sweating, rapid heartbeat, unconsciousness and even death. High blood sugar levels, or hyperglycemia, may also cause unconsciousness, although this usually develops much more slowly than hypoglycemia. Impaired consciousness underwater leads to almost certain death. Although hypoglycemia occurs most commonly in Type 1, it can also occur in individuals taking oral hypoglycemic medications. Hypoglycemia experienced during a deep dive may be wrongly perceived as nitrogen narcosis.

* Note: The acronym "IDDM" actually stands for the older term "insulin-dependent diabetes mellitus," although the newer term for this condition is termed "insulin-requiring diabetes mellitus," and is still represented as "IDDM." The diabetes community currently is in transition between nomenclatures.

Although hypo- or hyperglycemia can occur daily, other problems can develop over the long term, in persons with diabetes. These maladies include: retinopathy (alterations in visual acuity); disorders of the kidneys; coronary artery disease; and changes in the nervous system, including abnormal nervous conduction and atherosclerosis, that can cause poor circulation in the limbs.

Fitness and Diving: Divers with diabetes are at risk of sudden loss of consciousness. This carries the ultimate risk of drowning and implies additional risks for their dive buddies. Individuals with diabetes, however well the diabetes is controlled, should not be deemed as fit to dive without restriction. Those who meet certain criteria can dive provided they dive in accordance with detailed, specific procedures (see "Diabetes & Diving: Current practices demonstrate that many with diabetes do take the plunge — How safe is it?", referenced below). Divers with diabetes should be examined periodically for complications of their disorder that may disqualify them on the grounds of additional risk.

Medication Used in Treatment: Sulphonylureas (drugs that have a hypoglycemic action) such as glipizide, glibenclamide, chlorpropamide and tolbutamide may interact with numerous other drugs used to lower BG.

Biguanides (metformin) may cause self-limited gastrointestinal side effects and may cause problems* in individuals with renal, liver or heart diseases.

Acarbose (an alpha-glucosidase inhibitor) is also used in conjunction with other agents when the more simple sulphonureas do not work adequately to control blood glucose. Insulin acts to lower BG.

In general, diving with diabetes is not recommended. An additional consideration: insulin requirements may change substantially with demands of exercise and diving.

Additional Information:
• Diabetes.com — www.diabetes.com/
• The National Institute of Diabetes and Digestive and Kidney Diseases or (NIDDK) — www.niddk.nih.gov/
• "Diabetes & Diving: Current practices demonstrate that many with diabetes do take the plunge — How safe is it?" by Guy de Lisle Dear, *Alert Diver*, January/February 1997 (available on the DAN website at www.DiversAlertNetwork.org/medical/articles/index.asp).

There is a small risk of lactic acidosis which is markedly increased by any condition that reduces metformin clearance (acute or chronic renal impairment) or compromises oxygen delivery and predisposes to tissue hypoxia (acute or chronic respiratory or cardiovascular insufficiency) in persons with renal, liver or heart diseases.

Body System: Endocrine

THYROID

Condition: The thyroid is a vital gland that secretes a hormone (thyroxin) that helps regulate body metabolism. In excess quantities (hyperthyroidism), it can increase the heart rate or produce cardiac problems, affect respiratory rate, decrease body weight and even interact with the central nervous system. Symptoms of hyperthyroidism also include discomfort or anxiety. Cardiac effects include tachycardia (fast rate), serious dysrhythmias and heart failure. Hyperthyroidism also causes muscular weakness and periodic paralysis in individuals of Chinese descent. Lower-than-normal levels of thyroxin (hypothyroidism) may cause fatigue and slow or absent reflexes. Hypothyroidism is also characterized by a slow heart rate and slow metabolism; it may cause heart failure.

The thyroid gland's output can be controlled by medical intervention. It can be reduced by medication, radiation, radioactive iodine or surgery. Once the hormone level has been reduced to within the normal range (assessed by blood tests), and the signs and symptoms of hyperthyroidism have resolved, then a diver with a thyroid condition may resume diving. (Note: This assumes, however, that the diver has no other major health problems and the diver can achieve a suitable level of physical performance.)

Individuals who have been treated may eventually become truly hypothyroid (have reduced thyroid function) and may require supplemental thyroxine (Synthroid®) to raise their hormone level back into the normal range. It is vital for all individuals with thyroid ailments to have their thyroid function measured regularly by blood test. This can help check for hypo- or hyperthyroidism and can indicate the efficacy of treatment.

Fatigue sometimes occurs as a side effect of therapy: this may be a hurdle for a return to diving. Fatigue may lead to a decreased level of fitness, thus limiting endurance and stamina.

Fitness and Diving: Participation in recreational scuba diving is usually considered unsafe for individuals with hyperthyroidism. In untreated hyperthyroidism, thyroxin can be released in large quantities, causing debilitating symptoms for the submerged diver. Don't dive without treatment.

Medication Used in Treatment: Synthroid has no known interaction with decompression illness.

Additional Information:
- American Thyroid Association — www.thyroid.org/
- Thyroid Foundation of Canada — www.thyroid.ca/

Body System: All — Primarily Heart and Lungs

CYTOTOXIC DRUGS, CANCER EFFECTS

Condition: Cytotoxic drugs (cell-killing drugs) are used primarily for the treatment of cancer or some more serious generalized autoimmune diseases such as rheumatoid arthritis. As far as generalized fitness is concerned, the underlying disease may have more impact on diving than the treatment.

Cancer patients also often have lung problems such as: chronic lung diseases, opportunistic lung infections, lung metastases, radiation treatment to the lungs (causing fibrosis), pulmonary hemorrhage, pulmonary oxygen toxicity from oxygen therapy, pulmonary toxicity from blood component therapy and graft-versus-host disease.

Fitness and Diving: After cancer and its treatment, lung tissue is less able to stretch safely, and fibrosis caused by cytotoxics may render the diver more liable to a burst lung on ascent. Certain drugs, such as bleomycin, are contraindications to diving. Bleomycin causes a special type of serious lung fibrosis in response particularly to increased levels of oxygen. For anyone treated with this drug, any inspired oxygen level above 0.25 ATA should be avoided.

The cytotoxic drugs may leave residual effects even long after their withdrawal. Functional assessments of both cardiac and pulmonary status by formal testing are important before diving is considered. Life expectancy needs to be assessed before starting dive training.

Medication Used in Treatment: The incidence of either pulmonary or cardiac problems is shown in brackets.
- Bleomycin (pulmonary 1-10%);
- Busulfan (pulmonary 1-10%);
- Carmustine [BCNU] (pulmonary 2-30%);
- Cytarabine (pulmonary 20%);
- Mitomycin C (pulmonary 3-10%);
- Methotrexate (pulmonary, occasional);
- Chlorambucil (pulmonary, rare);
- Cyclophosphamide (pulmonary, rare);
- Procarbazine (pulmonary, rare),
- Adriamycin (cardiac).

Body System: Blood

SICKLE CELL ANEMIA

Condition: Sickle cell disorders are the most common hemoglobinopathies (abnormal red blood cells) encountered in the United States. Sickle cell anemia (HbS) results from a DNA mutation that changes one single amino acid molecule within the entire hemoglobin protein. Individuals that inherit the mutation from both parents develop sickle cell anemia.

Sickle trait (HbAS) is the mixed DNA or heterozygous (carrier) state; it can be precipitated by low oxygen levels. Sickle cell trait occurs in 8 percent of African Americans in the United States. Oddly enough, HbS confers a protective advantage against malaria infection and may be why it has survived as a genetic disease.

In general, however, sickle cell disorders have no advantages. Sickle cells are dehydrated, stiff and sticky: they flow poorly though small blood vessels, which can cause local hypoxia (low oxygen levels) and can lead to numerous complications.

Hypoxia, cold or dehydration can cause the RBCs to sickle. This may cause a sickle crisis, often manifested as pain. The sickle crisis may affect the bones, chest, abdomen and spleen. The pulmonary circulation is also particularly vulnerable to pulmonary vascular occlusion because it receives blood that has been deoxygenated, which allows sickling to happen. Chest symptoms may include pain and fever. Infections, such as pneumonia, meningitis and osteomyelitis are major problems. Effects on the central nervous system include stroke in about 8 percent of individuals with HbS. Red blood cell count (RBC) life span is shortened 5-8 times in all varieties of sickle cell disorders (normal RBC: 120 days). HbS patients commonly become severely anemic.

Fitness and Diving: Recurrent sickle crises can impair an individual's ability to exercise. Pain associated with sickle cell disorder can be confused with DCI. Pulmonary function is also affected by HbS. Local hypoxia and the occlusion of vessels can affect nitrogen loading and unloading during dive decompression. Diving may make HbS worse, too. For persons with sickle cell disorder, diving is not advised.

Medication Used in Treatment: The treatment of sickle cell syndromes includes hydration, oxygenation and analgesics for the painful crises. Some new research projects include attempts to prevent RBCs from sickling and to reduce the effects of sickled red cells on blood flow.

Additional Information:
Sickle Cell Information Center — www.scinfo.org/

Body System: Blood

LEUKEMIA

Condition: Leukemia is a blood cancer of white blood cells. It may occur as an acute or a chronic condition. Chronic lymphocytic leukemia (CLL) is the most common type of leukemia; it may account for approximately 10 percent of all leukemias.

The problems associated with leukemia depend on the stage of the disease present at the time of diagnosis, often made by chance on a routine blood count. Complications include anemia, low platelets and low white blood cell count. Although cures are unusual in chronic leukemia, a favorable response can be expected in most individuals treated with chemotherapy, radiation or both.

Acute leukemia accounts for 10 percent of all human cancers, and it is the leading cause of cancer deaths in adults younger than 35 years old. There are two main types: acute myelogenous leukemia (AML) and acute lymphoblastic leukemia (ALL). The cause of acute leukemia remains unknown. Treatment is usually by cytotoxic agents and / or by bone marrow transplantation.

Individuals with leukemia are very sensitive to infections because of their low white blood cell count. Unfortunately, for adults, the response to treatment is not good as with children with the same disease. Several adjunctive measures are useful to treat the diseases associated with leukemia: antibiotics and antifungal agents; blood cell growth factors; and blood transfusions, which may raise red cell and platelet counts.

Fitness and Diving: The leukemias, whether acute or chronic, are serious diseases that result in a limited life span. CLL patients may require no treatment and can do relatively well so they should be assessed on a case-by-case basis. Treatments have improved dramatically in recent years. However, unless acute leukemia is in full remission and exercise tolerance is acceptable, scuba diving is not recommended. The side effects of cytotoxic drugs and radiation treatments and other problems associated with the leukemia make continuation of diving — or its commencement — unwise.

Other factors to be considered include:
• Complications of the original disease,
• The effects and complications of secondary diseases such as pneumonia, and
• The effects of treatment.

Medication Used in Treatment: Cytotoxic drugs, blood transfusions, radiation therapy.

Additional Information:
Leukemia Society of America — www.leukemia.org/
National Marrow Donor Program — www.marrow.org

Body System: Liver

HEPATITIS

Condition: Hepatitis, or inflammation of the liver, is associated with a variety of diseases. Most commonly, it is related to a viral infection. The different forms of hepatitis include:

Hepatitis A — formerly called infectious hepatitis, is most common in children in developing countries, but it is seen frequently in adults in the Western world.

Hepatitis B — formerly called serum hepatitis, it is the most common form of hepatitis, with 300 million carriers in the world and an estimated 1.2 million carriers in the United States.

Hepatitis C — formerly called non-A, non-B hepatitis. More than 3.9 million Americans are carriers of the virus.

Hepatitis D — formerly called delta hepatitis, is found mainly in intravenous drug users who are carriers of the hepatitis B virus, which is necessary for the hepatitis D virus to spread.

Hepatitis E — formerly called enteric or epidemic non-A, non-B hepatitis, its symptoms resemble those of hepatitis A. It is caused by a virus commonly found in the Indian Ocean area, Africa and in underdeveloped countries.

Little is known of the three and possibly five other viruses identified recently. Other viruses, especially members of the herpes virus family, including the cold sore virus, chicken pox virus, infectious mononucleosis virus (EBV) and others, can also affect the liver.

Non-viral forms of hepatitis can be caused by drugs or chemicals, such as alcohol, or autoimmune processes. Alcoholic hepatitis is slow in onset but often fatal and cannot be reversed except by transplantation. Some parasites and bacteria can also cause hepatitis as a secondary effect.

About 26,000 Americans die each year from chronic liver diseases and cirrhosis. Deaths from liver and gallbladder diseases in 1993 reached 51,532, making hepatitis the seventh leading cause of death by disease. It is estimated that approximately 75 to 80 percent of cirrhosis cases could be prevented by eliminating alcohol abuse.

In 1994, an estimated 33,200 people were infected with hepatitis C virus (HCV). There are an estimated 3.9 million people chronically infected with hepatitis C, and about 12,000 die from it each year. The CDC (Centers for Disease Control and Prevention) estimate that annual deaths from hepatitis C will increase to 38,000 by 2010. Hepatitis B is responsible for 5,000 deaths annually: 3,000 to 4,000 from cirrhosis, 1,000 to 1,500 from primary liver cancer and 350 to 450 from fulminant, or severe, hepatitis.

Fitness and Diving: These diseases are serious and have variable infectivity. The fecal-oral or water-borne route can spread only hepatitis A and E. The oral route may transmit hepatitis B: the virus may be excreted in saliva. The most common symptoms are fatigue, mild fever, muscle or joint aches, nausea, vomiting, loss of appetite, vague abdominal pain and sometimes diarrhea. Many cases go undiagnosed because the symptoms suggest a flu-like illness or may be very mild or absent. Individuals with acute or chronic active hepatitis should not dive.

Medication Used in Treatment: Until recently, there has been no way to treat viral hepatitis. Interferon alpha-2b produces a remission of the disease in 30-40 percent of persons with chronic hepatitis B and 20-25 percent of those infected with chronic hepatitis C. However, once individuals stop taking the drug, 50 to 80 percent of them will suffer a relapse. Only 10 percent of hepatitis B cases are cleared of the virus.

For treatment of hepatitis C, another drug, ribavirin, is currently pending with the Food and Drug Administration. However, several available vaccines can prevent hepatitis B. They are all safe and effective, and they seem to prevent infection if begun within a few days of exposure.

Some mild types of cirrhosis can be treated, but there is no cure. Treatment is mostly supportive and may include a strict diet, diuretics, vitamins and abstinence from alcohol.

Additional Information:
The following websites have excellent information from which this summary was made, notably:
• The American Liver Foundation — www.liverfoundation.org/
• The Canadian Hepatitis Information Network — www.hepnet.com/

— September/October 1999

Body System: Generalized

LUPUS

By Dr. Martin Farber

Condition: Lupus erythematosus (LE) is a systemic inflammatory autoimmune disease of unknown causes. The symptoms of this disease are caused by the abnormal function of a class of white blood cells called "T" lymphocytes. There are three forms of LE: systemic, discoid and drug-induced. Systemic lupus, or SLE, is the most serious type. Onset is usually between the ages of 20-45 years but people of all ages can be afflicted. Approximately 90 percent of affected patients are female.

Because SLE is a systemic disease it can have many manifestations which may make it difficult to diagnose. Inflammatory joint disease is the most common symptom occurring in 90 percent of cases. Prolonged morning stiffness, warmth, redness and swelling are signs of joint involvement.

Another cause of joint pain in SLE is aseptic necrosis, a condition in which bone adjacent to a joint dies. Shoulders, knees, hips and wrists are the most common sites of involvement. Various studies have estimated the occurrence of aseptic necrosis in SLE as between 3 percent and 30 percent. Since corticosteroids (e.g., prednisone and others) are frequently used to treat SLE and these drugs are themselves risk factors for the development of osteonecrosis, the relative contribution of therapy to the incidence of osteonecrosis SLE is difficult to definitively know.

SLE can also affect the lungs and kidneys. Lung damage is estimated to occur in 50 percent of individuals with the disease. Severity ranges from having no symptoms to being life-threatening. Renal involvement can lead to kidney failure, requiring dialysis or transplantation if not treated quickly and aggressively. The disease can affect both the central nervous system, causing symptoms ranging from seizures to psychoses to stroke, and the peripheral nervous system, where paresthesias (loss of sensation) or focal muscle weakness can occur.

Fevers, malaise and rashes are also common with SLE. The so-called "butterfly rash" which extends over the bridge of the nose and onto both cheeks is typical but many other types of skin reactions can occur. Hyperkeratosis (thickening of the skin), follicular plugging, skin atrophy and alopecia (loss of hair) are common. Rashes, as well as other symptoms, are frequently exacerbated by exposure to sun. Patients with discoid lupus have symptoms limited to the skin and therefore have the best prognosis.

Lupus can be drug-induced, but in that case the disease is usually short-lived if the offending drug is recognized and removed. Drugs which may cause a lupus-like disease include isoniazid (used to treat tuberculosis), procainamide (used to treat some types of irregular heart rhythms) and hydralazine (used to treat hypertension).

Fitness and Diving Issues: The severity of symptoms in LE can vary ranging from mild to life-threatening. Clearly, evaluation of diving fitness in the patient with SLE is multifactorial. Both the severity of these symptoms must be considered as well as their effects on the individual's ability to respond to the exercise requirements of diving. A thorough evaluation to establish the extent of involvement in each organ system potentially affected by the disease should be performed in individuals seeking to be allowed to participate in unrestricted activities as potentially dangerous as diving. In individuals with mild or very well-controlled disease, diving may pose no additional risk if unrestricted activity is allowed by their personal physician. Consult DAN if needed.

Also, individuals with impaired pulmonary or cardiac function as well as active joint inflammation may carry additional risks of DCI due to impaired gas exchange. Though DCI is also a risk factor for osteonecrosis, it is not known whether this risk is higher in persons who have SLE or are being treated with steroids than for other divers. Individuals with a history of seizures, strokes (even if fully recovered) or other central nervous system manifestations of SLE may have a lower seizure threshold, increasing the risk of drowning. This may be especially important if diving with higher partial pressures of oxygen are being considered.

In addition, since much diving is done in tropical or subtropical climes, where sun exposure can be extreme, a diver with systemic or discoid lupus must be particularly concerned that this does not exacerbate or induce disease activity. The protection afforded by even the strongest sunscreen may be inadequate in sensitive individuals.

Medications and Treatment: Treatment of LE ranges from sunscreens and appropriate clothing for photosensitive rashes and other photosensitive symptoms to high-dose steroids and chemotherapy for severe disease. Non-steroidal anti-inflammatory drugs (including aspirin, naproxen and others) are frequently used to control pain and swelling from joint inflammation. Steroid creams can be helpful in controlling rashes though care must be taken when used on areas of sensitive skin such as the face.

Antimalarials such as hydroxychloroquine have been effective in controlling skin disease, joint disease as well as other mild systemic involvement. For serious involvement of the kidneys, lungs and nervous system high-dose steroids (frequently administered intravenously) and cytotoxic chemotherapeutic agents such as methotrexate, cyclophosphamide and azathioprine can be lifesaving.

In conclusion, while the diagnosis of SLE and its therapy presents many challenges, a thorough evaluation and careful therapy may allow the safe enjoyment of the diving experience.

Additional Information:
Arthritis Foundation — www.arthritis.org
American College of Rheumatology — www.rheumatology.org
Lupus Foundation of America — www.lupus.org

Martin Farber, M.D., Ph.D., is an active diver who is in private practice as a rheumatologist.

— From Alert Diver, March/April 2000

Diving After Bone Fractures

Is There a Greater Risk of Decompression Illness?

By James Chimiak, M.D.

Q: *Six months ago, during an automobile accident, I sustained multiple fractures in my left leg. The fractures did not require surgery, but I was hospitalized for five days and I wore a full-leg cast. I wore the cast for eight weeks, and I walked with a slight limp for two or three weeks after that. I experienced a little muscle fatigue and some swelling and stiffness in my ankle in the evenings, but I had no other trouble.*

I did go to physical therapy briefly to learn exercises for my leg muscles and joints. Two months ago, my doctor released me, allowing me to return to my regular activities. I have even started to jog on the treadmill. I have had no difficulties, but now I want to resume diving. I have heard that, because of the damage to my bones, I may have an increased risk for decompression illness (DCI). I think I am fine now, because I am doing all of my normal activities without a problem. Can I safely return to diving?

A: Three factors can affect your decision to return to diving: the acute loss of function, residual deficits and any additional risk of decompression illness (DCI).

Pain and acute loss of function impedes your ability to dive safely. Acute pain serves an important function since it limits the use of that limb to allow healing and prevent further injury. Thus, you should not dive with an acute fracture. Furthermore, swelling and changes in blood flow could impair the efficient release of nitrogen stored in the injured tissues, possibly increasing the risk of DCI.

Symptoms caused by the injury, such as pain and numbness, burning, itching or tingling could add diagnostic confusion if DCI is being investigated. However, after satisfactorily healing and rehabilitation and approval by the orthopedic surgeon, you can resume diving. Once complete healing has occurred, there is little or no evidence to suggest a higher risk of DCI.

If a diver experiences persistent pain, numbness or weakness, a dive physician should evaluate the diver's condition before any resumption of diving. If the diver returns to diving, the orthopedic surgeon must carefully document the diver's neurological, vascular and functional deficits. In many chronic pain states, no further injury occurs, and many studies report that, with increasing activity, subjects show improvement of overall function and a reduction in chronic pain.

— From Alert Diver, March 2001

Section 11

Nervous System

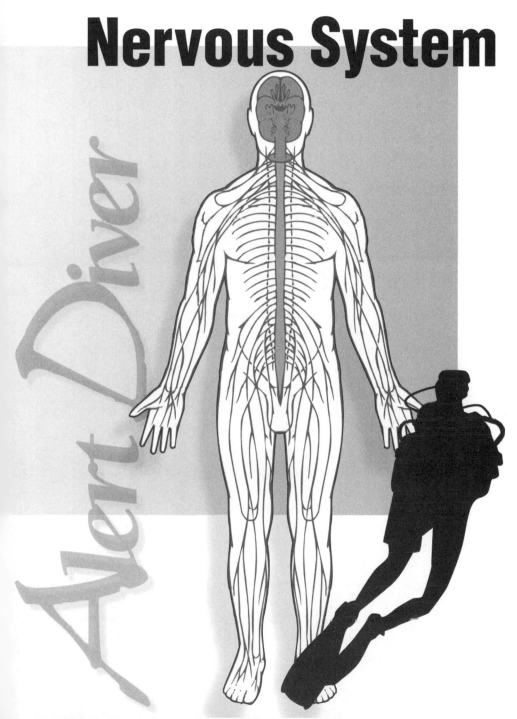

CNS Considerations in Scuba Diving

How Your Diving Fitness Can Be Affected By Your Central Nervous System Health

By Dr. Hugh Greer, DAN Southwest Regional Coordinator

Some of the most difficult questions DAN medics field every day are questions pertaining to the diseases and illnesses of the central nervous system and their relationships to scuba diving. By "central nervous system (CNS)," we mean the brain and spinal cord and the body functions they control.

What makes these questions so problematic? One reason is because the answers are so varied. First, many of the diseases and illnesses that affect the central nervous system produce symptoms that are the same as, and can be mistaken for, neurological decompression illness. Since DAN began collecting data on recreational divers, we have found that the central nervous system is affected in about 70 to 80 percent of all types and severities of decompression illness.

Diving with a disorder of the CNS has two important consequences: 1) the diver may have his DCI undertreated because he will ignore symptoms of DCI; or 2) the diver may have his DCI overtreated, as it is often difficult to know which symptoms are new when a physician with whom he is unfamiliar is treating him.

We don't know if individuals with chronic or long-term central nervous system problems are more susceptible to decompression illness. It does raise a concern that if DCI occurs, will the pre-existing illness be made worse by any additional injury?

Finally, we do not have a storehouse of data on the effects of scuba diving (or more specifically, the effects of high partial pressures of nitrogen) on the illnesses and diseases mentioned in this article. It would be unethical to perform experimental dives on individuals for the purposes of determining the risk of permanent or disabling injury for any given neurological disease.

That is why we have selected DAN's Southwest Regional Coordinator Dr. Hugh Greer, a practicing diving medicine neurologist and former Underwater Demolitions Team (UDT) officer to write on the topic of CNS consideration in scuba diving. His many years of evaluating and treating divers provide him with the knowledge and experience we need in order to answer questions in a very matter-of-fact fashion.

Whether you have experienced one of these conditions or if you have a student who has mentioned a central nervous system disorder, the decision to accept the risk of scuba diving with that condition should be an informed decision. And keep in mind that the assumption of risk is not purely personal: individuals with a CNS disorder must also be willing to let their buddies know that they have a condition that merits special consideration. In an emergency situation, it is assumed that a diver is capable of rendering assistance to a distressed buddy while underwater.

This article provides straightforward guidance for you, prospective divers, and for physicians. For those who may be turned away from a standard scuba training course because of physical limitations due to their medical condition, we offer a list of diver assisted organizations who offer special instruction and assistance for individuals who are determined to dive. DAN's role is to provide information needed to make an informed decision.

We have taken the top 11 questions relating to the central nervous system, to continue the series of DAN's most frequently asked questions.

— Joel Dovenbarger, BSN, Vice President, DAN Medical Services

Attention Deficit Disorder (ADD)

Condition: This brain disorder, usually recognized early in life, is manifested by an inability to concentrate or sustain attention. It may or may not be accompanied by physical hyperactivity. ADD is a significant (but over-diagnosed) cause of learning disability. The problem usually improves with age.

Fitness & Diving: At its worst, ADD can be so pronounced as to prevent a prospective student from learning the simple skills necessary for safety. This could present a significant hazard in many areas, including both driving and scuba diving. ADD is usually not that intense, however. Fitness to dive can best be assessed by looking at social, school, athletic and job performance. Note that because some ADD patients take medications, they should consider the potential impact of medications while diving.

Medication Used in Treatment: No testing has ever been done to determine interactions between high partial pressures of nitrogen and the medications used to treat attention deficit disorder. Two drugs currently in use are Ritalin® (methphenidate) and Dexedrine® (dextro-amphetamine). Both are heavy duty stimulants that leave most adults "wired." However, they often have a calming and somewhat paradoxical effect on children with attention deficient disorder. This desirable effect is less apparent as children grow older.

Post Brain Tumor Surgery

Condition: The type of brain tumor we're discussing here is one that is surgically treated or removed. This covers a lot of ground. Some brain tumors are benign — once it's removed, the person is cured of that particular tumor. Some brain tumors are cancerous and may return. Removal of either type of tumor — benign or cancerous — sometimes results in substantial loss of neurologic function and an ongoing risk of seizures; at other times there is no loss of function at all.

Fitness & Diving: This depends on all the factors above, and others, too. Individuals should be counseled that if cerebral DCI or AGE occurs, they may be at risk for significant residual symptoms due to pre-existing CNS problems. Another item to consider: Brain tumors may cause seizures, a definite contraindication for diving. Consider:

1. The extent of the physical handicap;

2. The presence of seizures or the need for anticonvulsant medication;

3. Surgery by itself does not constitute a diving hazard: when you dive, there is no pressure shift inside the head. The outside / inside pressure is the same, so no shift in structure occurs, and diving will have no effect on remaining tumor cells.

4. Surgery done through the nose (as in the removal of a diseased pituitary gland) may be a special case because of increased risk of barotrauma to the sinuses or nasal passages, which may have been traumatized during the procedure. However, surgery to the brain carries a risk of post-surgery seizures. Any loss of consciousness while underwater usually results in drowning. Accordingly, unless it can be assured that an individual does not have an elevated risk of seizures, he or she should not be encouraged to dive.

5. A defect in the skull itself may require special protection from physical trauma: piercing the skin over the defect while underwater poses a greater infection hazard than when at the surface.

Medication Used in Treatment: Some cancer treatment medications may affect the patient's lungs. A return to diving may necessitate a pulmonary evaluation.

Cerebral Vascular Accident

Condition: Stroke, or loss of blood supply to the brain, causes damage to part of the brain, or bleeding from a blood vessel in the brain, which results in similar injury. Strokes come in all sizes and shapes, and the resulting disability depends on size and location of the event.

Fitness & Diving:

1. Most strokes occur in older people. The stroke itself identifies the person as one who has advanced arterial disease, thus a higher expectation of further stroke or heart attack.

2. The extent of disability caused by the stroke (e.g., paralysis, vision loss) may determine fitness to dive.

3. Vigorous exercise, lifting heavy weights and using the Valsalva method for ear-clearing when diving all increase arterial pressure in the head and may increase the likelihood of a recurrent hemorrhage.

4. While diving in itself entails exposure to elevated partial pressures and elevated hydrostatic pressure, it does not cause stroke.

5. There is certainly increased risk in diving for someone who has experienced a stroke. Exceptional circumstances may exist, such as cerebral hemorrhage in a young person in whom the faulty artery has been repaired with little persisting damage. This type of recovery may permit a return to diving, with small risk. Each instance, however, requires a case-by-case decision, made with the advice of the treating physician, family and diving partners. Consulting a neurologist familiar with diving medicine is also advisable.

6. There is a concern for significant residual symptoms.

Cerebral Palsy

Condition: This describes brain injury, present at birth and which is manifested by some degree of weakness or incoordination. This includes a wide variety of clinical illnesses, ranging from "walks abnormally" to very severe and disabling handicaps. Some cases present accompanying seizures, learning disability and speech defect.

Fitness & Diving: Diving fitness depends entirely on the extent of disability in the individual case. Candidates with mild problems may qualify; candidates with more severe disabilities may qualify through one of the scuba programs for disabled people. The absence of seizures and the ability to master the water skills are particularly important. For participation in scuba, case-by-case selection is needed.

Epilepsy

Condition: This disorder of brain function causes episodic alterations of consciousness, called epileptic seizures. Abnormal electrical discharges in the brain cause these episodes; they may occur without warning, and they may vary in character from a brief loss of attention to violent, prolonged convulsion. People may outgrow the condition; it is often, but not always, controlled by medication.

Fitness & Diving: Loss of consciousness or loss of awareness while underwater carries a very high risk of drowning or embolism from an uncontrolled ascent. An analysis of motor vehicle operators with epilepsy has shown that a seizure occurring behind the wheel will result in an accident in nearly every instance, but no evidence exists that diving with compressed air scuba to the accepted 130 fsw limit increases the risk of epileptic seizures. One is no more likely to seize while diving than while driving: the risk is the same. There is no useful data to determine the potential for injury in divers with epilepsy.

Current doctrine among diving medicine physicians advises that individuals with epilepsy not dive. Those with childhood epilepsy, who have outgrown the condition and have been off medication for five years, still face a slightly increased risk of a seizure. To make an informed decision about diving, these individuals should discuss this with their personal physicians, families and diving companions.

Medication Used in Treatment: Anti-seizure medication acts directly on the brain and may interact with high partial pressures of nitrogen. This may produce unexpected side effects. (See nervous system medical effects, below.)

History of Seizures Without a Clear Diagnosis of Epilepsy

Condition: This is a cloudy question since many variables can cause transient alteration of consciousness. These alterations of consciousness include fainting, a reduction of blood pressure, which is very common in young people, an alteration in heart rhythm that is more common in older people, effects of medication and psychological events, such as hallucinations.

Fitness & Diving: As with epilepsy, any loss of consciousness underwater is likely to have a bad outcome. When diving using nitrox or mixed gas as a breathing gas, increased partial pressures of oxygen can increase the likelihood of seizures. Increased carbon dioxide may also increase seizure risk.

The best advice is to get a precise diagnosis of the cause of altered states of consciousness: effective treatment is often available. You cannot make a reasonable fitness-to-dive decision till this is sorted out. It may take some time and a visit to a neurologist or other specialists. Ask your doctor first.

General Concerns About Taking Medication While Scuba Diving

Condition: Many of the conditions discussed are treated with medication. These include anticonvulsants to prevent seizures, antidepressants and sedatives to alter behavior, pain medication and a host of others. In addition to the intended effect, many drugs have undesirable side effects, which vary from person to person and are not entirely predictable. The list of side effects, while far from complete, includes these most common states: drowsiness, dry mouth, blurred vision and slowness to urinate.

Additionally, these medications have not been tested in divers while diving or in a controlled hyperbaric environment: this type of assessment of risk for the diver cannot be performed. There may be an interaction between the medication and high partial pressures of nitrogen, producing an unexpected side effect such as anxiety or panic.

Fitness & Diving:

1. Alertness is important; medications while diving can affect a diver's alertness;

2. Increased pN2 (partial pressures of nitrogen) causes narcosis and can be expected to increase the drowsiness side effect of many drugs such as antihistamines and medications for motion sickness.

What to do:

1. Read the package insert of the drug you are taking;

2. Ask your doctor;

3. Pay attention. The medication may affect you in an unexpected way;

4. If you start a new medication, or change medications, don't dive until you have had a couple of days to feel it out. If your medication makes you drowsy on the surface, expect it may have greater effect at 75 fsw. In this case, you should either not dive, or discontinue using the medication. Always check with your physician before stopping a prescription medication.

The bigger question regarding diving on medication often relates to the reason why it is being taken. Taking aspirin for a previous stroke or heart attack is an example.

Head Trauma

Condition: "Head trauma" refers to a head injury sufficient to cause prolonged unconsciousness or persisting brain dysfunction. Mild head injury without unconsciousness rarely has lasting effects.

Fitness & Diving: Two principal concerns exist:

1. Post-traumatic epilepsy — This risk is directly related to the severity of the injury and the time elapsed between the injury and your plans to dive. Penetrating head wounds with brain disruption have a high risk of post-traumatic seizure; head injuries resulting in brief unconsciousness do not. With mild head injuries, risk falls sharply with time; with penetrating head wounds, long-term risk is less predictable.

2. Cognitive loss. Defects in memory, understanding and concentration are obvious risks in diving. This is best evaluated by social, school and job performances. If these skills are intact, there is probably no reason to restrict diving. Diving in itself does not worsen the effects of head injury.

Migraine Headache

Condition: A migraine headache is a periodic, usually one-sided, throbbing ache, sometimes preceded by warning signs and symptoms and of variable severity.

Migraine, though dreaded, is common. More than half the people in the world will have some experience with migraine during their lives, and about 5 percent will see doctors about it. A few of these will suffer significant disruption of their activities.

Fitness & Diving: Migraine as such poses little danger to divers. Even those with frequent migraine do not usually experience an increased incidence while diving. An elevated level of carbon dioxide in the blood, which occurs with decreased ventilation and breath-holding / hypoventilation, can theoretically precipitate a migraine headache because carbon dioxide (CO_2) causes vasodilation in the brain. Increased levels of oxygen in the blood (which occurs in diving as well as in hyperbaric chambers) has been used with variable success to treat severe migraine, because it is a powerful brain vasoconstrictor.

Very complex migraine, with visual loss or paralysis, might lead to confusion in diagnosing a diving accident. However, little data exists to suggest that migraine poses a significant hazard to divers. Severe and incapacitating migraine headaches while in the water would create a hazard for the individual. People with severe and incapacitating migraine should probably not dive.

Multiple Sclerosis (MS)

Condition: This immunologic disease occurring in young and middle-aged people is characterized by episodes of neurologic dysfunction, often separated by remission. The extent of disability is quite variable. Treatment has improved in recent years.

Fitness & Diving:
1. There is no evidence that diving in itself has an effect on the disease. About 20 years ago an unsuccessful effort was made to treat MS with hyperbaric oxygen. Patients neither suffered nor benefited from this treatment series.

2. Persons with MS are advised not to exercise to the point of exhaustion and to avoid becoming chilled or overheated. Diving candidates with MS should respect that advice.

3. In each individual case, consider whether the candidate can handle the physical load and master the water skills. Diving candidates should talk to their neurologist about diving.

Paraplegia

Condition: Paralysis (paraplegia) or weakness (paraparesis) of both legs may result from spinal cord injury such as accidental fracture, decompression sickness, muscle disease such as poliomyelitis or a brain injury such as cerebral palsy or stroke.

Fitness & Diving: Diving fitness depends on the cause and the extent of disability in each individual case. Considerations include:

1. The extent of physical disability that may determine whether the candidate can perform the required water skills. High spinal cord injury (closer to the head) may compromise breathing: Respiratory signals come from the spinal cord at the level of the 4th and 5th vertebrae, so a fracture at or above that level will likely paralyze the diaphragm. A fracture at the mid-thoracic (chest) level will paralyze the legs, while a fracture at the level of the 5th and 6th vertebrae will cause severe paralysis of the arms as well.

2. Diving in itself does not cause further injury unless the diver gets decompression sickness involving the spinal cord. In that case, because the spinal cord is already damaged, there may be an increased risk of residual disability, even after prompt treatment.

3. There are reliable programs (e.g., associations of disabled divers) designed to accommodate diving candidates with such problems. These programs emphasize the importance of avoiding DCS by careful diving practices.

4. As with multiple sclerosis and other CNS considerations, deciding on whether to dive with paraplegia requires a case-by-case decision. Decide after consultation with your physician.

Dr. Hugh D. Greer III was the DAN Southwest Regional Coordinator from 1981-2001, a practicing diving medicine neurologist and Underwater Demolitions Team (UDT) officer. He passed away on Oct. 2, 2001, at the age of 69. The DAN 2002 Report on Decompression Illness, Diving Fatalities and Project Dive Exploration was dedicated in his memory.

— *From Alert Diver, May/June 1999*

Section 12

Ophthalmology (Eyes)

High-Pressure Ophthalmology

DAN Answers Divers' Most-Asked Questions About Their Eyes

By Frank K. Butler Jr., Captain, Medical Corps, United States Navy

While working with Divers Alert Network as a consultant in ophthalmology over the past three years, I have had the opportunity to respond to many questions from DAN members concerning the eye and diving. This article discusses some of the most frequently asked questions on the topic.

A review of this topic entitled "Diving and Hyperbaric Ophthalmology" was published by Butler in the medical journal Survey of Ophthalmology (March/April 1995) and serves as a good additional reference on the subject of the eye and diving. If you'd like additional information regarding any of the questions in this article or if you have a question that was not addressed, this article may be helpful, or you can call DAN at +1-919-684-2948.

The Eye and Diving

Our eyes normally exist in a world where the pressure around them is the result of the combined weight of all of the gases in the earth's atmosphere. Diving exposes the eyes to increased pressures. While most of the time this has little or no negative effects on the diver, increased eye pressure in scuba diving can result in ocular decompression sickness and other dysbaric disorders. It may also raise new questions about the management of common eye conditions in divers. The issues discussed here, for the most part, have not been well addressed in ophthalmology literature.

1. Is it safe to dive after radial keratotomy?

Radial keratotomy (RK for short) is a surgical procedure designed to cure myopia (nearsightedness). In this operation, the surgeon makes a small number of radially-oriented incisions in the cornea of the eye. These incisions cause a decrease in the strength of the cornea and may increase the risk of serious injury if the eye is subjected to subsequent trauma, including barotrauma such as a facemask squeeze. Despite this theoretical risk, there have been no reports involving a traumatic rupture of the cornea resulting from diving after RK.

Divers who have had this procedure should wait at least three months after the surgery before returning to diving and should be careful to avoid a facemask squeeze — it's important to avoid imposing the "Boyle's Law Stress Test" on these corneal incisions.

If you are a diver and considering having this procedure done, I would recommend that you also ask your eye surgeon to discuss the potential advantages of photorefractive keratectomy, the alternative refractive surgical procedure discussed below.

2. Is it safe to dive after having had the new laser refractive surgery (LASIK or photorefractive keratectomy)?

Yes. These procedures use laser reshaping of the cornea instead of incisions to treat myopia. This method results in no decrease in the structural integrity of the cornea and no risk of corneal rupture as a result of facemask squeeze. It should be safe to dive approximately two weeks after this surgery. Discuss your plans with your physician and have a final evaluation before you dive.

3. What are the best contact lenses to wear underwater?

Divers who wish to wear contact lenses while diving should ask their ophthalmologists or optometrists to prescribe "soft" contact lenses. "Hard" lenses or rigid non-gas-permeable lenses have been found to sometimes cause symptoms of eye pain and blurred vision during and after deep dives. These symptoms occur as a result of gas bubbles forming between the cornea and the contact lens.

4. Can individuals who have had cataract surgery dive?

Yes. Most cataract surgeons now use surgical incisions designed to provide maximum post-operative wound strength. The recommended waiting time prior to returning to diving depends on exactly what type of incision was made. Ask your surgeon for recommendations for your particular type of surgery. For specific recommended waiting times prior to diving after this and other types of eye surgery, you may want to read "Diving and Hyperbaric Ophthalmology," the article mentioned at the beginning of this article.

5. Is it dangerous to dive if you have glaucoma?

Glaucoma, a disease in which increased pressure inside the eye, is associated with damage to the optic nerve and loss of vision. Because of this, physicians have voiced concern about the possibility that a hyperbaric environment might therefore cause increased damage to the eye. Although this would seem to be a logical conclusion, diving thus far has not been shown to be a problem for glaucoma patients. This is most likely because the damage associated with glaucoma is a factor of the difference between the pressure inside the eye and the surrounding pressure, rather than simply the absolute magnitude of the pressure to which the eye is exposed.

There are two important considerations for glaucoma patients who wish to dive. Some of the medications used to lower the pressure in the eyes of glaucoma patients may have adverse effects while diving. Timolol, for example, may result in a decrease in heart rate that could theoretically place a small percentage of divers at higher risk for loss of consciousness underwater; acetazolamide (diamox) may cause tingling sensations of the hands and feet that could be mistaken for symptoms of decompression sickness. These and other ocular medications are discussed in detail in the article mentioned in the introduction.

Certain types of glaucoma surgery (collectively called glaucoma filtering procedures) create a communication between the anterior chamber of the eye and the subconjunctival space to help lower the pressure in the eye. Facemask barotrauma may have an adverse effect on the functioning of the filter and result in a need for additional surgery or further damage to the eye from the glaucoma.

Individuals who have had glaucoma surgery or who are taking glaucoma medications should check with their ophthalmologist before diving.

6. Is it possible to get ocular (eye) decompression sickness?

Ocular decompression sickness is a relatively uncommon event, but one which does occur and it is very important that divers be aware of this possible presentation of DCS. *Symptoms may include:*
1. Loss of vision
2. Blurred vision (unless related to other causes — see below)
3. Diplopia (double vision)
4. Blind spots in your field of vision
5. Pain around the eye
6. Nystagmus (abnormal eye movements)

The presence of any of these symptoms following a dive should be evaluated as soon as possible by a physician knowledgeable about dive injuries, or the diver should call DAN.

7. I just came up from a dive and noticed that my vision is now blurry. What conditions could cause this symptom?

Possible causes of blurred vision after diving include:
1. Contact lenses which become tightly adherent to the eye during a dive. Try using lubricant eye drops to relieve this.
2. Displaced contact lens.
3. Corneal irritation from mask anti-fog solutions.
4. Ultraviolet or "sunburn" damage to the cornea.
5. Corneal irritation resulting from bubbles under hard or rigid gas-permeable contact lenses.
6. Use of transdermal scopolamine to prevent motion sickness.
7. Decompression sickness
8. Arterial gas embolism

If you are a contact lens wearer, I would first ensure that the lens is still in place and then instill some lubricant eye drops. If this is successful in restoring your vision to normal, then it is not necessary to seek medical attention. If you are not a contact lens wearer or these actions are unsuccessful, then you should have your symptoms evaluated by a physician knowledgeable about diving injuries. For a list of dive physicians in your area, call DAN.

8. I just came up from a dive and one of my eyes has a bright red spot on it. What could cause this? Do I need to see an eye doctor?
The most common cause of a red spot on the eye after a dive is a sub-conjunctival hemorrhage. This is a collection of blood over the sclera (white part) of the eye. It is usually caused by a mild facemask squeeze and does not require any treatment. A more severe squeeze could result in other injuries to the eye, however, so it is a good idea to see your eye doctor just in case. It is absolutely essential to see your eye doctor if you have eye pain, double vision, blind spots in your field of vision, or decreased vision after a dive or if you have a history of eye surgery in the past. (See related article, "Mask Squeeze," on Page 8.)

9. I am undergoing hyperbaric oxygen (HBO) treatments and notice that my vision is slowly getting worse. Why is this happening?
Hyperbaric oxygen therapy may cause a change in the way that the lens of the eye refracts light. This change occurs slowly and is usually not noticed until after a week or two of treatment. If the HBO therapy continues to that point or beyond, the patient may experience a slow myopic (nearsighted) change. This slow change typically continues as long as the HBO treatments continue. It is usually reversible after the treatments are finished, although there have been some reports in which this reversal did not occur or was incomplete.

10. What eye conditions would preclude someone from diving?
a. Gas in the eye (may be present after vitreoretinal surgery). Diving with gas in the eye may result in vision-threatening intraocular barotrauma due to the pressures of the surrounding water column.

b. Hollow orbital implants. The presence of a hollow orbital implant after an eye has been surgically removed because of injury or disease may preclude diving.

The increased pressures encountered while diving may cause a hollow orbital implant to collapse, resulting in cosmetic problems and a need for further surgery to replace the damaged implant.

Many ocular plastic surgeons are now using implants made of hydroxya-patite, a porous material which is not a contraindication for diving.

c. Acute eye disorders. Any acute eye disorder which produces significant pain, light sensitivity, double vision, or decreased vision is a contra-indication to diving. These symptoms may be produced by a number of ocular infectious, traumatic, or inflammatory conditions.

In general, it's best to wait until the underlying acute condition has resolved and there are no distracting or disabling ocular symptoms to contend with before returning to diving.

d. Recent eye surgery. After eye surgery, avoid diving prior to completion of the recommended convalescent period for your particular type of surgery.

e. Inadequate vision. There is a detailed discussion of visual acuity and diving in the article entitled "Diving and Hyperbaric Ophthalmology" mentioned in the introduction.

Deciding on your own level of visual acuity is primarily a judgment call, with few relevant scientific studies available to help resolve the issue. The approach taken in the article was to use statutory visual standards established for another hazardous activity — driving a car, for example — whose visual requirements are more demanding than diving. The recommendation made was that if you see well enough to qualify for a driver's license and operate a motor vehicle safely, then you should be able to see well enough to dive safely.

If a prospective diver has visual acuity which precludes him or her from being allowed to drive, then the fitness to dive decision needs to be individualized with the assistance of an eye physician and dive instructor.

f. Decreased vision. If your vision is impaired from previous episodes of decompression sickness or arterial gas embolism, don't risk further injury.

g. Some types of glaucoma surgery (see question #5).

A Final Word

Most of the restrictions to diving mentioned above do not apply to hyperbaric oxygen (HBO) therapy. According to "Diving and Hyperbaric Ophthalmology":

Hyperbaric exposures in a dry chamber "do not entail immersion of the eye or the possibility of facemask barotrauma. Only the presence of intraocular gas or hollow orbital implants remain as possible ocular contraindications to diving in these patients."

If you have concerns about your eyes and diving, if you're planning to have surgery, or if you have further questions, call DAN's Dive Safety and Medical Information Line at +1-919-684-2948.

Frank K. Butler, Jr., M.D., Captain, Medical Corps, U. S. Navy, is a staff ophthalmologist at the Naval Hospital in Pensacola, Fla., and an ophthalmology consultant for DAN. He also is the biomedical research director at Naval Special Warfare Command. His extensive service with the Navy has won him many military awards.

— *From Alert Diver, May/June 1998*

Eye Surgery for Divers

DAN Discusses Detached Retina Repair and Lasik

By Joel Dovenbarger, Vice President, DAN Medical Services

Q: *I recently had a detached retina repair. My vision has returned to normal, but I have a couple of black spots in my field of vision. My ophthalmologist has said that after two months I can return to all of my normal activities without restrictions. What is the waiting period before it is safe to return to diving?*

A: As divers (or any such groups) age, the risk of retinal detachment increases.

The eye's inner surface — the space between the retina in the back of the eye to the eye's lens through which images and light pass — is filled with a thick liquid called the vitreous humor. This fluid helps keep the retina in place.

As we get older, inconsistencies in the thickness of the vitreous humor can allow parts of the retina to pull away and even detach from the eye. Once this happens, the neural relays can no longer accurately relay to the brain what the eye sees. This may result in wavy, blurred vision or even loss of sight. Although you may suffer a retina detachment from severe nearsightedness or from trauma to the eye, aging is probably the best-known contributor.

The physician determines the means of reattachment, but vision usually returns to normal more quickly when individuals seek immediate evaluation and correction of the problem. After surgery, it is not unusual to see some black spots — small pieces of tissue from the retina called "floaters" that are suspended in the vitreous humor. They can be annoying, but they usually resolve over time.

Scuba diving neither causes nor contributes to retinal detachment in the normal eye. Without further problems, most divers can make a return to diving after a two-month waiting period.

Q: *I make 30-40 divers each year. I want to have my vision corrected with the new Lasik eye surgery. How long will I have to stay out of diving after the surgery?*

A: The Lasik (an acronym for *LASer In-situ Keratomileusis*) procedure, or laser eye surgery, has become a popular surgery. These procedures use laser reshaping of the cornea instead of incisions to treat myopia. This method results in no decrease in the structural integrity of the cornea and no risk of corneal rupture as a result of facemask squeeze. It should be safe to dive approximately two weeks after this surgery. Discuss your plans with your physician and have a final evaluation before you dive.

For more information on the eye, see "High-Pressure Ophthalmology" by Dr. Frank Butler on Page 151.

The Eyes Have It

By Joel Dovenbarger, Vice President, DAN Medical Services

Q: *One of my students reported that he was told to use a popular brand of dishwashing detergent as a mask defogger. Is there some danger in this?*

A: Liquid dishwashing detergent contains the basic element of all commercially available mask defoggers — either detergent or other surfactants, which stabilizes the wall of a bubble. Technically there is not much difference between liquid dish detergent and other forms of surfactant. Some may even feel that it ranks higher than spitting in your mask or using a sliced potato as a defogger.

There are real differences, however. Commercial anti-fogging solution is specifically made for mask defogging, usually with several hypo-allergenic ingredients. Dish liquids, on the other hand, may contain antiseptics, color dyes, scents and scent carriers that trigger allergic reactions. This is an important consideration for anything you place on the face and close to the eye.

Additionally, liquid soap in the eye can cause tearing and irritation, which can impair performance if it occurs when you're diving. Bacteria can live in detergent solutions once they have been contaminated — this is true of any liquid container that is not properly cared for or stored.

The economy may be in favor of using liquid detergent as a mask defogger, but we urge caution.

— From Alert Diver, September/October 1996

Section 13

Psychological

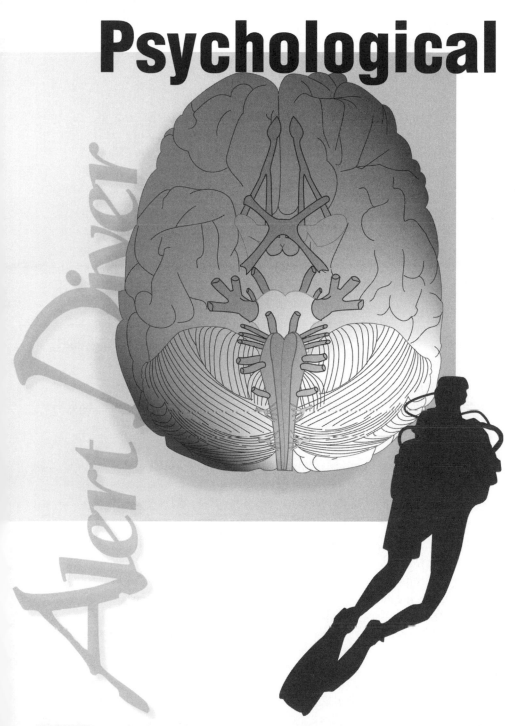

Psychological Issues in Diving — Part 1

DAN Explores Depression and Manic Depression and the Drugs Used as Treatment

By Ernest Campbell, M.D., FACS

Editors' Note: This is the first of three articles addressing psychological issues and diving. Part I discusses depression and manic depression; the second installment looks at anxieties, phobias, panic and narcolepsy; and Part III addresses schizophrenia, marijuana and alcohol use. Each section examines causes, symptoms, advice about diving and medications used for a particular disorder or habit.

Little research exists to characterize the relationship between mental conditions and scuba diving. Other than the obvious reasons people shouldn't dive — i.e., they are out of touch with reality, severely depressed and suicidal, or paranoid with delusions and hallucinations — many people with everyday anxieties, fears and neuroses can dive and do so safely.

Successful divers have psychological profiles that are positively correlated to intelligence and characterized by an average or below-average level of neuroticism. These divers generally score well on studies of self-sufficiency and emotional stability, according to diving physiologist Dr. Glen Egstrom.

Some actual psychological disturbances are well known, but, as for the risks of scuba diving, documented and studied cases are few in number. These include the depressions, bipolar disorder, anxiety and phobias, panic disorders, narcolepsy and schizophrenia.

In addition to the risks caused by the condition itself, we must add the possible hazards of the effects of medications taken singly or, even more dangerously, in combination. No scientific studies confirm the relative safety or danger of taking any given medication.

In terms of danger to divers, medications usually play a secondary role to the condition for which the medication is prescribed. Plainly a powerful drug, a mood-altering medication, should be used with care by divers. Drugs that carry warnings indicating they are dangerous for use while driving or when operating hazardous equipment should also be considered risky for divers; if they're dangerous for drivers, they're risky for divers. The possible interaction between the physiological effects of diving and the pharmacological effects of medications is usually an educated, yet empirically unproven, assumption. Each situation requires individual evaluation, and no general rule applies to all. Another unknown is the additive effect of nitrogen narcosis on the actual effects of the medication.

Finally, divers have different chemistries and personalities; because of the effects of various gases under pressure, each diver responds differently to abnormal physiological states and changes in their environment. Diving conditions such as decompression illness, inert gas narcosis, carbon dioxide toxicity, oxygen toxicity, high-pressure nervous syndrome and deep-water blackout all can cause reactions that are similar to a psychoneurotic reaction or an abnormal condition of the brain. Before advising for or against diving, the certifying physician must know all the possibilities and variations in each case of a diver with psychological issues.

DEPRESSIVE DISORDERS

Depression (Unipolar Disorder) and Manic Depression (Bipolar Disorder)

Overview of Depressive Illnesses and Their Symptoms

Depression and manic depression, two major types of depressive illnesses, are known as affective or mood disorders, because they primarily affect a person's mood. Different terms, respectively, for affective disorders include unipolar and bipolar disorders.

Depression is a persistent condition that can interfere with a person's ability to sleep, eat and hold a job and can last for weeks or months at a time. A depressed person almost always feels sad. It becomes difficult to feel any pleasure in life and the person can even become suicidal. Other symptoms include feelings of hopelessness and guilt, loss of interest in normal activities, reduced sex drive, changes in eating habits, insomnia, restlessness and poor concentration.

In this section, we will predominately discuss major depressive disorder and manic depression, encompassing symptoms of depression and mania, with wide mood swings, from deep sadness to the other extreme of elation, often losing touch with reality.

Each year, a large number of American adults — the figure varying from 10 million to 19 million according to the source — suffer from an affective disorder.

If you've never experienced depression, chances are that at some point in your life, you will. Women are twice as likely as men to experience major depression, while manic depression occurs equally among men and women. The highest percentage of these illnesses occurs between the ages of 25 and 44, according to Hopkins Technology, LLC.

Where do these illnesses come from? Genetic, biochemical and environmental factors each can play a role in the onset and progression of such illnesses. We all can experience occasional emotional highs and lows, but depressive disorders are characterized by extremes in intensity and duration. Hopkins records also indicate that people hospitalized for depression have a suicide rate as high as 15 percent.

Of all psychiatric illnesses, affective disorders respond best to treatment. If given proper care, approximately 80 percent of patients with major depression demonstrate significant improvement and lead productive lives, according to the National Institute of Mental Health (NIMH). Although the rate of treatment success is not as high for manic depression, a substantial number experience a return to a higher quality of life.

The Cause of Affective Disorders

Research shows that some people may have a genetic predisposition to affective disorders. If someone in your family has had such an illness, this does not necessarily mean that you will develop it. Moreover, if you do develop an affective disorder, a family history of depression does not explain conclusively why you did. However, having a family member with an affective disorder does increase your chances of experiencing depression of an endogenous, or biological, origin. Commonly called clinical depression, these disorders are distinguished from short-term states of depressed mood or unhappiness. Even if you don't have a genetic predisposition, your body chemistry can trigger the onset of a depressive disorder due to the presence of another illness, altered health habits, substance abuse or hormonal fluctuations.

Distressing life events can also trigger reactive depression. Losses and repeated disillusionment, from death to disappointment in love, can cause people to feel depressed, especially if they have not developed effective coping skills. If these symptoms persist for more than two weeks, with a leveling or increasing in intensity, this reactive depression may actually have evolved into a clinical depression. This should be distinguished from a normal grief response which can last several months.

Whatever the cause, the presence of depressive or manic-depressive illness indicates an imbalance in the brain chemicals known as neurotransmitters. This means the brain's electrical mood-regulating system is not operating as it should.

An episode of depression can usually be treated successfully with psychotherapy or antidepressant medication, or a combination of the two. The choice depends on the exact nature of the illness. With treatment, up to 80 percent of people with depression show improvement, usually in a matter of weeks, according to the NIMH.

Underlying their mood swings, most people with depression have anger and anxiety. Certifying or allowing a diver with depression to continue to dive carries with it significant dangers to the diver, his buddy and others on the dive excursion who may be attempting a rescue. It is possible that some scuba fatalities are actually suicides, apparently decided on the spur of the moment, but this is very difficult to prove.

Clearly, any condition that clouds a diver's ability to make decisions underwater poses dangers; diving under such conditions should not be allowed. In addition, we rarely have knowledge about drug changes resulting from the physiological effects of diving. Since such mood-altering drugs used to treat depression are clearly potent, people should use caution when they dive, paying particular attention to the warnings about use.

Discontinuing a drug to dive, even for a short period of time, may be unwise. The effects of a hiatus can play havoc with your body chemistry and affect your sense of well-being.

Depression

If symptoms of depression persist for longer than two weeks (see page 170 for a listing of the most commons signs), divers experiencing four or more of the symptoms of either depression, manic-depression or symptoms of both should seek professional help and stop diving until the problem is managed.

Divemasters and instructors should learn to recognize any changes in their divers' appearances, reactions and personalities and be quick to note any of the above signs and symptoms. Medical professionals should be alert to the dangers of diving for individuals who have these conditions or who take medications that might alter consciousness or affect a diver's ability to make decisions underwater.

Advice About Diving

Should a person with depression be certified as "fit to dive"? The merits of each case should be considered, including the type of drugs required, the response to medication and the length of time free of depressive or manic incidents. Most divers, particularly those who have responded well to medications over a long term, probably could receive clearance to dive.

We should also consider the following factors: decision-making ability, responsibility for other divers, and drug-induced side effects that could limit a diver's ability to gear up and move in the water.

In all cases, prospective divers should be mindful of the safety of buddies, dive instructors, divemasters and other individuals who might be affected if they were involved in a diving incident due to their condition. Prospective divers should provide full disclosure of their conditions and medications to the dive instructor and certifying agency.

MEDICATIONS

For depression and bipolar disorders (Note: In all cases, the generic name is first, followed by various brand names.)

Buprenorphine / Buprenex

Buprenorphine has been used to treat depression that has not responded to usual medication regimens, such as Prozac and Zoloft.
Possible side effects that may be adverse to diving:
• Drowsiness: A few patients may feel tired after taking buprenorphine.
• Low blood pressure: Avoid standing quickly from a sitting or lying position when using this medication.
• Headache.

Buproprion / Wellbutrin or Zyban

Buproprion is used to treat depression, attention deficit disorder, manic-depression and smoking cessation.
Possible side effect that may be adverse to diving:
• Increased incidence of seizure activity, dose-related.

Buspirone / Buspar

Buspirone, used to treat anxiety or depressive symptoms, aggressiveness, irritability or agitation. This medication may augment the effectiveness of an antidepressant by reducing anxiety, aggression and obsessive-compulsive symptoms.
Possible side effects that may be adverse to diving:
• Drowsiness: Occurs rarely. Make sure you know how you react to this medicine before driving or using dangerous machinery.
• Dizziness: This is uncommon, but may occur 30-60 minutes after taking a dose, with walking or standing.

Carbamazepine / Tegretol

This medication can prevent or reduce the severity of mood swings; it is also helpful in preventing the recurrence of depression.
Possible side effects that may be adverse to diving:
• Drowsiness: This is usually a problem only in the first few weeks. If this persists, use caution while driving or working with dangerous machinery.
• Dizziness: Usually temporary, this will disappear with continued use. Avoid this by rising or changing positions slowly.

Lamotrigine / Lamictal

Lamotrigine belongs to a group of medications called anticonvulsants, which are used to control seizure disorders. In psychiatry, lamotrigine may also be used to stabilize mood, especially in manic-depressive disorders.
Possible side effects that may be adverse to diving:
• Dizziness or drowsiness: Know how you react to this medicine before driving or operating dangerous machinery.
• Balance problems, dizziness, headache, blurred vision, tremor and nausea.

Lithium / Lithonate, Eskalith, Lithobid or Lithane

This medication has several uses. When taken regularly, lithium helps prevent or reduce the severity of mood swings. Lithium can also be used to augment the effectiveness of an antidepressant.
Possible side effects that may be adverse to diving:
• Muscular weakness: This usually diminishes with continued use of the medication.
• Drowsiness: This usually goes away with time. If you are drowsy, use caution with driving or operating dangerous machinery.
NOTE: Too much lithium can cause toxicity, with nausea and vomiting, diarrhea, tremor, dizziness, sleepiness, slurred speech and balance problems.

Monoamine-Oxidase Inhibitors (MAOIs): Phenelzine / Nardil and Tranylcypromine / Parnate

MAOIs are used to treat depression and anxiety disorders. This medication is usually well tolerated.
Possible side effects that may be adverse to diving:
• Dizziness: This may be due to low blood pressure. Dizziness may occur when one rises or changes positions too quickly. Arise or change positions slowly. This tends to occur only the first two months of treatment or with dosage increases. It may be helpful to take the entire dose at bedtime or taking several smaller doses during the day. Contact your physician before making any dosage changes.
• Drowsiness: This is usually transient, lasting up to several months, before the symptoms diminish.
• Tremor: This is an uncommon side effect that may improve with continued use.

Methylphenidate / Ritalin

Methylphenidate is used to treat attention deficit disorder and to augment the effects of antidepressants as a mood elevator.
Possible side effects that may be adverse to diving:
• Excessive stimulation: Consider decreasing the dose or wait longer between doses.
• Nervousness may occur when beginning this medication or when increasing the dose.
• Increased blood pressure. Check weekly while taking Ritalin.
• Increased resting heart rate returns to normal after a couple months.
• Infrequent side effects may include: headache, abdominal discomfort, fatigue.

Mirtazapine / Remeron

Mirtazapine is used to treat depressive and anxiety symptoms.
Possible side effects that may be adverse to diving:
• Drowsiness: Mirtazapine should be taken one hour before bedtime. Make sure you know how you react to this drug before driving or using dangerous machinery. Drowsiness often disappears with increased dose.
• Dizziness: Slowly rise from sitting or lying position.
• Dry mouth: Drink plenty of fluids. Chew sugarless gum or suck on sugarless candy to promote saliva production.

Venlafaxine / Effexor

Venlafaxine is used to treat depressive symptoms and attention deficit hyperactivity disorder.
Possible side effects that may be adverse to diving:
• Anxiety/restlessness, which may diminish with continued use.
• Drowsiness: Make sure you know how you react to this medicine before driving or using dangerous machinery.
• Dry mouth: This may diminish with continued use. Dry mouth may increase your risk for dental disease. Chew sugarless gum and brush at least daily with fluoridated toothpaste.
• Rare side effects include: Seizure, fainting, muscle tightness, menstrual changes, excitability, trouble breathing and swelling of feet or legs.

S-Adenosyl-L-Methionine (SAMe)

SAMe has been shown to alleviate depression, reduce symptoms of fibromyalgia, slow progress of osteoarthritis, improve memory, reduce alcohol-induced liver damage, and possibly reduce symptoms of attention deficit hyperactivity disorder.

Possible side effects that may be adverse to diving:
• Dry mouth: Drink plenty of fluids. Chew sugarless gum or suck on sugarless candy.
• Blurred vision: This is an unusual sign.
• Restlessness, anxiety or elation.
• Patients with manic-depression may change to a manic state.

Sertraline / Zoloft

Sertraline is used to treat depression, anxiety and obsessive-compulsive symptoms.

Possible side effects that may be adverse to diving:
• Anxiety / restlessness, which will usually diminish with continued use.
• Drowsiness: If this occurs, take this medication an hour before bed-time. This usually diminishes with continued use.
• Dry mouth: This may diminish with continued use. Dry mouth may increase your risk for dental disease. Chew sugarless gum and brush at least daily with fluoridated toothpaste.
• Tremor: This tends to diminish with continued use.
• Bruising / bleeding: Use of sertraline can slightly increase the risk of bruising and bleeding, but this can be significant when aspirin or non-steroidal anti-inflammatory drugs (e.g., naproxen, ibuprofen, ketoprofen, flurbiprofen, diclofenac, sulfasalazine, sulindac, oxaprozin, salsalate, piroxicam, indomethacin, etodolac) are also taken. Barotrauma to the middle ears, lungs, sinuses and any air-filled bodily cavity is also a hazard.

St. John's Wort

While the herb St. John's Wort is used to treat mild to moderate depression and possibly anxiety, it is not recommended for treatment of severe depression, including depression with suicidal thoughts, psychotic features (hallucinations, confused thoughts), or melancholia (weight loss, early morning awakening, very low energy).

Possible side effects that may be adverse to diving:
• Anxiety / restlessness, which will usually disappear with continued use.
• Fatigue, which is uncommon and usually disappears with continued use.
• Concentration: Some studies demonstrate improved concentration and attention.
• Dizziness: This is uncommon and usually goes away with continued use.

Tricylic Antidepressants — Tofranil, Elavil, Endep, Norpramine, Pertofrane, Pamelor, Aventyl, Surmontil, Vivactil, Adapin, Sinequan, Anafranil

In fixed-dose combination with other agents (e.g., Etrafon, Triavil, Limbitrol). Tricyclic antidepressants are used to treat depression, anxiety and chronic pain.

Possible side effects that may be adverse to diving:

• Drowsiness: This is usually a problem only during the first few days of starting or increasing the dose. Be cautious with driving and operating dangerous machinery until this symptom clears. If this occurs, take this medication an hour before bedtime. This usually goes away with continued use.

• Dizziness: This may occur when one rises too quickly or rapidly change positions. Avoid this by changing positions slowly, especially during the night.

• Dry mouth: This may disappear with continued use. Dry mouth may increase risk of dental disease. Chew sugarless gum, suck on sugarless candy, drink plenty of water, and brush at least daily with fluoridated toothpaste.

• Blurred vision: Usually temporary, rarely serious and diminishes with continued use.

Topiramate / Topamax

Topiramate belongs to a group of medications called anticonvulsants, used to control seizure disorders. In psychiatry, topiramate may also be used to stabilize mood, especially in manic depression.

Possible side effects that may be adverse to diving:

• Dizziness / drowsiness: Usually goes away with continued use.

• Difficulty concentrating: May not appear until after the first month of taking the medication.

• Tingling feelings of extremities: May disappear after first month of treatment.

• Double vision: May be temporary side effect.

Trazodone / Desyrel

Trazodone is used to treat depression, some sleep problems and agitation.

Possible side effects that may be adverse to diving:

• Drowsiness: You should not drive a car or operate dangerous machinery until you know how this drug affects you. Taking the evening dose 10 hours before rising in the morning may make this more tolerable.

• Dry mouth: Usually temporary. Suck on sugarless candy or chew sugarless gum. Use fluoridated toothpaste at least twice daily.

• Dizziness: May occur when one rises from a lying or sitting position too quickly, especially four to six hours after taking the medication. Rise and change positions more slowly to let your body adjust.

Valproic Acid / Depakote

Valproic acid belongs to a group of medications called anticonvulsants, used to control seizure disorders, but in psychiatry valproic acid may also be used to stabilize mood, especially in manic-depressives.
Possible side effects that may be adverse to diving:
• May cause drowsiness. Know how you react to this medicine before driving or operating dangerous machinery.

Nefazodone / Serzone

Nefazodone is used to treat depression and anxiety symptoms.
Possible side effects that may be adverse to diving:
• Drowsiness: Know drug's side effects for you when deciding to drive a car or operate dangerous machinery.
• Dry mouth: Usually temporary. Suck on sugarless candy or chew sugarless gum. Use fluoridated toothpaste at least twice daily.
• Dizziness: This may occur when you arise from a lying or sitting position too quickly, especially four to six hours after taking your medication. Rise and change positions more slowly to let your body adjust.
• Low blood pressure: Uncommon, it may subside with continued use.
• Blurred vision: Unusual, usually temporary, and usually subsides with continued use.

Paroxetine / Paxil

Paroxetine is used to treat depression, anxiety and obsessive-compulsive disorder.
Possible side effects that may be adverse to diving:
• Anxiety / restlessness: Usually disappears with continued use. If this causes difficulty, contact your psychiatrist.
• Drowsiness: If this occurs, take this medication one hour before bedtime. Disappears with continued use.
• Dry mouth: May disappear with continued use. Dry mouth may increase risk of dental disease. Chew sugarless gum and brush at least daily with fluoridated toothpaste.
• Blurred vision: Usually temporary, will diminish with continued use.
• Tremor: Tends to go away with continued use.
• Bruising / bleeding: Use of paroxetine can slightly increase risk of bruising and bleeding; can be significant when also taking aspirin or non-steroidal anti-inflammatory drugs (e.g., naproxen, ibuprofen, ketoprofen, flurbiprofen, diclofenac, sulfasalazine, sulindac, oxaprozin, salsalate, piroxicam, indomethacin, etodolac). This might be a danger if there is excessive bleeding due to the barotrauma of diving (e.g., middle ears, sinuses, lungs or any air-filled structure in the body).

For more information on depression and medications, consult with your doctor, with the DAN medical department by phone at 1-800-446-2671 or +1-919-684-2948 ext 222, by email at dan@DiversAlertNetwork.org, or register your questions with Dr. Campbell at his website, http://scuba-doc.com

DEPRESSION
Here are some of the symptoms:
- Prolonged sadness or unexplained crying spells
- Significant changes in appetite and sleep patterns
- Irritability, anger, worry, agitation, anxiety
- Pessimism, indifference
- Loss of energy, persistent lethargy
- Feelings of guilt, worthlessness
- Inability to concentrate, indecisiveness
- Inability to take pleasure in former interests, social withdrawal
- Unexplained aches and pains
- Recurring thoughts of death or suicide

MANIC PHASE OF MANIC DEPRESSION:
Here are some of the symptoms:
- Heightened mood, exaggerated optimism and self-confidence
- Decreased need for sleep without experiencing fatigue
- Grandiose delusions, inflated sense of self-importance
- Excessive irritability, aggressive behavior
- Increased physical and mental activity
- Racing speech, flight of ideas, impulsiveness
- Poor judgment, distractability
- Reckless behavior (spending sprees, rash business decisions, erratic driving, sexual indiscretions)
- In the most severe cases, hallucinations

REFERENCES
National Institute of Mental Health
Information Resources and Inquiries Branch
6001 Executive Boulevard, Room 8184, MSC 9663
Bethesda, MD 20892-9663
Telephone: +1-301-443-4513 or 1-866-615-NIMH (6464)
FAX: +1-301-443-4279
TTY: +1-301-443-8431
FAX4U: +1-301-443-5158
Website: http://www.nimh.nih.gov

National Alliance for the Mentally Ill
Colonial Place Three
2107 Wilson Blvd., Suite 300

Arlington, VA 22201-3042
+1-703-524-7600; 1-800-950-NAMI
Website: http://www.nami.org

Depression and Bipolar Support Alliance (DBSA)
730 N. Franklin, Suite 501
Chicago, IL 60610
1-800-826-3632; Fax: +1-312-642-7243
Website: http://www.ndmda.org

National Foundation for Depressive Illness, Inc.
P.O. Box 2257
New York, NY 10016
+1-212-268-4260; 1-800-239-1265
Website: http://www.depression.org

National Mental Health Association
 2001 N. Beauregard Street, 12th Floor
Alexandria, VA 22311
+1-703-684-7722; 1-800-969-6642
FAX: +1-703-684-5968
TTY: 1-800-433-5959
Website: http://www.nmha.org

Robins LN and Regier DA (Eds) (1990). Psychiatric Disorders in America, The Epidemiologic Catchment Area Study, New York: The Free Press.

(Glen Egstrom, PhD, Medical Seminars, 1994. Stress and Performance in Diving by Arthur J Bachrach, Glen H Egstrom, 1987.)

Frank E, Karp JF, and Rush AJ (1993). Efficacy of treatments for major depression. Psychopharmacology Bulletin, 29:457-75.

Lebowitz BD, Pearson JL, Schneider LS, Reynolds CF, Alexopoulos GS, Bruce MI, Conwell Y, Katz IR, Meyers BS, Morrison MF, Mossey J, Niederehe G, and Parmelee P (1997). Diagnosis and treatment of depression in late life: Consensus statement update. Journal of the American Medical Association, 278:1186-90.

Robins LN and Regier DA (Eds) (1990). Psychiatric Disorders in America, The Epidemiologic Catchment Area Study, NY: The Free Press.

Vitiello B and Jensen P (1997). Medication development and testing in children and adolescents. Archives of General Psychiatry, 54:871-6.

www.hoptechno.com/effect.htm

www.biopsychiatry.com/sameart.html

U.S. Department of Education, http://www.ldonline.org/ld_indepth/add_adhd/add_doe_facts.html#anchor550162

— *From Alert Diver, September/October 2000*

Psychological Issues in Diving — Part II

How Anxiety, Phobias and Panic Attacks Can Affect Our Recreation

By Ernest Campbell, M.D.

Anxiety

Anxiety is a normal human emotion we all experience when we face threatening or difficult situations. Associated with the secretion of catecholamines (adrenalin), fear or anxiety can help us avoid dangerous situations or get out of them. It can make us alert and it can spur us to deal with a threat or other problem rather than simply avoiding it (i.e., the "fight or flight" reaction). However, if feelings of foreboding become too strong or last too long, they can hold us back from many normal activities.

In abnormal situations, anxiety is manifested by apprehension and dread, though it cannot be attached to a clearly identifiable stimulus. Anxiety can be accompanied by worried feelings, tiredness, tension, restlessness, loss of concentration, irritability and insomnia. The physical effects of anxiety can range from irregular heartbeat, sweating, muscle tension and pain, heavy, rapid breathing, dizziness, faintness, indigestion and diarrhea, and they're produced by the effects of increased adrenalin.

People who are experiencing extreme anxiety can often mistake these signs and symptoms for evidence of serious physical illness, and worry about this can aggravate the symptoms.

A more intense form of anxiety is panic, a sudden, unexpected but powerful surge of fear. Panic can cause a wholesale flight from the immediate situation, a reaction that is especially dangerous for scuba divers. A diver who experiences panic at depth is subject to near-drowning, lung overexpansion injuries and death.

In susceptible people a heightened awareness of potential but definite dangers, complicated by a normal anxiety of being underwater, can cause a phobic anxiety state. The diver may then develop an actual fear of descending into the water. Some divers experience this while learning to dive, but other stronger motivating factors — finishing the class, spousal, parental or peer approval, an unwillingness to appear fearful to anyone else — can temporarily override their fears.

An overreactive anxiety state usually occurs in response to a mishap, such as a dive mask flooding with water. This may cause the diver to panic unnecessarily and behave irrationally. Often, this results in emergency ascents with the attendant dangers, frantic grabs for air supplies and lack of concern for the safety of others. This reaction is seen more often in those divers who have an above-normal tendency toward anxiety.

Phobias

A phobia is an objectively unfounded fear, an anxiety about particular situations or things that are not dangerous and which most people do not find troublesome. People with phobias have the intense signs of anxiety — e.g., irregular heartbeat, sweating, dizziness, etc., described above.

Phobias arise only from time to time, however, in particularly frightening situations. At other times, those who experience phobias don't feel anxious. If you have a phobia of dogs, you'll feel OK if there are no dogs around; if you are scared of heights, you're OK at ground level; and if you can't face social situations, you will feel calm when there are no other persons around.

A phobia will lead sufferers to avoid situations they know will provoke anxiety, but this will actually worsen the phobia as time goes on. It can also mean that the phobic person's life becomes increasingly dominated by the precautions taken to avoid the situation feared. Phobic individuals usually know that no real danger exists; they may note that they feel silly about their fears, but, still, they cannot control them. Notably, a phobia is more likely to fade away if it began after a distressing or traumatic event.

About one in every 10 persons will have troublesome anxiety or phobia at some point in life. However, most will never ask for treatment. Some divers have true claustrophobia, preventing their immersion into water or their entry into a recompression chamber. This syndrome may surface only during certain times of stress and diminished visibility, such as in murky water, during night diving or during prolonged diving.

This has no one cure, but treatments such as exposure therapy (see the website: www.phobialist.com/treat.html) expose the individual to the situation most feared. The two most popular forms of this therapy are "slow desensitization" and "flooding." Flooding is a rapid and more intense form of desensitization, without the relaxation techniques used in slow desensitization.

Through these treatments, phobia sufferers receive direct exposure to the fear until the anxiety subsides. One can imagine such direct exposure or can actually confront the phobia's trigger, the latter a dangerous method of treatment in the underwater setting.

An agoraphobic reaction in diving, often called blue orb or blue dome syndrome (see website: http://www.scuba-doc.com/bluorb.htm), is what a phobic diver can experience when he or she loses contact with both the bottom and the surface and becomes spatially disoriented.

Sensory deprivation — e.g., limited visibility, murkiness, loss of spatial orientation — can also cause illusions, particularly when visibility is impaired. Anxiety associated with this environment can cause heightened suggestibility and result in mistaking fish, other divers and objects for sharks or other threatening entities.

Panic Disorders

Recent studies suggest that episodes of panic or near-panic may explain many recreational diving accidents and the cause of some diving fatalities. Evidence also shows that individuals who have a high level of underlying anxiety are more likely to have greater responses when exposed to stresses, and, hence, this sub-group of the diving population will experience an increased level of risk. In a recent national survey, more than half of divers reported experiencing at least one panic or near-panic episode.

Panic attacks are often spurred by something that a non-diver would deem serious — entanglement, an equipment malfunction or being startled by some unexpected sea creature. These panic attacks can lead to irrational behavior. If divers and instructors knew more about the phenomenon, perhaps they could screen divers who might be susceptible to life-threatening panic attacks.

Panic attacks are not restricted to beginning divers; experienced scuba divers with hundreds of logged dives sometimes experience panic for no apparent reason. In such cases, it is believed that panic occurs because divers lose sight of familiar objects, become disoriented and experience sensory deprivation. However, among inexperienced divers, panic generally results from a specific reason, such as a loss of air or an encounter with a shark.

Panic can occur when divers reacts quickly but irrationally: their attention narrows, and they lose the ability to sort out options. If, for example, a problem develops with the regulator, the restricted air flow could prompt a panicked diver to ascend rapidly enough to cause an often-fatal arterial gas embolism (bubble) in the bloodstream. This would be considered a panic response if the diver had other safe options, such as access to a pony bottle (an emergency air supply) or was diving with others who could share their air supply, allowing a gradual ascent.

Some diving activities inevitably lead to anxiety: the stresses of equipment malfunctions, dangerous marine life (e.g., sharks), loss of orientation during cave dives, under-ice or wreck penetration dives, and other stress-laden situations. Diving with faulty or inappropriate equipment or performing high-risk dives has a greater potential to cause panic episodes; with appropriate training and cautionary actions, however, we can prevent or minimize these problems.

Trait Anxiety Versus State Anxiety

Trait anxiety is a psychological phenomenon regarded as a stable or enduring feature of personality; state anxiety is situational, or transitory. Individuals who score high on measures of trait anxiety are more likely to have an increased state of anxiety and panic during scuba activities, and they are at potentially greater risk than those scoring in the "normal" range.

Many dive physicians feel that such individuals probably should not dive. It has been found that interventions such as biofeedback, hypnosis, imagery and relaxation have not been effective in reducing anxiety responses associated with panic attacks. Psychological research has shown that hypnosis is effective in relaxing scuba divers, but it can also have the undesired effect of increasing heat loss in divers. Relaxation can lead to increased anxiety and panic attacks in some highly anxious individuals (this is known as relaxation-induced anxiety, or RIA). Individuals with a history of high anxiety and panic episodes should probably be identified if possible and counseled during scuba training classes about the potential risks.

Advice About Scuba Diving

In determining whether a person with anxiety, phobias and panic attacks should be certified as fit to dive, each case should be evaluated on its own merits, including the types of drugs required (if any), response to medication and the amount of time free of anxiety and phobia.

Individuals who score high on measures of trait anxiety most probably should not dive, but, if they choose to dive, they should be carefully monitored and fully informed of the risks, with special consideration to one's decision-making ability and responsibility to other divers.

In all cases, prospective divers should fully disclose their conditions and medications to the dive instructor and certifying agency. They should bear in mind the safety of their potential dive buddies, dive instructors, divemasters and other individuals who are affected by diving incidents.

MEDICATIONS
For Anxiety, Phobias & Panic Disorders
(Note: Many of the medications listed under "depression" are also used for anxiety. Generic names are listed first; common brand names follow).

Benzodiazepines

Medications in this group used to treat anxiety include: Alprazolam / Xanax; Chlordiazepoxide / Librium; Clonazepam / Klonopin; Clorazepate / Tranxene; Diazepam / Valium; Halazepam / Paxipam; Lorazepam / Ativan; Oxazepam / Serax; Prazepam / Centrax.
Side effects adverse to diving:
• Drowsiness: A common side effect. Be sure you know how you react to this medicine before driving or using dangerous machinery.
• Dizziness: Be careful about standing up quickly, going up and down stairs and driving.
• Difficulty learning: An unusual side effect, it tends to go away quickly with continued use.

Beta Blockers

Medications in this group used to treat anxiety include: Propanolol / Inderol; Pindolol / Visken; Atenolol / Tenormin; Acebutolol / Sectral; Betazolol / Kerlone; Bisoprolol / Ziac or Zebeta; Carteolol / Cartrol; Carvedilol / Coreg; Labetalol / Normodyne or Trandate; Metoprolol / Lopressor; Nadolol / Corgard or Corzide; Penbutolol / Levatol; Timolol / Blocadren or Timolide.
Side effects adverse to diving:
• Drowsiness: A common side effect. Make sure you know how you react to this medicine before driving or using dangerous machinery.
• Dizziness: Be careful about standing up quickly, going up and down stairs, and driving.
• Low blood pressure.
• Slow pulse: Particularly important to divers, as they may not be able to respond to exercise and stress.
• Breathing difficulty, wheezing, cough.
• Dry mouth: Drink plenty of fluids. Chew sugarless gum. Suck on sugarless candy. Pay special attention to dental hygiene (brush and floss regularly).

Patients with asthma or diabetes may develop special side effects while taking these medications. Also, physicians advise their patients to be aware that beta blockers can affect their tolerance to exercise.

Ed. Note: Regarding divers' use of beta blockers, here are some viewpoints.

Dr. Alfred Bove ("Diving Medicine," 3rd Edition, 1997) states the following about beta blockade: " . . . many cardiovascular drugs can alter exercise tolerance . . ." and "Patients using beta-adrenergic blocking medication will demonstrate some inhibition of the heart rate response to exercise." Dr. Bove also states: "Although the heart rate response is blunted this will rarely interfere with diving, because diving should not provoke maximum work demand."

To Dr. Bove's last statement Dr. Campbell, author of this article, advises: "There are occasions in which a diver will panic, have an anxiety attack or actually need to exert in dangerous situations and may be unable to have an adequate cardiovascular response." He adds: "Patients who have experienced adverse drug reactions from beta blockers due to combination therapy with calcium channel blockers or impaired metabolism due to renal or hepatic dysfunction should have their dosages adjusted or medications changed to avoid recurrent complications."

Dosages of beta blockers are not mentioned in Bove. "The usual therapeutic regimen" is mentioned.

Dive physician and author Dr. Carl Edmonds in "Diving and Subaquatic Medicine" (1992) cautions: "There should be an awareness of the effects of reduced exercise tolerance and autonomic system blockade," and "Beta blockers may also have other side effects such as bronchospasm."

Celexa / Citalopram

Celexa is used to treat depression, anxiety and obsessive-compulsive disorder.
Possible side effects adverse to diving:
• Anxiety / restlessness: This will usually go away with continued use.
• Drowsiness / dizziness: Avoid driving or working with dangerous machinery until the effect of this medication is known.
• Bruising / bleeding: Use of Celexa can slightly increase risk of bruising and bleeding, but this can be significant when aspirin or non-steroidal anti-inflammatory drugs (e.g., naproxen, ibuprofen, ketoprofen, flurbiprofen, diclofenac, sulfasalazine, sulindac, oxaprozin, salsalate, piroxicam, indomethacin, etodolac) are also taken. Barotrauma to sinuses, ears and lungs may cause significant hemorrhage because of this tendency for bruising and bleeding.

Fluoxetine / Prozac

Fluoxetine is used to treat depression, anxiety, and obsessive-compulsive disorder.

Possible side effects adverse to diving:

• Anxiety / restlessness: Goes away with continued use.

• Tremor: Tends to go away with continued use.

• Bruising / bleeding: Use of fluoxetine can slightly increase risk of bruising and bleeding, but this can be significant when aspirin or non-steroidal anti-inflammatory drugs (e.g., naproxen, ibuprofen, ketoprofen, flurbiprofen, diclofenac, sulfasalazine, sulindac, oxaprozin, salsalate, piroxicam, indomethacin, etodolac) are also taken.

Fluvoxamine / Luvox

Fluvoxamine is used to treat depressive, anxiety and obsessive-compulsive symptoms.

Possible side effects adverse to diving:

• Anxiety / restlessness: Will usually diminish with continued use. If anxiety causes difficulty, consult with your physician.

• Drowsiness: If this occurs, take this medication one hour before bedtime. Make sure you know how you react to this medicine before you drive or use dangerous machinery. Drowsiness usually diminishes with continued use.

• Tremor: Tends to diminish with continued use.

• Bruising / bleeding: Use of fluvoxamine can slightly increase risk of bruising and bleeding, but this can be significant when aspirin or non-steroidal anti-inflammatory drugs (e.g., naproxen, ibuprofen, ketoprofen, flurbiprofen, diclofenac, sulfasalazine, sulindac, oxaprozin, salsalate, piroxicam, indomethacin, etodolac) are also taken. Bleeding with barotrauma would be a concern.

Narcolepsy

A chronic disorder affecting the part of the brain where regulation of sleep and wakefulness take place, narcolepsy can be viewed as an intrusion by dreaming sleep (REM, or rapid eye movement) into the waking state.

Should people with narcolepsy become certified for scuba diving? No scientific studies exist on the subject: all that is written is pure supposition, based on knowledge of the condition and knowledge of what can happen to the diver with decreased awareness or consciousness.

Some individuals, no matter how much they sleep, continue to experience an irresistible need to sleep — these persons are narcoleptics. People with narcolepsy can fall asleep while working, talking or driving a car. These "sleep attacks" can last from 30 seconds to more than 30 minutes. They may also experience periods of cataplexy, or loss of muscle tone, which ranges from a slight buckling at the knees to a complete, "rag doll" limpness throughout the body.

In the general population, narcolepsy happens to one in every 2,000 people. It can occur at any time throughout life, but it will most likely begin during the teen years. Although narcolepsy has been found to be hereditary, some environmental factors contribute. Narcolepsy is a disabling and underdiagnosed illness: for sufferers, the effects can be devastating.

Studies have shown that even treated patients are often significantly psychosocially impaired in the areas of work, leisure and interpersonal relations, and they are more prone to accidents. These effects are even more severe than the well-documented deleterious effects of epilepsy when similar criteria are used for comparison.

Symptoms include excessive sleepiness, a temporary decrease or loss of muscle control (sometimes associated with getting excited), vivid dreamlike images when drifting off to sleep and waking up unable to move or talk for a period of time.

Narcolepsy and Driving

Several states have imposed driving restrictions on people with narcolepsy. These restrictions usually entail a narcolepsy-free period of one year after starting treatment and no drug-related symptoms. Although these restrictions do not extend to scuba diving, some dive physicians believe such guidelines may be advisable.

Side effects from the drugs used to combat the sleepiness of narcolepsy constitute another concern. Medications used to treat narcolepsy include stimulants, anticataleptic compounds and hypnotic compounds, some of which have definite effects and side effects that are definitely adverse for scuba divers.

Stimulants that increase the metabolic rate, as some narcolepsy-fighting medications do, can cause an increased risk of oxygen toxicity in divers using enriched air (nitrox). Any drug that affects the sense organs can also alter the decision-making process or increase risk-taking, and they are definitely adverse to divers.

Advice About Diving

The merits of each case, the drugs required, the response to medication and the length of time free of narcolepsy should determine each diver's fitness. How each diver copes with excitement, emotions and stressful situations are key considerations.

Any prospective diver should fully disclose this condition and any medications to the dive instructor and certifying agency. In addition, any prospective diver with narcolepsy should be mindful of the safety of buddies, dive instructors, divemasters and other individuals who can be affected by this causing a diving incident. Divers with this condition who choose to dive might consider using a full face mask to decrease the risk of drowning in case of unconsciousness during a dive.

— From Alert Diver, November/December 2000

Psychological Issues in Diving — Part III

'Scubadoc' Discusses Schizophrenia, Marijuana and Alcohol Use

By Ernest Campbell, M.D.

Little research exists to characterize the relationship between mental conditions and scuba diving. Other than the obvious reasons people shouldn't dive — they are out of touch with reality, severely depressed and suicidal or paranoid with delusions and hallucinations — many people with everyday anxieties, fears and neuroses can dive, and do.

Successful divers generally have profiles that are characterized by little or no neuroticism, and these divers score well on studies of self-sufficiency and emotional stability.

Some actual psychological disturbances are well known, but, as for their associated risks of scuba diving, they are poorly studied and documented. This group of disorders includes the depressions, bipolar disorder, anxiety and phobias, panic disorders, narcolepsy and schizophrenia. (Note: These were discussed in Parts I and II with the exception of schizophrenia, covered in this story.)

In addition to the risks caused by the condition itself, we must consider the possible hazards of the effects of medications — taken singly or in combination. In diving, medications play a secondary role to the condition for which they are prescribed. A mood-altering medication, for example, should be used with care in diving. Likewise, drugs that carry warnings as dangerous for use while driving or when using hazardous equipment should be considered dangerous for divers.

The interaction between the physiological effects of diving and the pharmacological effects of medications is usually an educated, yet unproven, assumption. Each situation requires individual evaluation: no general rule applies to all. Currently, there are no specific studies that indicate the safety or danger associated with drugs and diving.

Finally, divers have different personalities; each responds differently to abnormal physiological states and changes in the environment from the effects of various gases under pressure. Such states as inert gas narcosis, carbon dioxide toxicity, oxygen toxicity, high-pressure nervous syndrome (HPNS) and deep-water blackout all can cause reactions that are similar to a psychoneurotic reaction or an organic cerebral syndrome.

Before allowing or barring someone with psychological problems to dive, the certifying physician must know all the possibilities and variations in each individual case.

SCHIZOPHRENIA

Schizophrenia is a serious mental illness that affects one person in 100. It usually develops in the late teens or early twenties, though it can start in middle age or even much later in life. The earlier it begins, the more potential it has to damage the personality and the ability to lead a normal life. Although schizophrenia is treatable, relapses are common, and it may never resolve entirely. Sufferers typically have difficulty working and studying, relating to other people and leading independent lives. It causes great distress in families.

With this disorder, thoughts, feelings and actions are somewhat disconnected from each other. This may be easier to illustrate by describing the symptoms: Positive symptoms are abnormal experiences; negative symptoms are more an absence of normal behavior; and disorganized symptoms indicate the extent of disorganization of the patient's thought processes and vocalizations.

Positive Symptoms

We normally feel that we are in control of our thoughts and actions, but schizophrenia interferes with this feeling of being "the captain of the ship." It may feel as though thoughts are being put into the mind or removed by some outside, uncontrollable force. At worst, the whole personality seems to be under the influence of an outside force. This is a terrifying experience, which the person tries to explain according to education and upbringing.

Hallucination is the experience of hearing, smelling, feeling or seeing something that is not there. Voices are the most common hallucination, and they often appear so real that the hearer is convinced that they come from the outside — as if from loudspeakers or a spirit world. These voices are distressing, as they talk about the person as well as to the person.

Delusions, false and usually unusual beliefs, cannot be explained by the believer's culture or changed by argument. These ideas may be fantastic, as in "I'm God's messenger!" or apparently reasonable — "Everyone at work is against me." Persecutory delusions are especially distressing for the family if members are seen as the persecutors. Delusions may come out of the blue or may start as an explanation for hallucinations or the sensation of being "taken over."

Negative Symptoms

These affect interest, energy, emotional life and everyday activities. Those individuals with negative symptoms generally avoid meeting people, say little or nothing and may appear emotionally blank.

Disorganized Symptoms

Schizophrenia often interferes with a person's train of thought; it often becomes difficult to understand them. Those with schizophrenia will shout back at their voices or will comply with the instructions of the voices, often hurting themselves or others.

Some Background on Schizophrenia

The cause of this condition is unknown. However, approximately one in 10 persons with schizophrenia has a parent who suffers from the illness. The gene, or combination of genes, responsible has yet to be discovered.

An episode of schizophrenia can occur after a stressful event — and, though it cannot be the cause, it may help to bring on the illness. Long-term stress, such as family tensions, may also make it worse. Street drugs like ecstasy, LSD, amphetamines and marijuana (as well as hashish and ganja) are thought to help bring on schizophrenia in some individuals. There is no evidence that it is brought on by disturbed families.

Before the advent of the anti-psychotic drug Thorazine® in the 1950s, many people with schizophrenia spent most of their lives in mental hospitals. Things have changed since then, and most people with the illness are treated outside hospitals for most of their lives.

After a first episode of schizophrenia, about a quarter (25 percent) of the individuals experiencing it make a good recovery within five years; two-thirds (60-65 percent) will have multiple episodes with some degree of disability between these episodes; and 10-15 percent will develop severe continuous incapacity. Although the illness is severe and disruptive, many people who experience it are eventually able to settle down, work and build lasting relationships.

Medications

Since 1954, physicians have used a number of drugs to treat schizophrenia. Most work by blocking the path of dopamine, a particular chemical messenger in the brain. The drugs usually suppress the so-called positive symptoms, delusions and hallucinations. These symptoms gradually go away in a few weeks, but side effects can occur, causing stiffness and shakiness, like Parkinson's disease. These symptoms can be reduced by giving anti-Parkinsonian drugs.

Anti-schizophrenia drugs may also cause slowing up, sleepiness and weight gain. The worse consequence, unwanted and lasting movements of the mouth and tongue, is tardive dyskinesia (TD). This affects individuals who have taken anti-schizophrenia drugs for a year of more. This condition may not end even if the drugs are stopped.

Fortunately, new drugs block different chemical messengers, and they are much less likely to cause side effects. They may also help the negative symptoms, on which the older drugs have very little effect.

Because of the risk of repeated episodes, it is usually advisable to take drugs for years, if not for a lifetime. Although the dose is less than for an acute episode, some drugs can still cause side effects.

Advice About Diving

Merits of each case, the type of drugs required, the response to medication, and the length of time free of the disorder should determine whether a person with schizophrenia should be certified as fit to dive. Most probably should not consider diving.

However, some individuals who have responded well to medications over a long term may be considered for diving. Authorities should consider how one's decision-making ability, responsibility to other divers and any drug-induced side effects might limit a diver's ability to gear up and move in the water. Prospective divers should fully disclose such information to the dive instructor and certifying agency. Individuals responsible for divers should be alert to divers with inappropriate responses or activity, paranoid behavior or unusual ideas and be quick to ask about the possibility of schizophrenia.

MEDICATIONS FOR SCHIZOPHRENIA

NOTE: In all cases, the generic name is first, followed by various brand names.

Clozapine / Clozaril

Clozaril is used to treat nervous, mental and emotional conditions such as preoccupation with troublesome and recurring thoughts and unpleasant and unusual experiences such as hearing and seeing things not normally seen or heard.

Blood tests:
• Clozapine can cause a low white blood cell count in 1-2 percent of patients, which usually occurs between six to 18 weeks after starting Clozapine. White blood cells help to fight infections. Diving could possibly increase the risks of severe vibrio (aquatic bacteria) infection.

Possible adverse side effects for divers:
• Seizure: This has occurred in 1-2 percent of patients taking less than 300 mg / day; 3-4 percent taking 300-600 mg / day; and 5 percent over 600 mg / day. If a seizure occurs, contact your physician immediately.
• Increased saliva production: Most patients will experience this side effect, with some tolerance developing after eight-12 weeks. Increased salivation could increase the production of swallowed air, with attendant difficulty on ascent.
• Tiredness, dizziness: This usually improves or goes away in three to four weeks.
• Low blood pressure with standing: This condition usually improves over time. Discuss the dosage with your physician.
• Faster heartbeat: This usually is not serious, and tolerance may develop.
• Restlessness, tremors, stiffness, muscle spasms are uncommon, but can be treated.

Quetiapine / Seroquel

Quetiapine is used to treat psychotic symptoms and disorders.
Possible adverse side effects for divers:
• Low blood pressure: This usually occurs with standing from a lying or sitting position. Arise slowly and allow your body more time to adjust the blood pressure.
• Sleepiness: This is common, but usually mild and transient.
• Cataracts: One study with dogs showed a possible increase in cataract formation. This has not yet been reported in humans. You should have your eyes examined every six months.
• Other occasional side effects may include headache, dry mouth, dizziness, insomnia, constipation and agitation.

Quetiapine may cause muscle stiffness, hand tremors, face and mouth movements and, rarely, neuroleptic malignant syndrome, or high fever, stiffness, and flu-like symptoms. These symptoms occur less often than with older typical anti-psychotic medications.

Risperidone / Risperdal

Risperidone is used to treat nervous, mental and emotional conditions such as preoccupation with troublesome and recurring thoughts and unpleasant and unusual experiences such as hearing and seeing things not normally seen or heard.

How does it work?
The effects of this medication appear to be related to reducing activity of dopamine in the brain. It also blocks some serotonin activity in the brain. Some of the benefits may occur in the first few days, but it is not

unusual for it to take several weeks or months to see the full benefits. In contrast, many of the side effects are worse when you first start taking it. *Possible adverse side effects for divers:*
• All medications that act on dopamine can sometimes have side effects involving muscle coordination or muscle tension. It appears that risperidone is somewhat less likely to cause this type of side effect than others. Examples can include stiffness in the arms, back or neck. Sometimes patients experience shakiness or problems with muscle coordination.
• Some people who take risperidone may become more sensitive to sunlight. When you first begin taking this medicine, avoid too much sun and do not use a sun lamp until you see how you react, especially if you tend to burn easily. If you burn easily or have a severe reaction, contact your physician.

New Drugs for Schizophrenia

Atypical antipsychotic drugs on the market currently include clozapine, risperidone (described above) and olanzapine (described below). Use of these medications in selected patients who do not benefit from, or cannot tolerate, traditional agents is an important step in improving their lives.

The use of traditional antipsychotic medications has been limited — by their substantial side effects and the failure in some cases to achieve long-term control of symptoms. New "atypical" antipsychotic drugs show promise for the treatment of resistant cases of schizophrenia and improvement in patient tolerance and compliance. These medications have been more successful than traditional antipsychotic drugs in treating the negative symptoms of schizophrenia, such as social withdrawal and apathy.

The atypical antipsychotic drugs produce fewer side effects and no tardive dyskinesia or abnormal tonicity in muscles. However clozapine can produce fatal agranulocytosis, an acute condition where there is a great reduction in the production of white blood cells.

Olanzapine / Zyprexa

Olanzapine is used to treat psychotic symptoms and disorders.
Possible adverse side effects for divers:
• Tiredness, dizziness, insomnia, nervousness, restlessness, nausea, vomiting, constipation, dry mouth, runny or stuffy nose, increased salivation, weight loss or gain, increased heart rate and low blood pressure withstanding.

• Olanzapine may cause muscle stiffness, hand tremors, face and mouth movements, and rarely neuroleptic malignant syndrome (high fever, stiffness, and flu-like symptoms). These symptoms occur less often than with older typical anti-psychotic medications.

OTHER AGENTS AFFECTING THE CNS: ALCOHOL

Research has shown that one's ability to process information diminishes, particularly in tasks that require undivided attention for many hours, after the blood alcohol level has reached 0.015 percent. This means that the risk for injury of a hung over diver increases significantly, particularly if high blood alcohol (BAC) levels were reached during the drinking episode.

The American Medical Association (AMA) upper limit of the BAC for driving a vehicle in the United States is 0.05 percent. Surely diving with any alcohol on board would be foolish, considering the alien environment (water) and the complex skills required to follow no decompression procedures.

Alcohol Impairment

The following behavioral components required for safe diving diminish when alcohol is on board or has been on board in the previous 24 hours:
• Reaction time
• Visual tracking performance
• Concentrated attention
• Ability to process information in divided attention tasks
• Perception (judgment)
• The execution of psychomotor tasks.

The individual who has alcohol on board may not feel impaired or even appear impaired to the observer, but that person definitely is impaired. This can persist for extended periods. The use of alcohol, even in moderate doses, clearly carries a self-destructive aspect of behavior and leads to higher probabilities for serious accidents.

Alcohol is a Diuretic

In addition, alcohol produces dehydration, which is a major contributor to decompression illness. In any form, alcohol has a direct effect on the kidneys, causing an obligatory loss of body fluids.

Many divers appreciate a cool beer, but drinking and diving can turn a safe sport into a nightmare for partners in the dive. They should think twice before drinking alcohol before diving.

Recent discussions in scuba magazines, chat rooms and scuba forums have concluded that it's OK to drink beer between dives during a surface interval. Some divers insist on drinking beer before and after their dives. Does drinking alcoholic beverages and diving pose any danger? The short answer is this: By drinking alcohol before and during diving trips, a diver severely endangers not only himself but his buddy!

A study by Perrine, Mundt and Weiner found scuba diving performances significantly degraded at blood alcohol levels of 40 mg / dl (0.04 percent BAC). The study also cites a clear increase in the risk of injury at this level, which can be reached by a 180-pound / 81-kilogram man who ingests two 12-ounce / 336-gram beers in one hour on an empty stomach. This study once again points out that one experiences a diminished awareness of cues and reduced inhibitions at relatively low levels of blood alcohol. Their study used well-trained divers who were being paid to do their best; their diving performances were being videotaped.

Dr. Glen Egstrom, Ph.D., has stated the problem succinctly: his review of more than 150 studies on the effects of alcohol on performance has resulted in the following observations:

1. Ingestion of even small amounts of alcohol does not improve performance; to the contrary, it degrades performance.
2. While certain variables can speed up or delay the onset of the effects of alcohol, they are minor issues, which do not overcome the decrements to the central and peripheral nervous system.
3. Alcohol can be cleared from the blood at a predictable rate, usually .015 BAC per hour. This does not necessarily mean that the diminished performances have been completely eliminated in that time.
4. Alcohol, a depressant drug, slows certain body functions by depressing the entire central nervous system. Effects are noticeable after one drink.
5. The effects are mood elevation, mild euphoria, a sense of well being, slight dizziness and some impairment of judgment, self control, inhibitions and memory.
6. Increases in reaction time and decreases in coordination follow the dose / response curve quite well.
7. Alcohol is involved in roughly 50 percent of all accidents involving persons of drinking age.
8. Persons who have been drinking alcohol consistently underestimate its deleterious effects on performance.
9. Alcohol affects divided attention tasks to a greater degree than those tasks requiring a single focus of concentration. For example, a diver will be affected to a greater degree by a shallow water head-first dive, which required many interrelated decisions necessary to a successful dive, than by lifting a heavy weight.

Naltrexone / Revia

Naltrexone is used to treat alcoholism, by diminishing craving and the effect of alcohol. It is also used to decrease impulsivity associated with self-destructive behaviors.

Possible adverse side effects for divers:

• Dizziness: This is a fairly common side effect, which often disappears with continued use.

• Less common side effects may include: headache, constipation, nervousness, fatigue, insomnia, limb or abdominal pain, and weight loss.

Haloperidol / Haldol

Haldol is a butyropherone derivative with antipsychotic properties that have been considered particularly effective in the management of hyperactivity, agitation and mania.

MARIJUANA

• Marijuana is a psychoactive, sedating drug.

• The more marijuana is used, the shorter its effects last.

• Tolerance to the psychoactive effects develops with continued use.

• Psychological and mild physical dependence gradually occurs with regular use.

Withdrawal symptoms include:

• Restlessness, insomnia, nausea, irritability, loss of appetite, sweating.

• Risk of adverse reactions is greater for persons who have had schizophrenia or other psychotic disorder, depression, dysthymia (mood disorder), and bipolar disorder (manic depression).

• Tar content of marijuana is significantly greater than cigarettes, with more carcinogens (substances producing or inciting cancer).

Potentially harmful effects to divers include:

• Accidents and deaths caused by distortions in perception of time, body image and distance.

• Impairment of recent memory, confusion, decreased concentration.

• Decreased muscle strength and balance.

• Decreased blood flow in brain.

• Impaired ability to perform complex motor tasks.

• Poor memory.

• Amotivational syndrome.

• Depression, especially in new users.

• 50 percent of users will have a "bad trip," a severe panic reaction with fear of dying or losing one's mind.

• Fast heart rate and lower exercise tolerance.

• Dry mouth and throat.

High doses may cause:
• Hallucinations.
• Depersonalization.
• Paranoia.
• Agitation.
• Extreme panic.

Chronic use may cause:
• Bronchitis, sinusitis, pharyngitis (inflammation of the mucous membrane and underlying parts of the pharynx), chronic cough, emphysema, lung cancer.
• Poor immune system functioning; severe marine infections.
• Poor motivation, depressed mental functioning.

ABOUT THE AUTHOR
Ernest S. Campbell, M.D., FACS is the Webmaster at Diving Medicine Online. Contact him at scubadoc@scuba-doc.com, or visit the website: http://scuba-doc.com

— From Alert Diver, March 2001

Section 14

Respiratory (Breathing)

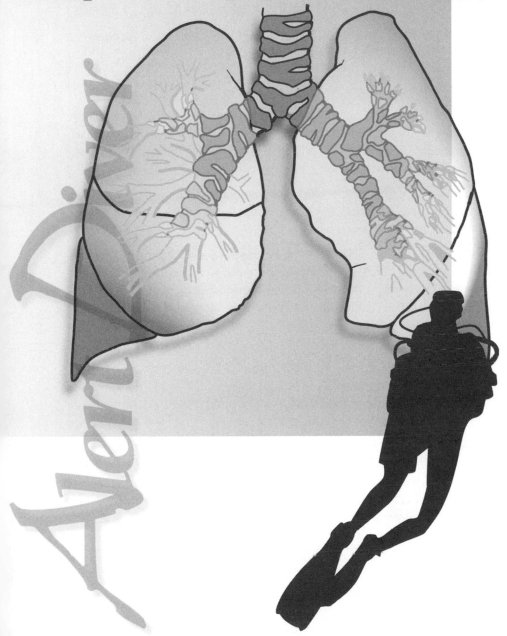

Pulmonary Considerations in Diving

DAN Medical Director Dr. Richard Moon discusses lung diseases that prospective divers must consider when choosing to dive

By Dr. Richard Moon, DAN Vice President and Medical Director

The human body consists of several different body systems, and each serves a specific purpose. For example, the central nervous system carries all our neural messages, from balance to sight and hearing, touch, smell and taste. We could not navigate our environment without our nervous system.

Thousands of diseases can affect the systems in our bodies, but remarkably, enough reserve seems to be built into our systems that we can easily survive many traumas. Even with the removal of part of a body system, like part of the intestines, a kidney or even a lung, we can live on.

Today, with modern medicine and science on our side, we change our participation in very few activities to accommodate disease. After disease, people can maintain active lifestyles.

With specific diseases, however, we need to be aware of the systems they affect. If we're involved with scuba diving, for example, we should pay special attention to diseases of the lungs. Although some divers may continue diving actively with little or no limitations after disease or other trauma, scuba diving carries a special risk for those who have suffered some types of lung disorders.

When they're engaged in diving, scuba divers can usually tolerate the small changes that occur in the lung air spaces. In certain lung diseases such as sarcoidosis*, however, lung tissue can stiffen, causing potential problems for scuba divers. For anyone who wants to take up diving or continue diving after illness, any condition that restricts or impedes the flow of air into and out of the lung can be problematic.

Dr. Richard Moon, DAN's Medical Director and Professor of Anesthesiology at Duke University Medical Center, has explained the basic physiology of the lung and associated diseases we must consider when we choose scuba diving as a recreational activity. Although incomplete, the list of lung diseases does refer to the most commonly asked questions that DAN receives about lung disease. Healthy lungs are essential for safe diving.

— Joel Dovenbarger, Vice President, DAN Medical Services

* Sarcoidosis: A disease of unknown cause, it results in inflammation and scarring in the lung tissue.

The human body consumes oxygen to generate energy from foods such as glucose; it also produces carbon dioxide as a byproduct of this activity. The lungs, vital to this process, add oxygen to the blood and remove carbon dioxide.

To accomplish this, gas must move into and out of the lungs (i.e., breathing, or ventilation) at a rate governed by the level of exertion. At rest, in normal breathing, gas moves at a rate of around 5 liters per minute, but during heavy exercise, the body accommodates an increased requirement for oxygen and greater production of carbon dioxide. This may increase the ventilation rate to about 100 liters per minute. Since the muscles of respiration, such as the diaphragm, can move as much as 150 liters of gas into and out of the lungs per minute, a reserve usually exists.

Breathing Capacity and Limits

However, during diving, two factors can limit the breathing capacity. First, the density of the breathing gases increases. At 33 feet / 10 meters, the density is twice as high as at the surface; at 66 feet / 20 meters, it is three times as high, and so on. Higher gas density increases the breathing resistance, which in turn reduces the maximum ventilation. In a dry hyperbaric chamber, experiments have demonstrated that at 130 feet / 40 meters a person's maximum ventilation is reduced by 40 percent.

Additionally, immersion in water can further reduce breathing capabilities. This effect, mostly due to movement of blood from the legs into the vessels of the lung, causes the lungs to become slightly more stiff, and thereby increases the mechanical load on the breathing muscles.

Also, the breathing resistance of the regulator can reduce a diver's ventilation. At high levels of exertion under water, maximum sustainable ventilation can be reduced below the level required for adequate carbon dioxide exchange. When this happens, the diver may experience shortness of breath and subsequent panic. Carbon dioxide levels in the blood rise and can exacerbate nitrogen narcosis. During extreme exertion, high levels of carbon dioxide may even cause unconsciousness.

For healthy divers, this is likely to occur only during heavy exertion at depths below 100 feet / 30 meters. However, lung disease, which can reduce maximum breathing capabilities even at the surface, may limit ventilation even during moderate exertion at shallower depths. Lung diseases such as asthma, emphysema, sarcoidosis and other diseases that affect large proportions of the lung can reduce maximum ventilation. A physician can quantify breathing capacity using a pulmonary function test.

Diving and Asthma

A medical conference on diving and asthma in 1995 recommended that a prospective diver should have normal spirometry, or pulmonary function test, before and after a maneuver that typically exacerbates asthma, such as exercise (see Elliott, D.H., ed. "Are Asthmatics Fit to Dive?" Kensington, MD: Undersea and Hyperbaric Medical Society, 1996).

The consensus was that divers with chronic asthma should dive only if they meet these guidelines: 1) that they have no symptoms (e.g., wheezing, cough, shortness of breath); and 2) that they have normal breathing function (determined, for example, by using a personal instrument such as a peak-flow meter).

In the United States, every diver does not need a pulmonary function test, but it is recommended that prospective divers with any lung disease that may affect breathing capacity receive a formal assessment of pulmonary function by a physician.

Formerly, individuals who suffered asthma of any kind were advised not to dive. However, if symptoms are eliminated and breathing capacity is normal, the evidence suggests that the risk of diving is not excessive.

For more information on this topic, see "Asthma & Diving" by Guy de Lisle Dear, M.B., FRCA, DAN Assistant Medical Director, in the January/February 1997 issue.

Pulmonary Barotrauma

Another issue is the ability of the lungs to exhale gas during ascent. In training, divers learn that breath-holding during ascent can cause the pressure in the lungs to increase, producing rupture of air sacs. This in turn causes lung collapse (pneumothorax), entry of air into the tissues surrounding the heart (pneumomediastinum) or the skin (subcutaneous emphysema or crackly skin). Air can also track into the tissues around the larynx (causing an abnormal voice) and the pulmonary blood vessels (arterial gas embolism).

These three situations are referred to as pulmonary barotrauma. Some lung diseases can lead to pulmonary barotrauma during ascent, even if the diver does not engage in breath-holding. Examples include lung conditions in which there are cysts, or balloon-like extensions of air sacs (known as blebs or bullae). Because these sacs are thin-walled, and tend to empty their air slowly, pressure can build up during ascent and they may rupture, causing lung collapse.

Other conditions that have an increased risk of pulmonary barotrauma include:

• lung diseases that cause obstruction of air passages (such as asthma that is not optimally medicated);

• certain diseases in which there is scarring or inflammation of the lung tissue (such as sarcoidosis, eosinophilic granuloma, interstitial fibrosis or scarring due to other causes); and

• previous spontaneous pneumothorax — anyone who has previously experienced a spontaneous (i.e. without diving) pneumothorax or pneumomediastinum faces heightened risk of this injury.

For individuals with any lung condition that has an increased risk of pulmonary barotrauma, diving physicians recommend that they avoid scuba diving.

In addition, individuals who have experienced arterial gas embolism, pneumothorax, pneumomediastinum or subcutaneous emphysema should not dive until they have been evaluated by a physician. Sometimes a specialized scan of the lungs (computed tomography, CT or CAT scan) can be used to look for a small bleb that cannot be seen on a plain chest X-ray. However, whether some people can be predisposed to one of these problems and yet still have a normal CT scan is unknown.

Some lung infections such as tuberculosis can cause scarring of the lung and enlargement of lymph nodes in the chest. This condition in turn could compress airways and predispose an individual to pulmonary barotrauma. Individuals who have had successful treatment of tuberculosis should get a chest X-ray and consult a physician prior to being evaluated to scuba dive.

Some individuals who have experienced two or more episodes of spontaneous pneumothorax have had surgery to reduce the probability of a future occurrence. This surgery may entail either removal of visible blebs (and hence the inciting factor) or introducing an irritant material between the two layers of pleura (called pleurodesis), rendering complete lung collapse impossible.

Another type of operation aims to prevent pneumothorax by surgically removing or stapling visible blebs. However, two instances of serious arterial gas embolism in divers who have had surgery for recurrent pneumothorax have been reported to DAN. Thus, although pneumothorax may be prevented by such operations, it appears that gas embolism in divers can still occur.

Other Risk Factors: Surgery, Trauma, Smoking, Colds

Pneumothorax can also occur due to trauma, either penetrating (e.g., from a stab wound) or blunt trauma (e.g., a non-penetrating external blow to the chest). Lung surgery requires that the tissue enveloping the lung (the pleura) be cut. Neither of these situations is likely to increase the risk of pneumothorax (lung collapse), but some diving physicians believe that a surgical incision into the lung causes an increased risk of arterial gas embolism. With any of these conditions, consultation with a diving physician is recommended.

After lung surgery (for example, lobectomy or pneumonectomy, removal of a portion of the lung or the entire lung, respectively) there may be some reduction in maximum breathing capacity, which could impair a diver's ability to tolerate exertion underwater.

Smoking can cause chronic bronchitis, emphysema and atherosclerosis. In addition, it exacerbates asthma. While smoking is not recommended, there is currently little evidence that smoking by itself predisposes anyone to diving-related illness, unless it has produced or exacerbated lung disease.

After a respiratory infection such as a cold, bronchitis or pneumonia, some people develop an increased tendency for the airways to constrict, as with asthma. This often lasts for a few weeks after resolution of the infection. It can manifest as a cough, shortness of breath or wheezing. During this time there may also be excessive mucus in the airways, which could cause gas-trapping during ascent. Because of this, diving physicians recommend that diving should be postponed after a respiratory infection until all symptoms, including cough, have completely resolved.

Scuba Diver's Asthma Attack Linked to Pollen in Air Tank

A scuba diver's life-threatening asthma attack some 27 meters (almost 90 feet) below the surface was apparently caused by exposure to pollen from the Mediterranean nettle *Parietaria*, Italian researchers believe.

Investigators warn divers who are allergic to pollen to use a filter to remove allergens from air used in air tanks.

Reporting in the September issue of the *Journal of Allergy and Clinical Immunology*, Dr. Gennaro D'Amato and colleagues, of Azienda Ospedaliera ad Alta Specialita A. Cardarelli, Naples, note that their patient had had "long experience of underwater diving, without unto-ward effects."

The diver, a 37-year-old man, also had bronchial asthma and had tested positive for allergy to the nettle, including "positive skin test responses and a high concentration of specific serum IgE to *Parietaria* pollen allergen, together with .... symptoms in the *Parietaria* pollen season."

Before the dive in question, the diver used a new supplier to recharge his air tanks. When investigators later inspected the premises of this supplier, they found that "the compressor was not fitted with an air filter and the area was rich in *Parietaria* plants," suggesting that air containing pollen from the plant was used to fill the tanks.

In subsequent experiments using air from tanks and pollen traps, D'Amato's team detected "damaged granules of *Parietaria* pollen" that could have released specific allergens responsible for the diver's asthma.

The evidence that the asthma attack was pollen-related is "very persuasive," D'Amato and colleagues say. They advise divers at risk for pollen-induced breathing disorders "to check that air used to recharge their tanks is filtered to prevent the passage of respirable pollen grains."

— Reuters Health News Service
SOURCE: Journal of Allergy and Clinical Immunology 1999:710

— From Alert Diver, July/August 2000

Breathing Easy

DAN Explores Respiration & Diving Safety

By Dr. Richard Vann, Vice President, DAN Research

Let's face it: Breathing is not something we have to think about — it's an involuntary process. This involuntary process topside at sea level is not the same during diving: breathing through a regulator is a bit of an unnatural act.

But divers are an adventurous lot, we'll all agree. And breathing through a regulator is part of the adventure of scuba diving.

Let's take a look, however, at this "unnatural" part of diving.

When you are resting in warm water at shallow depth, diving is relaxing and relatively safe. But say you'd like to visit a wreck at 130 feet / 40 meters: As depth and workload increase, breathing through a regulator can expose you to abnormal levels of oxygen, carbon dioxide and nitrogen. This in turn can make your respiratory system act quite differently than what you're accustomed to on land.

Bottom line: When you're diving, be aware of your breathing. You should monitor and adjust both your breathing and exertion level in order to avoid panic from becoming out of breath or drifting into an altered state of consciousness. Here's how it works.

Divers who panic because of breathing problems and make emergency ascents are at risk of arterial gas embolism or decompression sickness, and divers who lose consciousness are at risk of drowning. Loss of consciousness when breathing air or nitrox has been called "deep-water blackout," while "shallow-water blackout" generally occurs with oxygen rebreathers.[1]

The causes of panic or unconsciousness in diving can be difficult to determine, but injury and fatality reports and unplanned laboratory incidents suggest that respiration plays an important role. Knowledge of the underlying mechanisms is incomplete because experimental investigations of the problem are understandably rare.

The automatic act of breathing is designed to maintain physiologically acceptable levels of oxygen and carbon dioxide in the blood and tissues. You do not normally think about it — you just breathe. A healthy person breathing fresh air at sea level unconsciously adjusts his or her ventilation to match physical exertion. This is not always so during diving where non-physiological levels of oxygen, nitrogen and carbon dioxide may have independent, cumulative or interactive effects that are exacerbated by depth, work, breathing resistance and gas density. Don't ignore your breathing when you dive.

Incident One — Carbon Dioxide Retention and Dyspnea[2]

"We were testing a new bicycle ergometer at 7.8 ata (67 msw / 224 fsw) in the dry chamber. Nitrogen narcosis is very evident on air at that pressure, but we were doing OK until we started breathing on the measuring circuit that gave us only about half the air we needed.

"Herb stopped pedaling after about three minutes, out cold with his eyes rolled back. I took the bike. I knew I wasn't getting nearly enough air, but I was too narked to think straight and was determined to finish the test.

"I pedaled myself right into oblivion and, coming around slowly afterward, I experienced the most horrible feeling of my life, the sense of near-suffocation. Both of us surely would have drowned if such a thing had happened when we were under water."

— *Diving Physiologist Edward Lanphier, M.D.*

Carbon Dioxide Retention and Dyspnea:[3]
A Cause for Panic

Diving gases almost always have more oxygen than needed. The primary stimulus for breathing when you dive is an elevated level of carbon dioxide.

Diving gases are hyperoxic, i.e., they have greater than the normal oxygen partial pressure of 0.21 atm, and the blood was not designed to carry oxygen and carbon dioxide at hyperoxic pressures. Most of the oxygen in the blood is carried in reversible chemical combination with hemoglobin in the red blood cells, while most carbon dioxide is physically dissolved in the blood. At sea level, where the amount of oxygen in the venous blood is low, carbon dioxide (CO_2) is tightly bound to hemoglobin, but at higher oxygen partial pressures during diving, carbon dioxide is loosely bound. This causes the carbon dioxide level in the blood and tissues to rise.

Under normal conditions, a high level of CO_2 causes a person to breathe more vigorously, and the increased ventilation eliminates the excess CO_2. If the carbon dioxide level is not reduced, breathlessness or dyspnea is the usual outcome.

Carbon dioxide can be retained in the body for various reasons. At sea level, the heart limits a person's maximum exercise capacity, but during diving, the respiratory system is usually the limiting factor. Immersion in water causes blood to shift from the legs to the lungs, which reduces both lung volume and maximum breathing capacity. The breathing capacity is decreased further by greater "work" of breathing from resistance to gas flow in the airways and regulator. This resistance increases with gas density at greater depths and with more physical activity.

Regulators generally require extra inspiratory effort before they deliver air, although this is usually not a problem for a resting diver with most modern, well-maintained regulators. A difference in depth between the lungs and the regulator second stage (called the "static lung load") increases the work of breathing as well, because the regulator is not compensating fully for the pressure that the lungs are breathing against.

Carbon dioxide can also be retained in the body during diving if a stimulating environment, frightening experience or, possibly, nitrogen narcosis inhibits ventilation. In addition, divers sometimes consciously override the desire to breathe caused by high CO2 and "skip-breathe," or hypoventilate, to conserve air. Skip-breathing can be responsible for post-dive headaches because it induces high carbon dioxide levels that cause the blood vessels in the brain to dilate — similarly to migraine.

Dyspnea, Panic and Rapid Ascent

Excess carbon dioxide usually causes a feeling of breathlessness or dyspnea that, as indicated by Incident #1, is a frightening experience with panic as a common response. As the oxygen partial pressure increases, however, carbon dioxide becomes less effective in signaling the need for increased ventilation, which allows the carbon dioxide level to increase further. The importance of adequate respiration is not always emphasized during initial diver training, and newly trained divers are particularly susceptible to making rapid ascents as the result of the panic caused by dyspnea. These divers risk air embolism, decompression sickness or both.

Divers who expect the same respiratory performance at depth as on land may be surprised when a real or perceived emergency causes an urgent need to breathe. Although an episode of respiratory distress underwater can be a learning experience, it is certainly not ideal. Since a person's normal automatic regulation of respiration at sea level may be compromised at depth, divers should be sure to ventilate adequately and minimize exertion to avoid dyspnea.

If sudden, unexpected activity is necessary, a diver should increase ventilation by breathing deeply. This is the best way to avoid the terror of being unable to breathe. What if breathlessness does occur? The best way for an "out-of-breath" diver to avoid panic is to stop all activity, relax and let breathing return to normal.

Fatalities, Injuries and Safe Dives

Direct evidence linking respiration, panic and rapid ascent is under-standably rare, but data published in the DAN *Report on Decompression Illness, Diving Fatalities and Project Dive Exploration* for Year 2000 suggests that rapid ascent may have a role in both injuries and fatalities. Figure 1 (below) compares the incidences of rapid ascent in dives that resulted in injury or death with the incidence of rapid ascent in safe dives that were monitored by PDE.

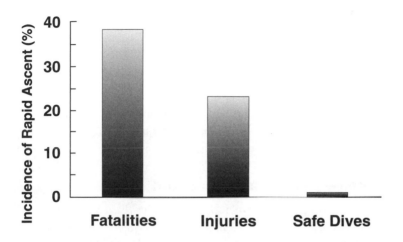

FIGURE 1: Rapid ascent was 38 times more common after fatal dives than after safe dives, and 23 times more common after dives resulting in injuries than after safe dives. These observations were based on 26 fatalities, 431 injuries and 5,908 safe dives collected during PDE.

Rapid ascent was reported in 38 percent of fatal dives, in 23 percent of dives resulting in injury, and in 1 percent of safe dives.[4] These observations do not prove "cause and effect," but they do deliver the message that any circumstance with the potential to cause rapid ascent should be viewed with caution.

Rapid ascent can occur for many reasons, including loss of buoyancy control or running out of air. In Figure 2, for example (see next page), running out of air was reported in 24 percent of fatalities, 5 percent of injuries, but in only 0.3 percent of safe dives.

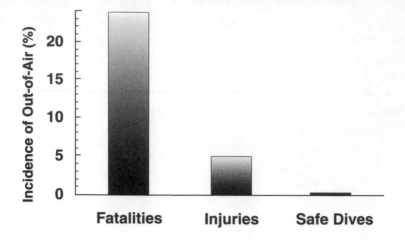

FIGURE 2: Running out of air was 79 times more common after fatal dives than after safe dives, and 17 times more common after dives resulting in injuries than after safe dives.

Incident Two — Deep-Water Blackout

During a dive to 54 msw / 180 fsw in a "wetpot" (a water-filled hyperbaric chamber) at Duke University Medical Center, a diver performed moderate exercise by swimming against a trapeze attached to a weight; his oxygen consumption was 2 liters per minute. The diver used a closed-circuit rebreather that recirculated his exhaled gas after scrubbing the carbon dioxide and adding oxygen.

The oxygen partial pressure was maintained at 1.4 atm. The remaining gas was nitrogen with a narcotic effect equivalent to breathing air at 53 msw / 178 fsw. The diving supervisor observed the diver to steadily increase his work-rate despite orders to slow down until, without warning, the diver became unconscious. He revived immediately when he was removed from the water. Had the incident occurred during an open-water dive, the consequences might have been more serious, as in Incident #3. (following)

Incident Three — Deep-Water Unconsciousness and Death[5]

Two experienced divers explored the wreck of the Chester Polling at a depth of 42-51 msw / 140-170 fsw off the Massachusetts coast. After 15 minutes at depth, one diver signaled to his buddy that he was in trouble, and they began to ascend together.

At 24 msw / 60 fsw, the affected diver lost consciousness and dropped his regulator. The buddy attempted to replace the regulator but failed, and at 5 msw / 17 fsw, inflated the other diver's buoyancy compensator. The diver died from apparent drowning. An autopsy revealed no cardiac abnormalities.

Impaired Consciousness and Interactions Among Gases[6]

Greater work of breathing at increased depth can heighten a diver's carbon dioxide retention. For the reasons described earlier, carbon dioxide retention worsens at elevated oxygen partial pressures such as 1.4 atm. Carbon dioxide levels equivalent to about 10 percent on the surface are narcotic and can affect consciousness. This is an obvious problem for a diver at depth.

Carbon dioxide narcosis and nitrogen narcosis are additive; this means that when both occur at the same time, a diver is at greater risk of altered consciousness. Nitrogen narcosis, heavy work, breathing resistance, high oxygen partial pressures, and carbon dioxide retention were all present in Incidents 1, 2 and 3. Elevated carbon dioxide also increases cerebral blood flow and raises oxygen delivery to the brain, thereby increasing the risk of central nervous system (CNS) oxygen toxicity.

The combined effects of nitrogen narcosis, carbon dioxide intoxication and oxygen toxicity can impair consciousness in divers. These effects are exacerbated by exercise and gas density, which further increase carbon dioxide retention. Figure 3 illustrates the effects of gases, exercise and depth on the risk of unconsciousness.

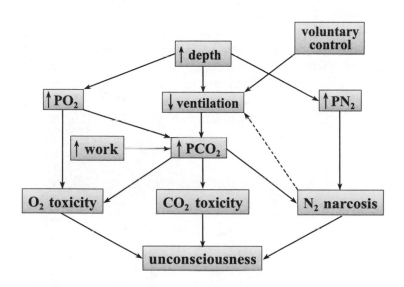

FIGURE 3: Divers should approach deep air or nitrox diving with caution because interactions of depth, work, oxygen, nitrogen and carbon dioxide can affect respiration and consciousness. Carbon dioxide is the primary factor controlling respiration during diving in the presence of oxygen partial pressures above 0.21 atm.

Some divers reduce their ventilation voluntarily to save gas, while others increase their ventilation very little in response to elevated CO2. Work of breathing increases with gas density and depth; this makes ventilation more difficult and causes carbon dioxide retention. In the presence of elevated oxygen levels, dyspnea caused by excess CO2 is less effective as a warning of altered consciousness.

Carbon dioxide itself is narcotic, and elevated CO2 exacerbates both nitrogen narcosis and oxygen toxicity of the central nervous system (CNS). Anesthetic gases depress breathing; nitrogen narcosis also may depress breathing, although this has been difficult to separate from the effects of increased density. (This hypothetical effect is shown as a dashed line.)

Individual Susceptibility to Impaired Consciousness

Susceptibility to carbon dioxide retention, oxygen toxicity and nitrogen narcosis can vary widely from one individual to another. Some divers have poor ventilatory response to inspired carbon dioxide — i.e., they increase their ventilation to a lesser extent than do most people when exposed to elevated levels of carbon dioxide.

These divers are known as "carbon dioxide retainers."[3] Diving physiologists believe that such people are at elevated risk of central nervous system oxygen toxicity because of greater cerebral blood flow. In addition to the variation in individual response to carbon dioxide, there is evidence of wide differences in susceptibility to CNS oxygen toxicity. Studies by the British during World War II, for example, found that the time to symptom onset (e.g., seizures) varied randomly from 7 to 145 minutes for a single diver who made 20 exposures at 21 msw / 70 fsw while breathing 100 percent oxygen at a partial pressure of 3.1 atm (Figure 4).[6]

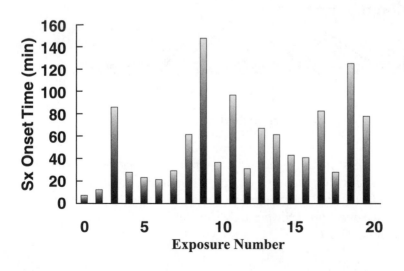

FIGURE 4: The variation in individual susceptibility to symptoms of CNS oxygen toxicity.7 The time to symptom onset is illustrated for a single individual who was exposed to 100 percent oxygen at 21 msw / 70 fsw) on 20 days over a three-month period. The average onset time was 44 minutes, with a range of 7-148 minutes.

A few individuals have made air dives to depths of 90-150 msw / 300-500 fsw and have returned safely despite nitrogen and oxygen stresses that would incapacitate most people. Other divers have developed severe decompression illness or have not returned, perhaps due to loss of consciousness.

Individual differences in susceptibility to carbon dioxide toxicity, oxygen toxicity and nitrogen narcosis exist among divers, but at present, we cannot predict who is susceptible or resistant or how individual susceptibility varies from day to day.

In summary, pay attention to your breathing when you dive: stay in the ranks of safe dive statistics.

Avoiding Nitrogen Narcosis and Reducing Carbon Dioxide Retention

Unconsciousness from nitrogen narcosis, oxygen toxicity and carbon dioxide intoxication becomes inevitable as air dives become deeper and deeper. For divers who want to make deep dives, "heliox" (He/O2 mixtures) or trimix (He/N2/O2 mixtures) will help avoid nitrogen narcosis and will reduce carbon dioxide retention. Of course, these exotic mixes introduce new hazards, requiring specific training, experience, equipment and work-up dives.

REFERENCES
1. Lanphier EH, ed. "The unconscious diver: respiratory control and other contributing factors." Bethesda: Undersea Medical Society; 1982. Publication Number 52WS (RC) 1-25-82.
2. Lanphier E. The story of CO2 build-up. "AquaCorps J." 1992; 3(1): 67-69.
3. Lanphier EH, Camporesi EM. Respiration and exertion. In: Bennett PB, Elliott DH, eds. "The Physiology and Medicine of Diving." London: Saunders, 1993: 77-120.
4. The DAN "Report on Decompression Illness and Diving Fatalities Based on 1998 Data," 2000.
5. Menduno, M. 1992. Safety first: an analysis of recent diving accidents. "Technical Diver." 3(2): 2-10.
6. Bennett PB. Inert gas narcosis. In: Bennett PB, Elliott DH, eds. "The Physiology and Medicine of Diving." London: Saunders, 1993: 170-193.
7. Donald KW. "Oxygen and the diver." Harley Swan, UK: The Spa Ltd, 1992.

— From Alert Diver, July/August 2000

Tight Squeeze

Discomfort in a diver's lungs and windpipe can come from a number of irritating sources

By Joel Dovenbarger, Vice President, DAN Medical Services

Q: *I am 36 years old and have logged about 750 dives, most at less than 50 feet / 15 meters. My problem occurs during the lobster season. At average depths of 22 feet / 7 meters, I am swimming, ducking, looking, twisting and reaching as fast as I can for lobster. I can catch my entire limit and am relied upon to do that because my buddies don't have the same skill level.*

After two or three dives, or up to three hours in the water, I can't take a deep breath due to discomfort in my lungs and windpipe. About one day later, though, everything is back to normal.

I know the answer might be to just slow down and not exert myself so much, but if I'm fine physically and in good shape, why do I need to slow down?

A: This is an interesting question — given the details of this particular case, it is impossible to determine the exact cause and effect for your symptoms. Here are some possible explanations.

You may be experiencing some saltwater aspiration while you are breathing and rapidly changing the depth of your dive. Since salt water is hypertonic — in this case, loaded with sodium chloride or salt — tracheobronchial irritation can occur. This may be the cause of your discomfort when taking a deep breath. It should subside relatively shortly after your dive.

It may also be due to an irritating substance in your air supply. Any type of contaminant or residue from solvents, lubricants or combustible materials can irritate the mucus membrane lining when inhaled. If you obtain your air from the same source each time you dive for lobsters, this may be possible; if you buy your air from a single source each and every time you dive, including your lobster diving, this solution is not as reasonable.

Hyperventilation is another possible irritant. Breathing dry, compressed gas for two to three hours a day can dry the airway (assuming your activity does require an increased respiratory effort). The mucus membrane in the airway is responsible for providing moisture to humidify the dry, compressed scuba gas. It is possible to breathe dry gas at an accelerated rate (while exercising) that outstrips the airway capacity to humidify the air — which creates the irritation of the throat and airway.

This condition should also readily resolve once scuba diving has ceased.

Your discomfort might be due to mild barotrauma to your airway and lung tissue. Usual indications range from air bubbles under the skin (subcutaneous emphysema), to a collapsed lung (pneumothorax), to arterial gas embolism (AGE).

Barotrauma results from the overinflation of the lungs when the gas volume expands against the soft tissues. This may occur when divers unintentionally hold their breath while changing the depth of their dive. In this case, we don't know if breath-holding occurred while breathing scuba or what depth changes, if any, occurred when pursuing lobsters. Mild barotrauma, however, is not a completely satisfactory answer, since gas volume changes seem to be small.

You may have some pre-existing condition that causes these symptoms, such as asthma. Before you go diving again, I suggest that you undergo exercise testing to check for it.

Note: If you or anyone else has noted similar chest discomfort after diving send us a note describing your activity, depths and times, as well as any contributing factors, such as rapid ascents, strong currents, rough surface conditions, or exertion. Tell us if this condition occurs frequently or only if you perform some special task. A compilation of individual descriptions may help DAN researchers to explain this phenomenon.

—*From Alert Diver, May/June 1996*

Section 15

Women's Issues

DAN Explores Fitness and Diving Issues for Women

By Donna M. Uguccioni, M.S.; Dr. Richard Moon, Vice President and Medical Director; and Dr. Maida Beth Taylor

When I first began working with Divers Alert Network some 13 years ago, there was one group of questions that presented a special challenge to me: they were about women and some of their unique characteristics as divers.

At the time, it seemed that the answers provided by the diving medical community were not based predominantly on information or evidence that supported these responses, but rather on long-held biases with little substance. Women, for example, were considered to be more susceptible to decompression illness because they had more body fat than men. Adipose tissue takes longer to offgas after a dive, so the more fat, the greater the chance of decompression illness, right?

Not necessarily. Many other individual and environmental factors must be taken into account.

Women, in fact, generally do have more body fat than men; but somewhere along the line, the connection was made that this was the cause of decompression illness in women. If that extra bit of body fat caused DCI in women, then it follows that men who have extra adipose tissue should run the same risk. This simply isn't the case.

When we break down dive injuries by the sex and experience of the diver, we find a much stronger relationship between females and their dive experience: women who have been diving for less than two years generally account for 39 percent to 50 percent of all injuries in female divers.

Many other questions remain about women's issues in diving: for example, what about pregnancy, breast-feeding, breast implants?

Of the many questions commonly asked by or about women and diving, we have selected 11 of the most frequently asked. The following article is a collaboration of three main authors: Donna Uguccioni, M.S., DAN's diving physiologist and researcher on women-and-diving issues; DAN Medical Director Dr. Richard Moon; and Dr. Maida Beth Taylor, who is an expert on the topic of women and diving and an author on these issues. These experts have produced the most current, realistic and logical answers for DAN's most commonly asked questions on women and diving. Dr. Taylor has added additional text and references for some questions that cannot be easily answered. We think the answers here can help dispel many unsubstantiated opinions in the diving community.

Although we don't have all the answers for women-and-diving issues, DAN continues to research these topics and promote safer, healthier diving.

— Joel Dovenbarger, BSN, Vice President, DAN Medical Services

Breast Cancer, Cancer & Surgery

The Condition: Tumors in the breasts are not uncommon, especially after age 30. Tumors may be cancerous (malignant) or non-cancerous (benign). Approximately one in nine women will develop breast cancer. Early detection can be made with regular, manual self-examinations of the breasts, but not all tumors can be detected in this manner. Mammography (X-ray of the breast) can detect tumors that manual examination cannot.

The American Cancer Society recommends the following:

1. Women 20 years of age and older should perform breast self-examination every month.
2. Women ages 20-39 should have a physical examination of the breast every three years, performed by a healthcare professional such as a physician, physician assistant, nurse or nurse practitioner.
3. Women 40 and older should have a physical examination of the breast every year, performed by a healthcare professional such as a physician, physician assistant, nurse or nurse practitioner.
4. Women 40 and older should have a mammogram every year.

Tumors are often removed surgically and treatment of malignant tumors may involve surgery, radiotherapy, chemotherapy — or a combination of two or three of these procedures.

Both chemotherapy and radiotherapy can have toxic effects on the lung, surrounding tissue and body cells that have a rapid growth cycle such as blood cells.

Fitness and Diving Issues: Cytotoxic drugs (chemotherapy) and radiation therapy can have unpleasant side effects such as nausea and vomiting, and a prolonged course of therapy can result in greatly decreased energy levels. This makes diving while experiencing such side effects inadvisable. Radiation and some chemotherapeutic drugs can cause pulmonary toxicity.

An evaluation to establish the safety of a return to diving should include an assessment of the lung to ensure that damage likely to predispose the diver to pulmonary barotrauma (arterial gas embolism, pneumothorax or pneumomediastinum) is not present.

Finally, before diving, healing must have occurred, and the surgeon must be satisfied that immersion in salt water will not contribute to wound infection. Strength, general fitness and well-being should be back to normal. The risk of infection, which may have increased temporarily during chemotherapy or radiotherapy, should have returned to normal levels.

Ovarian Tumor

The Condition: Ovarian tumors may be malignant (cancerous) or benign (non-cancerous). Tumors may be solid or a hollow sac (cysts). Cysts are sometimes filled with fluid and usually are the non-cancerous form of an ovarian tumor. There is no reliable testing or screening for ovarian cancer. Diagnostic tests CA 125 and ultrasound are often recommended but have a very high rate of false positive and false negative; both tests may register as abnormal in many other diseases besides ovarian cancer. Pap smears occasionally can have pieces of calcium on them called psammoma bodies, which can be indicative of ovarian tumors.

Fitness and Diving Issues: With respect to diving, the major issues are the effects on the body from the surgery and/or radiation/chemotherapy treatments (See "Breast Cancer and Cancer in Women").

Pregnancy

The Condition: Being pregnant means there's a developing embryo or fetus in the body. The duration of pregnancy, from conception to delivery, is approximately 266 days, or nine months.

Fitness and Diving Issues: There are few scientific data available regarding diving while pregnant: much of the available evidence is anecdotal. Laboratory studies are confined to animal research, and the results are conflicting. Some retrospective survey-type questionnaires have been performed, but these are limited by data interpretation.

Nevertheless, researchers theorize that diving is in some ways similar to taking a drug: the pharmacological effects of nitrogen or other inert gases and high oxygen partial pressure on a developing fetus are not completely known.

There is the possibility that diving may induce bubbles in the fetus. Also, fluid retention during pregnancy may cause nasopharyngeal swelling, which can lead to nose and ear stuffiness and the risk of ear or sinus squeezes. Pregnant women experiencing morning sickness, coupled with motion sickness, may have to deal with nausea and vomiting during a dive. This is at best an unpleasant experience, and it could lead to more serious problems if the diver panics.

Due to the limited data available and the uncertainty of the effects of diving on a fetus, it is recommended that scuba diving should be postponed until after the pregnancy.

Return To Diving After Giving Birth

The Condition: Diving, like any other sport, requires a certain degree of conditioning and fitness. Divers who want to return to diving postpartum (after having a child) should follow the guidelines suggested for other sports and activities.

Fitness and Diving Issues: After a vaginal delivery, women can usually resume light to moderate activity within one to three weeks. This depends of several factors: prior level of conditioning; exercise and conditioning during pregnancy; pregnancy-related complications; postpartum fatigue; and anemia, if any. Women who have exercise regimens prior to pregnancy and birth generally resume exercise programs and sports participation in earnest at three to four weeks after giving birth.

Obstetricians generally recommend avoiding sexual intercourse and immersion for 21 days postpartum. This allows the cervix to close, decreasing the risk of introducing infection into the genital tract. A good rule of thumb is to wait four weeks after delivery before returning to diving.

After a cesarean delivery (often called a C-section, made via a surgical incision through the walls of the abdomen and uterus), wound-healing has to be included in the equation. Most obstetricians advise waiting at least four to six weeks after this kind of delivery before resuming full activity. Given the need to regain some measure of lost conditioning, coupled with wound healing, and the significant weight-bearing load of carrying dive gear, it's advisable to wait at least eight weeks after a C-section before returning to diving.

Any moderate or severe medical complication of pregnancy — such as twins, pre-term labor, hypertension or diabetes — may further delay return to diving. Prolonged bed rest in these cases may have led to profound deconditioning and loss of aerobic capacity and muscle mass. For women who have had deliveries with medical complications, a medical screening and clearance are advisable before they return to diving.

Additional Information: Caring for a newborn may interfere with a woman's attempts to recover her strength and stamina. Newborn care, characterized by poor sleep and fatigue, is a rigorous and demanding time in life.

Breast-Feeding

The Condition: A mother may choose to breast-feed her infant while maintaining an otherwise active life. This may continue for weeks or months, depending on the mother's preference.

Fitness and Diving Issues: Is it safe to scuba dive while breast-feeding?

From the standpoint of the child, the mother's breast milk is not unduly affected. The nitrogen absorbed into the body tissues is a component of breathing compressed air or other gas mixes containing nitrogen. This form of nitrogen is an inert gas and plays no role in body metabolism. Although nitrogen accumulates in all of the tissues and fluids of the body, washout after a dive occurs quickly. Insignificant amounts of this nitrogen would be present in the mother's breast milk; there is, however, no risk of the infant accumulating this nitrogen.

From the mother's standpoint, there is no reason for a woman who is breast-feeding her child to avoid diving, provided there is no infection or inflammation of the breast.

Endometriosis

The Condition: With endometriosis, the tissue containing typical endometrial cells occurs abnormally in various locations outside the uterus. During menstruation this abnormally occurring endometrial tissue, like the lining of the uterus, undergoes cyclic bleeding. The blood in this endometrial tissue has no means of draining to the outside of the body. As a result, blood collects in the surrounding tissue, causing pain and discomfort.

Fitness and Diving Issues: Because endometriosis can cause increased bleeding, cramping, amount and duration of menstrual flow, diving may not be in a woman's best interest when she experiences severe symptoms. Nevertheless, there is no evidence that a woman with endometriosis diving at other times is at any greater risk of diving-related disease than a person without this condition.

Hysterectomy

The Condition: This is a surgical procedure in which the entire uterus is removed through the abdominal wall or through the vagina.

All that has been said about diving after a cesarean section (see "Return to Diving After Giving Birth") applies to diving after general surgery, including a hysterectomy.

Women may resume diving after a hysterectomy, but they should wait until they have recovered general strength and fitness before they take the plunge — usually six to eight weeks, and sometimes longer.

Fitness and Diving Issues: As far as it relates to scuba diving, a hysterectomy is considered major surgery. It is recommended that anyone undergoing an abdominal surgery allow six to eight weeks of recovery before resuming diving. If the procedure is complicated in any way, by infection, anemia or other serious issues, it may be wise to further delay diving.

These recommendations apply to all types of hysterectomy:

1. Removing the uterus abdominally (total abdominal hysterectomy);
2. Removing the uterus vaginally (vaginal hysterectomy);
3. Removing the uterus plus the tubes and ovaries (hysterectomy plus salpingo-oophorectomy);
4. Removing the top of the uterus, but leaving the cervix intact (subtotal hysterectomy).

Breast Implants

The Condition: Silicone and saline implants are used for cosmetic enhancement or augmentation of the normal breast size and shape of reconstruction, particularly after radical breast surgery for cancer or trauma.

In one study, by Dr. Richard Vann, Vice President of Research at DAN, mammary (breast) implants were placed in the Duke University Medical Center hyperbaric chamber. The study did not simulate the implant in human tissue. Three types were tested: silicone-, saline-, and silicone-saline-filled. In this experiment, the researchers simulated various depth / time profiles of recreational scuba diving.

Here's what they found: There was an insignificant increase in bubble size (1 to 4 percent) in both saline and silicone gel implants, depending on the depth and duration of the dive. The least volume change occurred in the saline-filled implant, because nitrogen is less soluble in saline than silicone.

The silicone-saline-filled type showed the greatest volume change. Bubble formation in implants led to a small volume increase, which is not likely to damage the implants or surrounding tissue. If gas bubbles do form in the implant, they resolve over time.

Fitness and Diving Issues: Once sufficient time has passed after surgery, when the diver has resumed normal activities and there is no danger of infection, she may begin scuba diving.

Breast implants do not pose a problem to diving from the standpoint of gas absorption or changes in size and are not a contraindication for participation in recreational scuba diving.

Avoid buoyancy compensators with constrictive chest straps, which can put undue pressure on the seams and contribute to risk of rupture.

Additional Considerations: Breast implants filled with saline are neutrally buoyant. Silicone implants are heavier than water, however, and they may alter buoyancy and attitude (trim) in the water, particularly if the implants are large. Appropriate training and appropriate adjustment of weights help overcome these difficulties.

Menstruation During Diving Activities

The Condition: Menstruation is the cyclic, physiologic discharge through the vagina of blood and mucosal tissues from the non-pregnant uterus. The cycle is controlled hormonally and usually occurs at approximately four-week intervals.

Symptoms may include pain, fluid retention, abdominal cramping and backache.

Fitness and Diving Issues: Are women at greater risk of experiencing decompression illness (DCI) while menstruating? Theoretically, it is possible that, because of fluid retention and tissue swelling, women are less able to get rid of dissolved nitrogen. This is, however, not definitively proven.

One recent retrospective review of women divers (956 divers) with DCI found 38 percent were menstruating at the time of their injury. Additionally, 85 percent of those taking oral contraceptives were menstruating at the time of the accident. This suggests, but does not prove, that women taking oral contraceptives are at increased risk of decompression illness during menstruation. Therefore, it may be advisable for menstruating women to dive more conservatively, particularly if they are taking oral contraceptives. This could involve making fewer dives, shorter and shallower dives and making longer safety stops. Four other studies have provided evidence that women are at higher risk of DCI, and in one study of altitude bends, menses also appeared to be a risk factor for bends.

Are women at an increased risk of shark attacks during menstruation? There are few reported shark attacks on women, and there are no data to support the belief that menstruating females are at an increased risk for shark attacks. The average blood lost during menstruation is small and occurs over several days. Also, it is known that many shark species are not attracted to the blood and other debris found in menstrual flow.

In general, diving while menstruating does not seem to be a problem as long as normal, vigorous exercise does not increase the menstrual symptoms. As long as the menstrual cycle poses no other symptoms or discomforts that affect her health, there is no reason that a menstruating female should not dive. However, based upon available data, it may be prudent for women taking oral contraceptives, particularly if they are menstruating, to reduce their dive exposure (depth, bottom time or number of dives per day).

Premenstrual Syndrome

The Condition: Premenstrual Syndrome, or PMS, is a group of poorly understood and poorly defined psychophysiological symptoms experienced by many women (25-50 percent of women) at the end of the menstrual cycle, just prior to the menstrual flow.

PMS symptoms include mood swings, irritability, decreased mental alertness, tension, fatigue, depression, headaches, bloating, swelling, breast tenderness, joint pain and food cravings. Severe premenstrual syndrome has been found to exacerbate underlying emotional disorders. Although progesterone is used in some cases, no consistent, simple treatments are available.

Fitness and Diving Issues: Research has shown that accidents in general are more common among women during PMS. If women suffer from premenstrual syndrome, it may be wise to dive conservatively during this time. There is no scientific evidence, however, that they are more susceptible to decompression illness or dive injuries / accidents.

Also, individuals with evidence of depression or antisocial tendencies should be evaluated for their fitness to participate in diving: they may pose a risk to themselves or a dive buddy.

— *From Alert Diver, January/February 1999*

Decompression Illness & Symptom Recognition

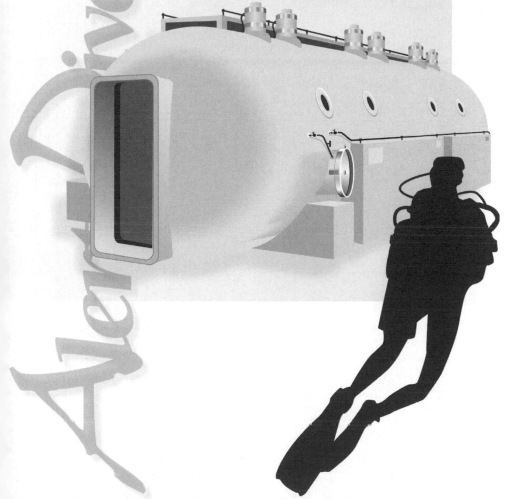

Decompression Illness and Symptom Recognition

By Joel Dovenbarger, Vice President, DAN Medical Services

Decompression illness (DCI) occurs in approximately 1,000 U.S. scuba divers each year. Exposure to high partial pressures of nitrogen during scuba diving results in the accumulation of nitrogen in the body. After a reduction in ambient pressure, body tissues can become supersaturated with nitrogen; at this juncture, bubbles may form, causing damage.

Individual differences may cause some individuals to experience DCI despite having similar profiles to symptom-free divers. Factors such as dehydration or certain medical conditions that limit blood flow could contribute. Rapid ascents can augment the degree of supersaturation in body tissues and increase the risk of pulmonary barotrauma and arterial gas embolism.

Prior to the use of the term DCI, dive injuries were reported in the following ways: arterial gas embolism (AGE); Type I decompression sickness (pain only or skin bends); or Type II decompression sickness (neurological or cardiorespiratory DCS). Although the cause of injury is different in AGE and DCS, symptoms are often similar. This clinical similarity and the fact that treatment is largely the same for both conditions have popularized the term, DCI, which refers to conditions due to either the cause of injury. DCI is now more commonly used to describe and classify bubble-related disease in divers.

DAN has published a great deal of information about DCI, especially in the annual *Report on Decompression Illness, Diving Fatalities and Project Dive Exploration* and in the DAN *Dive and Travel Medical Guide*. For consistency, this article will paraphrase some of that information.

Diagnosing DCI

The DCI diagnosis is based largely on a recent history of scuba diving and the onset of symptoms shortly after diving. DCI can be mild, severe or even life-threatening. Approximately 58 to 62 percent of initial symptoms will occur in the first six hours after the dive, but symptoms can occur up to 24 or more hours later, particularly if there has been an altitude exposure.

It may take hours for bubbles to gradually increase in size and produce symptoms in the diver. Additionally, 10-17 percent of divers continue to dive after they have already developed symptoms, thereby exacerbating symptoms. Commercial airline flights may also bring on symptoms a day or longer after diving. As ambient pressure in the aircraft is reduced, existing non-symptomatic bubbles enlarge.

DCI cases are typically classified by the descriptive nature of the signs and symptoms found, such as "musculoskeletal DCI," "neurological DCI," lymphocutaneous DCI, etc. Neurological symptoms occur in 65-70 percent of all reported cases each year. The second most common form of DCI is musculoskeltal or "pain-only" DCI.

Pulmonary barotrauma of ascent usually causes arterial gas embolism (AGE), which might affect the brain (cerebral AGE or CAGE) or coronary arteries. In this condition, symptoms originate according to the sites where bubbles damage or obstruct blood vessels. This causes a reduction in blood flow to tissue downstream from the bubble-related obstructions.

Rapid ascent made by the diver while breath-holding is the primary cause of pulmonary barotrauma. Obstructive lung disease can also cause AGE. Symptoms, which are usually neurological, resemble an acute stroke and occur within minutes of the diver's reaching the surface. Cerebral gas embolism is responsible for about 10 percent of all DCI cases each year, but it has decreased significantly from 20 percent of all cases in the late 1980s and early 1990s.

Signs and Symptoms

After evaluating signs and symptoms, a physician makes a diagnosis of DCI. A symptom such as "pain," "tingling" or "numbness," is a subjective complaint. A sign is an objective observation by someone other than the diver. Signs include abnormal reflexes, decreased strength or inability to differentiate between a sharp and dull sensation.

For divers to recognize DCI, they should know DCI symptoms. The following symptom descriptions are based on cases of DCI in the DAN recreational scuba injury database.

Symptom Description

Numbness and Tingling (paresthesia): This sensation is generally referred to as "pins and needles." A diver may complain of a sensation similar to striking the "funny bone" or the extremity "falling asleep." The sensation might feel like the numbness following a shot of Novocain from a dentist. This sensation occurs only in combination with joint pain and most commonly affects a single extremity. The feeling may also be described as coldness, or a heavy, swollen sensation. Numbness and tingling is reported in 35-46 percent of all cases.

Pain: Pain usually refers to a dull, sharp, boring or an achy sensation similar to "toothache" in or around any joint or muscle. It often starts gradually and builds in intensity. Movement of the affected joint or limb rarely affects the severity of the pain. The pain is also disproportionate to the amount of exercise or strain incurred by the diver. It may be described as unusual or just a "different" type of discomfort. Pain, which most commonly occurs in one arm, is reported in 30-50 percent of all DCI cases.

Extreme Fatigue: It is not uncommon to be tired after a scuba dive or other physical exertion; however, the fatigue associated with DCI is unusual. The diver may complain of being "dead tired" or may want to lie down and sleep shortly after entering the boat, ignoring personal responsibilities such as stowing or cleaning equipment. Behavior may seem to be out of character or unusual for the diver and for the amount of effort or work performed. Importantly, extreme fatigue, which may precede more serious signs and symptoms, is associated with about 20 percent of all DCI cases.

Dizziness: Fifteen percent of divers with DCI report symptoms of dizziness; however, dizziness is a non-specific term that may encompass any subjective feeling of unsteadiness. Vertigo, a particular form of dizziness, occurs when the diver or the environment appears to be spinning. Often accompanied by deafness, loss of balance, nausea and vomiting, vertigo has many causes. Because it represents damage to either the brain stem or the inner ear, it is considered a serious manifestation of DCI.

Headache: A headache after diving can have several causes: sinus barotrauma; temporomandibular joint (TMJ) pain caused by clenching the mouthpiece tightly; and carbon dioxide retention (caused by "skip breathing"). Rarely is headache a symptom of carbon monoxide poisoning and DCI of the central nervous system. In the latter, other signs and symptoms usually accompany it. Headaches are reported in 10-12 percent of all cases of DCI.

Nausea: Nausea, the overwhelming feeling of illness that occurs prior to vomiting, can indicate seasickness, middle- or inner ear barotrauma or gastrointestinal problems. When it occurs in conjunction with vertigo or unsteadiness, it can be a symptom of DCI. Nausea and vomiting is reported in about 10 percent of all DCI cases.

Rash: Rash is most commonly caused by a skin reaction to a dive suit (suit squeeze or allergy) or contact with marine life. It may also be due to DCI – called "skin bends" – which can exist in several forms. The most common rash is red, slightly raised and patchy, usually on the torso.

Another disorder, characterized by diffuse itching, may not be accompanied by a visible rash. This type of skin bends, which is believed to be due to inert gas supersaturation caused by direct uptake through the skin, only occurs in drysuits or dry chamber dives.

In a third type that looks like hives (urticaria), small raised areas may be accompanied by itching. This type, which is rare, is usually observed in chamber or bell decompressions in which the breathing gas is different from the ambient chamber gas. A fourth type, sometimes called "guinea pig skin" (cutis marmorata), has a marbled, "bruised" appearance. This form may be a harbinger of more serious DCI. Rash and itching are reported in 6-8 percent of all cases.

Serious Symptoms

The average diver can easily recognize various very severe symptoms as being probable symptoms of DCI. These include loss of or altered consciousness, seizure, muscle weakness, difficulty walking or total paralysis. These symptoms or signs all indicate involvement of the central nervous system. A subtle but serious indicator of spinal cord damage is the inability to urinate despite having a full bladder. For all serious symptoms, administration of oxygen and transport to a treatment facility should not be delayed. Such manifestations occur in fewer than 5 percent of all cases.

Prevention

For divers, a small but inevitable risk exists. Following the principles of safe diving is important, but that still offers no guarantee of symptom-free or risk-free diving. Individuals who have been within the limits of their dive computers or tables have reported many cases of DCI. Although much is still unknown about why divers get injured without table violations, divers can take additional measures to decrease their risk.

Even though recreational diving doesn't usually require in-water decompression stops, this does not mean that decompression is not required. Decompression occurs during any ascent to the surface and, in the period between dives, further desaturation occurs as excess nitrogen continues to leave the body. Decompression sickness is a disease of decompression. Therefore, the only way for divers to reduce risks of developing DCS is to pay attention to their exposure to nitrogen and the manner in which they decompress to the surface.

Divers can take a basic preventive measure by limiting their exposure to high partial pressures of nitrogen. They can perform fewer dives in a single day, take longer surface intervals between dives, spend less time spent at maximum depth and make shallower dives.

To offgas nitrogen effectively, divers must be well hydrated. Adequate circulation of blood and elimination of nitrogen from tissues both depend upon an adequate blood volume. Scuba diving *per se* and sun exposure can cause significant loss of body fluid. This reduction in blood volume impairs the elimination of nitrogen during and after ascent, making fluid replacement with water or non-dehydrating fluids advisable.

Once divers know the risks of scuba diving, they should take the logical next step and make concerted efforts to manage those risks. For their health and for injury prevention, divers should have physical examinations from a dive physician. Some pre-existing conditions may limit a diver's physical or mental abilities to dive, and fitness to dive should therefore be assessed in light of such concerns. Additionally, as divers grow older, many want to continue diving. This changing health status and common temporary restrictions such as infections or injuries require evaluation and advice from a knowledgeable source.

The Case Reports

Approximately 1,000 U.S. citizens receive treatment annually for decompression illness in the United States and overseas, according to reports by the DAN worldwide network of referral hyperbaric chambers.

Many cases of decompression illness demonstrate similar patterns of symptoms and presentation, but dive profiles are often quite diverse. Instances of DCI can range from mild pain-only cases to severe neurological symptoms or complete paralysis. Despite similar symptoms, the cases which follow had different responses to recompression. Why some cases are more resistant to treatment is not completely understood.

Surprisingly, although decompression illness and its symptoms are well known to most divers, these divers are often hesitant to report their symptoms or seek evaluation. The more moderate or mild symptoms can be confused easily with pre-existing injuries or other recent activities and may also contribute to the delay.

The following case reports from the last few years are illustrative of the variety of symptoms in decompression illness, symptom severity and outcomes after treatment for DCI incidents treated by U.S. and nearby recompression chambers. Although complete dive profiles are not given here, they generally help in making a definitive diagnosis.

For more DCI cases, visit www.DiversAlertNetwork.org and download the most recent edition of the DAN annual *Report on Decompression Illness, Diving Fatalities and Project Dive Exploration*. Divers who have symptoms or suspect DCI should call the DAN 24-Hour Diving Emergency Hotline at +1-919-684-4326 (4DAN) collect or -684-8111.

Case 1
Neurological DCI After Repetitive Diving Complete Resolution with Treatment

The diver was a 38-year-old male in good health. Diving for two years, he had completed about 15 dives per year. After a check-out dive on the first dive day, he made repetitive dives on the following two days without incident. On the fourth day of diving, the diver made two dives: 95 feet / 29m for 35 minutes with a safety stop; a one-hour surface interval; and then a dive to 50 feet / 15m for 44 minutes, with a 20-foot / 6m safety stop. All of his dives were within acceptable decompression limits according to his dive computer. He had made one dive during the previous evening and afterward consumed six beers.

Approximately one hour after the last dive of the day, he noticed the sensation of weakness in his left hand. Over the course of the next hour he experienced tingling in his left hand, which extended from his fingertips to his forearm. A generalized feeling of weakness and fatigue followed, making him feel as though he had made a great exertion.

The diver's symptoms persisted for another hour, and he contacted a local physician for evaluation. He was placed in a chamber and recompressed according to U.S. Navy Table 6. After the treatment, he experienced partial relief of weakness and tingling in his left wrist, and is generalized weakness had resolved. He was treated the following day with a U.S. Navy Treatment Table 5, with complete relief of his remaining symptoms.

Dehydration after beer consumption could have played a role in this DCI event. The onset of symptoms within two hours after surfacing is fairly typical. Early treatment after symptom onset likely contributed to his complete recovery.

Case 2
Symptoms Mimicking Other Conditions

The diver was a 69-year-old, 5-foot-8, 170-pound male in reasonable health, although taking "stomach medication" and two medications for elevated blood pressure. He also reported a history of arthritis in his neck and lower back, but with no pain or symptoms at the time of the injury. He was an open-water diver with 30 years of diving experience, having made 400-plus dives in the previous five years and 80 dives in the last 12 months.

On the first day of diving he performed three multilevel dives to 120-130 feet / 36.5-40m. Dive times ranged from 30-40 minutes. The following day he dived to 110 feet / 33.5m for 40 minutes.

After a surface interval of one hour and 20 minutes, he made a dive to 96 feet / 29m for 40 minutes. After a surface interval of four and a half hours, he went to 113 feet / 34m on a multilevel dive for 45 minutes. All dives were within acceptable limits according to his dive computer.

Within 30 minutes after his last dive, he developed a sharp pain in his left shoulder and a tenderness in the back of his neck. Since he was accustomed to experiencing occasional pain associated with his arthritis, he treated himself with a non-steroidal anti-inflammatory medication that he commonly used. Over the next two days his neck pain gradually resolved, but his shoulder pain persisted. He also noted that the painful area in his left shoulder appeared swollen, and that his left arm was weaker than his right. He had no other symptoms suggestive of decompression illness, such as numbness, tingling or extreme fatigue.

On the third day the diver was evaluated by his physician, who, despite unremitting shoulder pain, found no evidence of weakness or swelling of the left shoulder. The diver was compressed using U.S. Navy Treatment Table 6 approximately 72 hours after his symptoms first began, and he experienced complete resolution of all symptoms.

Symptoms that mimic other conditions, particularly if they are similar to pre-existing diseases, may not be recognized as decompression illness.

Case 3
Neurological Decompression Illness: Followed by a Case of Cerebral Decompression Illness

The diver was a 37-year-old male (6 feet, 185 lbs.) who had been certified for two and a half years. He had made a total of 100 dives, with 50 dives in the past year. He was in good health, a non-smoker with no current or previous medical problems.

He made four dives to maximum depths of 60-80 feet / 18-24 m. The following day he made an 80-foot dive, followed by two 60-foot dives. He made a safety stop on the first five dives, while the last two required mandatory decompression according to his dive computer. The diver was cold and slightly nauseated at times on the dive vessel, although his dives were largely uneventful. The exception was a slight sensation of numbness in his right leg between the third and fourth dives: at the time, he did not believe this was DCI.

After his last dive, he again felt a numbness in his right leg. It spread to his entire leg over the next two hours. He went to a local hospital, where he provided 100 percent oxygen. He was transferred by helicopter to a local hyperbaric facility. There he received a U.S. Navy Treatment

Table 6 for five consecutive days (one each day). His symptoms resolved after the fifth treatment.

The diver resumed diving three and a half months later at the same location over a two-day weekend. He made two dives with no problems, both to 60 feet with safety stops.

When he awoke the following morning, however, some 12 hours after his last dive, he had a headache, weakness down the right side of his body, slurred speech and altered mental status. During an extended U.S. Navy TT6, he experienced complete resolution. He remained overnight for observation; he did not return to diving.

Case 4
Symptoms after Diving and Commercial Air Travel

The diver was a 41-year-old male (5 feet 9 inches, 192 lbs.) in good health. His medical history included allergies, for which he took antihistamine medication. He had just finished open-water certification and was on a diving excursion to the Caribbean. In nine dives over four days, he never exceeded 70 feet / 21 m; he did make safety stops, used a dive computer, and had no decompression violations. His last dive was to 42 feet / 12.7 m.

Within 30 minutes after surfacing from his last dive, he experienced mild numbness (light paresthesia) in his left hand and forearm. He also noted transient numbness around his right index finger, lasting about five minutes. He mentioned this to no one, and the numbness subsided after about an hour and a half. He continued his normal activities without recurrence.

Some 26 hours after his last dive, he left for home by commercial airline and noted a return of the left arm paresthesia, with extension to his upper arm and a heaviness and aching in his joints. These symptoms remained unchanged during a second flight. The following day, he experienced light-headedness and elbow pain as well. He went to his personal physician with these complaints. After ECG and chest X-rays were found to be normal, he was referred to a local hyperbaric physician.

Approximately 55 hours after his last dive, he was recompressed on a U.S. Navy Treatment Table 6 with two extensions. His symptoms gradually resolved, and he was symptom-free at the end the six-hour treatment. He was advised not to dive for a month, pending evaluation by his personal physician.

Case 5
Spinal Cord Decompression Illness

The diver was a 55-year-old female (5 feet 2 inches, 135 lbs.). She was certified as a basic open-water diver seven years previous to the dives in question but had not been diving for three years and had fewer than 20 lifetime dives. She had a history of pneumonia, lower back surgery, and had just recovered from a relapse of hepatitis C but was very active despite these conditions.

During a weeklong vacation, she made one uneventful 50-foot / 15-meter dive for each of three days. On the fourth day, her dive depth was 110-120 feet / 33-36 m; she followed another diver's computer, making a safety stop at 15 f / 4.5 m. During the safety stop, she lost bladder control.

While relaxing on the boat, she had sudden onset of right shoulder pain radiating down her arm, leg, chest and back; she felt numbness in her legs that progressed to weakness so severe that she could stand without assistance. Within minutes, she was unable to walk. Surface oxygen was unavailable. She was taken to a local hospital, where a physician untrained in diving medicine examined and released her after hydration and a multivitamin shot.

Because she remained weak in her lower extremities and unable to stand or walk, her traveling companion arranged for medical evacuation by pressurized aircraft to the United States. The diver had no memory of these events.

On examination in a diving medical facility, she had weaknesses (paresthesias) in her arms and legs, pain in both shoulders and back, could stand only with assistance and was unable to walk. She had had no bowel or bladder function since the dive. She was treated on a U.S. Navy Treatment Table 6 about 30 hours after symptom onset with little improvement. She had resolution of her joint and muscle pain and a decrease in the paresthesias of her arms and legs after a second Table 6.

Another Table 6 and a Table 5 treatment produced further improvement, and on the fifth day of treatment, she began twice-a-day hyperbaric oxygen therapy at two atmospheres for two hours. After her tenth treatment, her leg strength had returned to about 90 percent of its undamaged state, but she still had transient paresthesias and was unable to urinate spontaneously. Due to the severity of her injury and residual symptoms, she was advised to never dive again.

At her 12-month follow-up, she continued to have short-term memory loss, bowel and bladder incontinence, balance difficulties, chronic leg pain, paresthesia and general fatigue.

Case 6
Neurological DCI With Complete Resolution in Three Recompressions

The diver was a 34-year-old female (5 feet 6 inches, 118 lbs.) and in excellent health. She had made 12 dives since her open-water certification two months earlier. Her last dive was three weeks prior to a trip to Mexico, where she was injured after seven dives in three days.

Her first dive, which was to a depth of 90 feet / 27 m, was followed by two shallower dives. On the second day, she made an 80-foot / 24-meter dive, followed by a shallower dive. She had no symptoms after the first two dive days. On the third day, she made an 80-foot dive for 35 minutes followed by a 60-minute surface interval and a 50-foot / 15-meter dive for 45 minutes.

Approximately one hour after the last dive, she developed a sense of generalized fatigue followed by an overall sense of weakness. Within a half hour, these symptoms began to interfere with her ability to stand and walk. Two hours after the dive, she contacted the dive operator, who made arrangements to take her to the local chamber.

Her weakness increased over the next two hours, and she developed a headache and general aching similar to muscle soreness from the flu. She received her first recompression treatment in a hyperbaric chamber four hours after the dive, with complete resolution after three treatments.

Case 7
Arterial Gas Embolism (AGE) and Neurological Injury Leading to Residual Symptoms

The diver, a 45-year-old female (5 feet 6 inches, 150 lbs.), was in good health. She had advanced certification and had made more than 90 dives in five years, with 15 dives during the previous year. The last dive before her injury on a Caribbean vacation had been four months earlier.

She began her first day with a dive to 69 feet / 21 m, which was followed by a second, shallower dive. She experienced no problems or symptoms. Well-rested on the second day, she went to 88 feet / 26.4 m with a multilevel ascent. At about 30 feet / 9 m and 30 minutes into the dive, she made a rapid ascent. This was the result of a strong current and difficulty in reaching the dump valve of her new buoyancy compensator, with which she was unfamiliar.

Before reaching the surface, she felt weak and unable to move her legs, and she lost consciousness soon after surfacing. When she awoke during the ride to the chamber, she experienced nausea, weakness, fatigue and paralysis from the waist down.

She was recompressed within one hour on an extended treatment table and had some improvement. She received a second treatment with minimal gain and remained paralyzed. After air evacuation to the United States, she underwent an additional 57 hours of recompression and improved gradually. One year after her injury, she still had weakness and numbness in her legs.

Unconsciousness immediately after a rapid ascent is associated with 50-60 percent of all case in the DAN database diagnosed as AGE, arterial gas embolism. Even with a rapid and aggressive treatment, signs and symptoms may not completely resolve.

Case 8
A Recurrence of Pain-Only DCI
With Resolution Upon Recompression

The diver was a 35-year-old male (5 feet 11 inches, 185 lbs.) in excellent health. A divemaster, he had received certification 15 years earlier. He had made 350 dives in the past five years and 30 dives during the previous year. His last dive was two weeks prior to the day of his injury.

The diver made a one-day ocean excursion near his home on the East Coast of the United States. His first dive was to 115 feet / 34.5 m with a safety stop. Shortly thereafter, he noted pain in his left arm. The pain subsided during the surface interval required by his dive tables.

His second dive was to a maximum depth of 75 feet / 22.5 m. He had no difficulties until an ascent to a 10-foot / 3-meter decompression stop, during which the pain in his left arm returned with twice the intensity: the muscles between his shoulder and elbow, and between his elbow and wrist, were affected.

Upon surfacing, he breathed 100 percent oxygen with little improvement. The pain persisted through the afternoon and evening, which eventually led him to a local emergency room and recompression chamber. The pain resolved within 10 minutes of recompression.

There are many causes of pain, but if it occurs after diving, it's reasonable to suspect DCI. In this case, seek medical evaluation by a diving physician as soon as possible. Early recompression offers the greatest possibility for full recovery and return to diving.

Index